T0302079

HUMANOMICS

While neoclassical analysis works well for studying impersonal exchange in markets, it fails to explain why people conduct themselves the way they do in their personal relationships with family, neighbors, and friends. In *Humanomics*, Nobel Prize-winning economist Vernon L. Smith and his long-time co-author Bart J. Wilson bring their study of economics full circle by returning to the founder of modern economics, Adam Smith. Sometime in the last 250 years, economists lost sight of the full range of human feeling, thinking, and knowing in everyday life. Smith and Wilson show how Adam Smith's model of sociality can re-humanize twenty-first century economics by undergirding it with sentiments, fellow feeling, and a sense of propriety – the stuff of which human relationships are built. Integrating insights from *The Theory of Moral Sentiments* and the *Wealth of Nations* into contemporary empirical analysis, this book shapes economic betterment as a science of human beings.

Vernon L. Smith is the George L. Argyros Endowed Chair in Economics and Finance at Chapman University, California. He was awarded the Noble Prize in Economic sciences in 2002 for, 'having established laboratory experiments as a tool in empirical economic analysis, especially in the study of alternative market mechanisms'. He is a founding member of Chapman University's Economic Science Institute and Smith Institute for Political Economy and Philosophy, and is a Distinguished Fellow of the American Economic Association.

Bart J. Wilson is the Donald P. Kennedy Endowed Chair in Economics and Law at Chapman University, California. He is a founding member of the Economic Science Institute and founding member and Director of the Smith Institute for Political Economy and Philosophy. He has been co-teaching humanomics courses for nearly a decade with professors in the Departments of English and Philosophy.

CAMBRIDGE STUDIES IN ECONOMICS, CHOICE, AND SOCIETY

Founding Editors

Timur Kuran, *Duke University*
Peter J. Boettke, *George Mason University*

This interdisciplinary series promotes original theoretical and empirical research as well as integrative syntheses involving links between individual choice, institutions, and social outcomes. Contributions are welcome from across the social sciences, particularly in the areas where economic analysis is joined with other disciplines such as comparative political economy, new institutional economics, and behavioral economics.

Books in the Series:

Humanomics

*Moral Sentiments and the Wealth of Nations
for the Twenty-First Century*

VERNON L. SMITH AND BART J. WILSON

CAMBRIDGE
UNIVERSITY PRESS

CAMBRIDGE
UNIVERSITY PRESS

University Printing House, Cambridge CB2 8BS, United Kingdom

One Liberty Plaza, 20th Floor, New York, NY 10006, USA

477 Williamstown Road, Port Melbourne, VIC 3207, Australia

314-321, 3rd Floor, Plot 3, Splendor Forum, Jasola District Centre, New Delhi - 110025, India

79 Anson Road, #06-04/06, Singapore 079906

Cambridge University Press is part of the University of Cambridge.

It furthers the University's mission by disseminating knowledge in the pursuit of education, learning and research at the highest international levels of excellence.

www.cambridge.org
Information on this title: www.cambridge.org/9781107199378
DOI: 10.1017/9781108185561

First published 2019

A catalogue record for this publication is available from the British Library

ISBN 978-1-107-19937-8 Hardback
ISBN 978-1-316-64881-0 Paperback

Cambridge University Press has no responsibility for the persistence or accuracy of URLs for external or third-party internet websites referred to in this publication, and does not guarantee that any content on such websites is, or will remain, accurate or appropriate.

To Nicholas Phillipson,

historian, scholar of the Scottish Enlightenment,

biographer of David Hume and Adam Smith

Contents

Figures

Tables

Preface

Each of us, as coauthors of this book, have been reading and citing Adam Smith (1759), *The Theory of Moral Sentiments* (hereafter, *Sentiments*) for well in excess of a decade.* Our comprehension, though, is much younger. It took time to gradually assimilate Smith's thinking and modeling, and we had to realize the limitations of our own earlier partial understanding. Our economic education and modeling traditions handicapped us from the start. Yet we were strengthened by nagging unanswered questions. Experimental evidence in two-person games, such as the well-known ultimatum game, had a falsifying confrontation with economics in the 1980s and 1990s, from which economic theory had not recovered by the early 2000s. Many important empirical findings followed that confrontation, but economists had not integrated the advances into a satisfactory theoretical framework.

There existed two disparate collections of evidence. Anonymously paired people were predominantly caring, other-regarding, interdependent actors in the personal, social exchange context of trust games in the laboratory. Trusting actions generated substantial trustworthiness in response. In ultimatum games proposers offered generous splits of twenty dollars in direct violation of the self-interested prediction, and responders accepted generous offers while rejecting stingier offers that were often much better than zero earnings from rejection. Contrastingly, buyers and sellers in laboratory markets were predominantly self-interested, own-regarding pursuers of utility maximization – "Max-U" – defined only over their own private outcomes.

---

* Beginning with Vernon L. Smith, 1998, "The Two Faces of Adam Smith," Southern Economic Association Distinguished Guest Lecture, *Southern Economic Journal*, 65 (1), pp. 1–19. Wilson first read *Sentiments* cover to cover in the summer of 2006 with four precocious high school students (two of whom eventually received PhDs in economics).

Economists offered a solution to this dichotomous representation of the human personality in two widely accepted but unsatisfactory forms. The first was to add other, as well as own, outcomes to the individual characterizations of Max-U. Thus, in ultimatum games the proposer and the responder each have the other's, as well as their own, payoff in their respective utilities for the joint outcome. This logically circular reduction appeared to neatly and comfortably rescue the neoclassical Max-U model, legitimizing it as a theory of everything, provided only that you used the right just-so utility representation of other as well as their own outcomes. More sophisticated empirical explorations further unearthed features to be added to Max-U theory. If someone found that human intentions, or some particular context mattered, then in the venerable tradition of Ptolemaic curve-fitting, they added the finding to the utility function as a new parameter. A larger theoretical pre-experiment framework did not guide or predict the empirical discoveries.

The second form was to recognize that social transactions were just special forms of economic exchange that were reciprocal. By analogy with trade in goods and services, people exchange favors across time in life, and people reciprocate trust with trustworthiness in laboratory trust games. As another exercise in circular reasoning, this solution simply offered to assign a name to the robust empirical regularity that people responded to good things done to them by doing good things in return.

Missing in both adaptations was a more fundamental rethinking of human sociability. Why does the payoff to the other person appear in one's own utility function? How did it get there? It is not there in three-year-olds, not in sociopaths, and certainly not in psychopaths. Alternatively, why do people respond trustworthily to trusting actions when it is a convenient opportunity to gain from another's largess, as she will never know your identity? And why, when you go to the clothing store or the supermarket or Amazon, do you show so little regard for helping them by buying the highest marked-up items?

Sentiments changes all of that. Smith models human relationships as expressed in families, extended families, among neighbors, friends, and acquaintances, radiating outward until it bumps into those who are personally unknown to us. In these communities, general rules govern an inveterate commitment to sociability that characterizes relationships within which all the little utilitarian services are exchanged. Fundamentally, it is the human capacity for sentiment, fellow feeling, and a sense of propriety that is the stuff of which human relationships, and the general rules-to-be-followed, are made. Sentiments, fellow feeling, and a sense of propriety are also the building blocks with which Smith develops an overarching theory that encompasses, by definition, the broad types of players observed in laboratory experiments that do not conform to Max-U predictions. Such player types come from Smith's propositions governing the feelings-expressed calculus of gratitude-reward or resentment-punishment. In concrete applications in the laboratory, these types (subject to errors of self-command, reading the context, self-deceit, etc.) have been called altruists or conditional cooperators or punishers of defection or rejecters of unfair offers. Such types so named enable Max-U to continue working as a superficial explanation.

But sociality and our general rules of conduct must all be learned.

We begin as children with none of these proclivities but with an inherited capacity to upload the programming scripts for social competence. Parents, knowing of our ignorance, indulge our want of self-command, restraining us enough for safety. Then at school age we mix with equals, who as Smith says, "have no such indulgent partiality." The child soon learns that things go better with playfellows if one moderates anger. Thus, the child "enters the great school of self-command" and maturation has begun in earnest.

Such rules of conduct are general, meaning that they arise, either from actions intending to do good things for others, leading to gratitude and a proportionate urge to reward, or actions intending to do bad things to others, leading to an asymmetric outsized urge to punish in proportion to the resentment felt. The former concerns beneficence, the latter justice achieved through mechanisms that limit and control the expression of injustice. Hence, the two great pillars of society: beneficence and justice. Beneficence constitutes the virtues we celebrate and applaud: courtesy, kindness, thoughtfulness, compassion, honor, and integrity. These features of good conduct cannot be extorted, coerced, or legislated. The end of justice is to nip hurtful action in the bud, to be neither excessive nor inadequate to restrain and protect the innocent while pointing the aggressor to a better way. For no society can subsist if all descend into mutually destructive injury.

Smith's propositions in *Sentiments* explain the earlier two-person game outcomes that had falsified the standard socioeconomic model of science while fully accommodating market Max-U analysis. This book develops that resolution but also offers several new experimental designs based on *Sentiments* that yield robust results commensurate with the predictions or that rationally reconstruct the outcomes in terms of sources of error or uncertainty in the model.

This new synthesis, made of old elements, points to a neoclassical tradition that swung too far in displacing, rather than more modestly supplementing, Smith's classical systems-oriented thinking. The new equilibrium concepts were defined too narrowly over outcomes, a substitution that seemed superior in the context of institution-free general equilibrium market analysis and the partial-partial equilibrium analysis of game theory. At some point even the human being was dropped as the subject of our general inquiry as a social science. Whereas the opening sentence of *Sentiments* situates the entire project as about humankind, rarely in almost any graduate or intermediate level textbook in economics can you find something that distinguishes in kind its application of consumer theory to humans, chimpanzees, or pigeons. As long as the choices are consistent with a set of axioms, everything follows for any species. In contrast, the opening title of book 1 of Smith's other great book, published to broad acclaim in 1776, is universally about people, not any or all beings, but human beings. Even his little known essay which only Smithian scholars read, "The History of Astronomy," opens with twenty pages not about astronomy, the science, but about humankind and why there is indeed such a line of inquiry called astronomy (our curious disposition and our sentiments of wonder, surprise, and admiration). We economists have lost sight of an elementary understanding of the social and economic range of human action. We have lost sight of the fellow feeling by which human beings gravitate toward one another, and we have lost sight of the sentiments that excite human beings to act and by which human beings judge their own and one another's conduct. Studying Adam Smith has humanized our study of economics as we hope it will do for yours, for much work remains to examine the potential for applying modern (equilibrium) analysis to the rule-space of human conduct, both social and economic, but which is moral all the way down.

Acknowledgments

Many events and people were in the background that has culminated in our contributions to the content and form of this book. We should first mention the Liberty Fund colloquia that concentrated on Adam Smith's *The Theory of Moral Sentiments* in which we have been privileged to participate for many years. These probing discussions of Smith's first book eventually awakened in us the unexpected prospect that Smith's penetrating work on moral sentiments could illuminate our comprehension of the mainsprings of human action and its expression in experimental economics. In these colloquia we met Adam Smith scholars like Ryan Hanley, Daniel Klein, Leonidas Montes, James Otteson, Maria Pia Paganelli, Eric Schliesser, Michelle Schwarze, and other participants who made their mark on us. We have also been privileged to read and discuss Adam Smith's ideas with many undergraduate, graduate, and law students at George Mason University and Chapman University. Their refreshing observations and dedication to reading eighteenth century texts made for stimulating learning experiences all around.

VERNON SMITH

Ryan Hanley invited me to contribute to his masterful collection, *Adam Smith: His Life, Thought and Legacy* (Princeton: Princeton University Press, 2016). My essay, "Adam Smith and Experimental Economics: *Sentiments* to *Wealth*" (pp. 262–279), speaks to some aspects of my coming of age with Adam Smith. I am indebted to a great many individuals, universities, and conference organizers who invited me to give public lectures on Adam Smith. These adventures contributed to my gradual comprehension and development of Smith's way of thinking about the human social enterprise. One such occasion was a Mises Conference in

Sestri Levante in October 2011, arranged by Alberto Mingardi, director of the Bruno Leoni Institute, where I chose the title "How Social Norms Emerge Spontaneously: Adam Smith, Moral Sentiments and Property." There, I had the great pleasure of meeting Nick Phillipson, who remarked that he had never heard anyone offer these particular observations on Smith's contributions. If such be the case, it derived from unanswered questions arising from what Bart and I felt was the failure of economists, cognitive psychologists, experimentalists, and behaviorists to account for the experimental games and results that constitute much of this book.

BART WILSON

In 2013 Pat Lynch invited me to co-lead with David Alvis a weeklong Liberty Fund colloquium on Adam Smith's entire corpus of writing. Those formal and informal discussions left me with an indelible understanding of Adam Smith as a systems thinker and polymath. Pete Calcagno twice invited me to the College of Charleston to lecture during Adam Smith Week, which provided timely opportunities in 2017 and 2018 to experiment with and rework our ideas. I was fortunate in January 2017 to co-teach an intensive four-week course on Adam Smith with my colleague Keith Hankins, who helped me see new things right when I needed to see them. During the spring and summer of 2017, Jim Murphy and the Department of Economics at the University of Alaska Anchorage generously hosted me as the Rasmuson Chair in Economics while I worked on substantial portions of the book. There is nothing like a "spring" trip to Nome and Utqiaġvik to see and hear firsthand how people interweave the social and the economic.

Finally, both of us would like to sincerely thank Gabriele Camera, Yvonne Durham, Deirdre McCloskey, Andreas Ortmann, Jan Osborn, and Maria Pia Paganelli for carefully reading and comprehensively commenting on early and late drafts of the book.

Cover Art Note

The Age of Enlightenment – Adam Smith is one of five pieces in Yinka Shonibare's 2008 series of life-size fiberglass mannequins with Dutch wax printed cotton. His sculpture is as legible as it is beautiful. The vivid colors and meticulous print finish catch our eyes, and with a momentary hold on our gaze, Shonibare reveals an uncomfortable truth in visual metaphor: Adam Smith has a hunched back. In Smith's reaching for his magnum opus, *An Inquiry into the Nature and Causes of the Wealth of Nations*, Shonibare suggests that the rationality of classical economics is subject to the frailties of being human. Shonibare also uses the physical disability, in his own words, "as a device for showing how these figures, who were partly responsible for defining otherness in the context of the Enlightenment, could also be 'othered' in the context of disability."[*] With a close reading of Adam Smith's other great but not well-known book, *The Theory of Moral Sentiments*, we endeavor to add exclamation points – and question marks – to both thought-provoking ideas.

---

[*] Downey, Anthony. 2008. "Setting the Stage," in *Yinka Shonibare MBE*. Rachel Kent, Robert Hobbs, and Anthony Downey. New York, NY: Prestel Verlag, p. 45.

Note on the Text

We have reused, reconsidered, and reworked the following papers in writing this book:

Osborn, Jan, Bart J. Wilson, and Bradley R. Sherwood. 2015. "Conduct in Narrativized Trust Games," *Southern Economic Journal* 81(3): 562–597 (in Chapter 12). Reprinted with permission.

Smith, Vernon L. and Bart J. Wilson. 2014. "Fair and Impartial Spectators in Experimental Economic Behavior," *Review of Behavioral Economics* 1(1–2): 1–26 (in Chapters 1, 7–9, 11). http://dx.doi.org/10.1561/105.00000001. Reprinted with permission.

Smith, Vernon L. and Bart J. Wilson. 2017. "*Sentiments*, Conduct, and Trust in the Laboratory," *Social Philosophy and Policy* 34(1): 25–55 (in Chapters 3–4, 6). Reprinted with permission.

Smith, Vernon L. and Bart J. Wilson. 2018. "Equilibrium Play in Voluntary Ultimatum Games: Beneficence Cannot be Extorted," *Games and Economic Behavior* 109: 452–464 (in Chapter 9). Reprinted with permission.

Wilson, Bart J. 2010. "Social Preferences Aren't Preferences," *Journal of Economic Behavior and Organization* 73(1): 77–82 (in Chapter 3). Reprinted with permission.

1

Humanomics Spans the Two Worlds of Adam Smith

Sociality and Economy

A persistent conflict in modern human life arises from living simultaneously in two worlds governed by distinct rule systems. Human beings
are first governed by the caring other-regarding rules of our close-knit
social groups, like our families, extended families, neighbors, and friends.
We do good things for such people, and we refrain from doing bad things
to such people because we personally know them. On an individual level,
we specifically know how to be helpful, kind, and compassionate to them.
They have names like Candace and Ryan, Stephanie and Steve, Caroline
and Kyle, and we have firsthand knowledge about them. We know such
mundane things as which friend can take which jokes (and which ones
cannot take jokes at all) and such poignant things as what our neighbor
needs right now is someone to sit with while she copes with some trauma-
tizing news. With love and solidarity we treat those people personally
known to us as the dear individuals they are.

Because we cannot possibly know the specific circumstances of everyone
beyond our circle of kith and kin, the extended order of markets treats
everyone we do not personally know precisely the same. We do not
personally know which farmer or wholesaler or trucker or grocer will
best serve us in delivering food from the farm to our kitchen table, so we
open it up for competition to decide who will serve us well. Wisconsinites,
Kansans, Canadians, Mexicans, Chileans, New Zealanders, Czechs, and
even the French all vie to supply us with what we desire: cheese and wheat,
pork and tomatoes, grapes and kiwis, beer and wine. The same rules apply
to everyone whom we do not personally know – do not harm by stealing,
deceiving, or breaching a promise – and we let freedom of choice among
them, called competition, do the rest. Whoever supplies the tastiest cheese
at the best prevailing prices gets our money. Today that might be Robert
Wills from Cedar Grove Cheese in Plain, Wisconsin, but next week it

might be Will and Hilary Chester-Master from Abbey Home Farm in Cirencester, United Kingdom. If specifying the actual names of cheesemakers googled from the Internet feels a bit too particular, that is our point. We do not personally know the names of the multitudes of people who produce the far greater part of those daily goods and services we stand in need of.

If the solidarity and love for our fellow compatriots that we do not personally know led us to forbid the importation of goods from other producers that we also do not personally know – say, like those in Asia or Europe – we would destroy the ability of markets to support specialization and thereby create wealth and human betterment. Such conflict prominently takes the form of sharp controversies over inequality in the distribution of income and wealth, and whether or to what extent wealth creation generates inequality through innovation and the subsequent diffusion of its benefits.[1]

Similarly, applying impersonalized rules of competition, like that of "today you win my patronage, tomorrow you lose" to our more intimate social groupings would crush the ability of friends, family, and neighbors to forge and strengthen the bonds of human sociality. Imagine how many friends we would have if we treated them like we treat the owners of restaurants that we patronize: *No, I'm sorry, your taste in wine is not a good fit for dinner this week; the Johnsons are coming over. Maybe next week, though?* "So," says the economist and social philosopher F. A. Hayek, "we must learn to live in two sorts of world at once" (1988, p. 18).

Although Hayek articulated the idea of living in two different worlds, and the conflict it engenders, the origin, substance, and functioning of these two parallel worlds was made comprehensible originally in two books written over two centuries ago by Adam Smith, *The Theory of Moral Sentiments* in 1759 (hereafter *Sentiments* in the text, and TMS in citations) and *An Inquiry into the Nature and Causes of the Wealth of Nations* in 1776 (hereafter *Wealth* in the text, and WN in citations). We use the neologism "humanomics" to refer narrowly here to the study of the very *human* problem of simultaneously living in these two worlds, the personal social and the impersonal economic.

In the roots of their common origin in human life, Adam Smith's work enables us to understand these two worlds as one. He modeled both worlds in a manner that we believe seamlessly connects the two in a unified social and ethical science of human beings. It is our aim to further develop,

---

[1] Thomas Piketty (2014) and Deirdre McCloskey (2016).

articulate, and demonstrate that model for contemporary social science theory and experiment. *Sentiments* did not fare well in the academy; *Wealth* fared far better. The two works were once even seen as contradictory. Jacob Viner, for example, a leading scholar in the intellectual history of economics, could write, "But it can be convincingly demonstrated, I believe, that on the points at which they come into contact there is a substantial measure of irreconcilable divergence between the *Theory of Moral Sentiments* and the *Wealth of Nations* with respect to the character of the natural order" (Viner 1991, p. 93). And again, "Many writers, including the present author at an early stage of his study of Smith, have found these two works in some measure inconsistent" (Viner 1991, p. 250). This so-called Adam Smith problem was corrected in a revisionist literature that greatly elevated the status of Smith's first book.[2] These corrections in the intellectual understanding of Smith, coming two centuries after *Wealth* was published, and a century after the neoclassical marginal revolution do not close the immense gap between how Smith and modern scholars think about human action.[3] Our own experience is that of having stumbled into a gradually deepening appreciation of the unifying principles of social science in Smith's two great works. That path began and received illumination from unanticipated and unpredicted results in experimental studies. First in markets, where the standard self-interest model of action under strict private information predicted outcomes far more accurately than was thought possible by contemporary professional economists; and second, the same utility maximizing model of action in simple ultimatum and trust games failed decisively to predict

---

[2] Leonidas Montes (2003, 2004) examines this literature and other aspects of Smith's thought.

[3] In the last edition of *Sentiments,* Smith stated that in the first edition he had indicated his intention "to give an account of the general principles of law and government, and of the different revolutions which they had undergone in the different ages and periods of society; not only in what concerns justice, but in what concerns police, revenue, and arms, and whatever else is the object of law. In ... [*Wealth*] ... I have partly executed this promise.... What remains, the theory of jurisprudence, which I have long projected, I have hitherto been hindered from executing, by the same occupations which had till now prevented me from revising the present work. Though my very advanced age leaves me, I acknowledge, very little expectation of ever being able to execute this great work to my own satisfaction; yet, as I have not altogether abandoned the design, and as I wish still to continue under the obligation of doing what I can, I have allowed the paragraph to remain as it was published more than thirty years ago, when I entertained no doubt of being able to execute every thing which it announced" (Adam Smith 1790). We do not know whether that plan, if followed, would have brought a fuller integration of Smith's remarkable two books, and a less ambitious attempt by neoclassical economists to reduce all human action to an exercise in utility maximization.

systematically replicable results.[4] This book is largely a consequence of our attempt to give meaning to this disjunction, where none of the attempts to do so have been satisfactory. *Sentiments* gave us an unexpectedly fresh framework.

SOCIAL ORDER

Contrary to popular belief, Adam Smith does not argue, famously or infamously, that humans are primarily motivated by self-interest. Even in *Wealth*, he speaks not of self-interest but of one's "own interest," which includes prudence but is always mediated by what "other men can go along with."[5] Smith renownedly says that "it is not from the benevolence of the butcher, the brewer, or the baker, that we expect our dinner, but from their regard to their own interest. We address ourselves, not to their humanity but to their *self-love*, and never talk to them of our own necessities but of their advantages" (WN, pp. 26–7, our italics).[6] But acting in one's "own interest" need not entail putting one's own interest above another's interest in commerce, which is what acting with self-interest quite fundamentally means then and now. In *Sentiments* Smith often uses "selfish" to clearly demark the narrower meaning of self-interest.

A deeper reading of *Wealth* reveals Smith's qualification of the meaning of "own interest." Appealing to the self-love of the butcher, the brewer, and the baker means "allowing every man to pursue his own interest his own way, *upon the liberal plan of equality, liberty and justice*" (WN, p. 664, our italics). If that qualification is unpersuasive, he elaborates later when discussing competition: "Every man, *as long as he does not violate the laws of justice*, is left perfectly free to pursue his own interest his own way, and to bring both his industry and capital into competition with those of any other man, or order of men" (WN, p. 687, our italics). As part of acting in one's own interest, we, like the political theorist Ryan Hanley, read Adam Smith as having a commitment to the equality and dignity of all

---

[4] F. A. Hayek (1945) is an exception; the results from market experiments demonstrate Hayek's interpretation of the role of prices in coordinating economic activity. See Vernon Smith (1982).

[5] Tellingly, book 5 in volume 2 of *Wealth* is the first and last time Smith uses the word "self-interest," and then it is to describe "the industry and zeal of the inferior clergy [in Rome]" (p. 789).

[6] In the same paragraph, preparing us for this quotation, we find an echo from *Sentiments*: "In civilized society he (man) stands at all times in need of the cooperation and assistance of great multitudes, while his whole life is scarce sufficient to gain the friendship of a few persons . . . and it is in vain for him to expect it from their benevolence only" (WN, p. 26).

people.[7] Thus, if the modern economist espouses naked self-interest as the foundation for economic decision-making, she does so incompatibly with the founder of the discipline and more generally with the genius of the Scottish Enlightenment. There are moral rules, just rules, that govern our conduct in impersonal markets.

Smith's friend David Hume likewise circumscribes market behavior within rules when he distinguishes interested commerce (what the economic historian Douglass North calls impersonal or market exchange) from disinterested commerce (what North calls personal or social exchange).[8] Samuel Johnson's *A Dictionary of the English Language*, published in 1755, offers four meanings for *interest* in eighteenth-century usage; while the first meaning of *interest* is "concern, advantage, good," the fourth meaning, which applies here, is "regard to private profit."[9] Hume recognizes that promises were invented for interested commerce to "bind ourselves to the performance of any action" (1740, p. 335). While with disinterested commerce we "may still do services to such person as I love, and am more particularly acquainted with, without any prospect of advantage; and they may make me a return in the same manner, without any view but that of recompensing my past services," the same is not true of our impersonal intercourses. We precisely engage in mutually benefiting and impersonal exchange for the distinct prospect of a private profit, and we voluntarily do so only with promises, "the sanction of interested commerce of mankind" (p. 335).

Smith's first and lesser known work *Sentiments* is a deep and insightful study in disinterested commerce that creates human social betterment and also explains the origin of justice. In *Wealth* we learn that the pursuit of private benefit, under the governing rules of justice, is what enables specialization and wealth creation for human economic betterment. Smith sees these two forms of human betterment as the result of gradual socioeconomic development. In this our project dovetails with Deirdre McCloskey's grander narrative in *Bourgeois Equality* (2016, pp. 203–4):

Smith had two invisible hands, two outcomes of (in his uncharacteristically clumsy phrase) "the obvious and simple system of natural liberty." One was the invisible hand of the marketplace, whose effects are occasionally noted in [*Wealth*]. For example, to mention Smith's most original economic contribution, the marketplace in labor equalizes the wage-plus-conditions in Scotland with those in England, within social and legal limits, because people move from one place to

---

[7] See Ryan Hanley (2009) and also Samuel Fleischacker (2004).
[8] Douglass North (1990, 2005).   [9] Samuel Johnson (1755).

the other until it is so, as though directed by an invisible hand. Likewise the invisible hand gently pushes people out of their solipsistic cocoons to consider what is valued in trade by other people. "Every individual . . . neither intends to promote the public interest, nor knows how much he is promoting it." . . .

[The other was the invisible hand of the impartial spectator,] the social one as against the economic. We become polite members of our society by interacting on the social stage – note the word, "inter-acting." Smith in [*Sentiments*] did not believe, as his teacher Hutcheson did, that in achieving social peace and prosperity we can depend on natural benevolence. . . . Nor did he believe, as many economists still understand him to do, in a fuzzy version of Mandeville's hardwired opposite of cooperation, a macho competiveness, greed is good.

Against inherited niceness or nastiness, as I have noted, Smith repeatedly emphasized in [*Sentiments*], as he did also in [*Wealth*], that during their lives people change, shaped by society and, it may be, by their own impartial spectator. In the phrase appropriate to a time of apprenticeships, people were "brought up to a trade."

Smith's aim in *Sentiments* is to understand how and why personal forms of other-regarding or moral action emerge and are sustained in our more intimate groupings and constitute the substance of human sociality. It is a work in psychology and economics applied to social interaction well before either had been established as independent fields of inquiry. Smith was yet to write *Wealth*, often identified with the founding of economics, but it would take another 125 years for psychology to be founded as separate and distinct from philosophy. To understand *Sentiments* we must learn the meaning conveyed in the eighteenth-century words and concepts Smith used, thereby enabling us to learn to think in his language, important in engaging the substance of his thought, the topic of Chapter 2.

SENTIMENTS PREDICTS WHERE THE NEOCLASSICAL MODEL FAILS

Neoclassical economics, with its firm methodological foundations in utility maximization ("Max-U"), received unexpectedly strong evidential support from the study of experimental markets beginning in the 1960s.[10] In these experiments participants are identified as either buyers or sellers in a series of trading periods. Buyers are assigned private values for units of the item they could buy or attempt to buy in each trading period. Multiple units have declining values reflecting diminishing marginal utility – the key

---

[10] So abbreviated and further discussed by Deirdre McCloskey (2006). The original experiments are reported in Vernon Smith (1962); see Douglas Davis and Charles Holt (1993) for a summary of the many subsequent such experiments; for a discussion of why the results were "surprising," see Vernon Smith (2008a, pp. 193–197).

contribution of the neoclassical marginal revolution.[11] A buyer earns a profit on each unit purchased from a seller equal to the difference between the value to the buyer and the price paid for the item. Sellers are assigned units with values representing their cost of supplying units to the market. Sellers' profits are the difference between selling price and personal cost. Hence, buyers are motivated to buy at low prices, and sellers to sell at high prices. Max-U is achieved simultaneously for all buyers and sellers at the competitive market clearing price where the quantity sellers could profitably sell equaled the quantity buyers could profitably buy.

Trading in the experimental market is organized using the two-sided "double auction" procedure common in early commodity and securities market trading. Buyers announce bids to buy, sellers announce asks to sell, with contracts effected either by a buyer accepting the lowest ask price, or a seller accepting the highest bid price. From the first experiments down to the present day, these markets converge quite rapidly and robustly to the competitive equilibrium price under repetitions across time. This victory for the application of Max-U theory to markets is somewhat marred, however, in that Jevons believed that such results only obtain if all participants in the market have complete and perfect information on supply and demand and therefore the clearing price. But in the experiments, each buyer and seller possess only private decentralized information on the small fragment of the total supply and demand that defined their part of the overall market. Consequently, the experimental results not only confirm the efficacy of Max-U to markets but under far weaker conditions than Jevons, and the generations of economists that followed him, thought necessary.

Jevons and neoclassical economists erred in thinking that the participants in markets needed the same information that Max-U theorists needed to compute an equilibrium. In effect they impose their mental model of market outcomes on the behavior of the market participants. Adam Smith did not make this error in either *Sentiments* or *Wealth*. His modeling perspective is first that of the actor, her feelings, reactions and

---

[11] William Stanley Jevons (1862, 1871) was particularly influential in the English-speaking world in propagating the Max-U calculus of supply and demand theory. From Richard Howey (1989), we learn that in 1862 Jevons sent his paper "Notice of a General Mathematical Theory of Political Economy" to the British Association for the Advancement of Science; though the paper was read, only a short abstract was published in the proceedings. But the event clearly established Jevons's priority for the first articulation of the marginal utility and general equilibrium theories that became part of the 1870s neoclassical revolution. Serendipitously, Smith (1962) published experimental tests of supply-and-demand theory on the centenary year of Jevons's contribution.

interactions, and second the consequences for society or economy of that perspective.

Max-U in the neoclassical vision is proffered not only as a theory of markets but as the modeling foundation for all human decision-making. The model fails decisively to predict the extent of cooperation in the study of two-person interactive games, including ultimatum and trust games, beginning in the 1980s and popular in laboratory experiments ever since the 1990s.[12] *Sentiments* reconciles the discordant results between market and two-person interactive experiments, and provides fresh insight into the observed personal social conduct in the two-person games. Smith was not a utilitarian in the neoclassical sense of Max-U. (In what follows we use "utilitarian" in the sense of pertaining to utility, not in the sense of pertaining to the philosophical doctrine of utilitarianism.) For Smith "self-love" is necessarily at the core of our being, but in the responsible individual's prudent maturation, conduct is shaped by learnt other-regarding rules of social order originating in our capacity for mutual sympathetic fellow-feeling.

Behavioral and experimental economists offered other ways of reconciling the predictive failures of Max-U in the form of "social preference" and "reciprocity" theories.[13] Since neither of these ex post resolutions are appropriate for characterizing Smith's model, *Sentiments* deserves our careful attention if we are to understand why and how modern thinking turned away from the classical tradition, ill-preparing us for the disruptive discoveries in two-person interactive games. It is an error common to the modern mind to suppose that any insightful earlier conceptual breakthrough in understanding must surely have been integrated into the subsequent literature. Indeed many of the insights in *Sentiments* were subsequently discovered, and the psychology of sentiment has been independently reevaluated.[14] But we will show that the model in *Sentiments* – the thought framework – is distinctive and relevant for a twenty-first-century social science of human beings.

MODELING HUMAN ACTION

A good place to start in getting a grasp on Smith's model and manner of thinking is to examine his opening sentence: "How selfish soever man may

[12] For summaries, see Colin Camerer (2003, chapters 1, 2) and Smith (2008b, chapters 10, 11, 12).

[13] See, e.g., Armin Falk, Ernst Fehr, and Urs Fischbacher (2008) and Kevin McCabe, Mary Rigdon, and Vernon Smith (2003).

[14] See, e.g., Daniel Kahneman and Cass Sunstein (2005).

be supposed, there are evidently some principles in his nature, which interest him in the fortune of others, and render their happiness necessary to him, though he derives nothing from it except the pleasure of seeing it" (TMS, First.I.I., p. 3).[15] For economists trained in the neoclassical utilitarian tradition and the psychologists influenced by it, "pleasure" automatically implies utility, while a concern for the fortune (and happiness) of others is about altruism. Smith is neither a utilitarian in the modern sense, nor is he writing here about altruism. The word *altruism* did not enter the English language for another century.[16] Smith's conception of "pleasure" refers to the feeling of something good, not the mere ordinal ranking of alternatives meant by modern utility maximization. In Smith's model, we feel good about "mutual sympathy," which is being in a harmonious or resonant relationship with others. Smith's relationship involves what the modern reader would call "mutual empathy" although the word *empathy* would not enter English for another 150 years. Empathy involves a capacity to comprehend by your imagination what you would feel if you were in another person's situation. But Smith's use of "fellow feeling" is especially self-evident in conveying the meaning we want to capture, and we will use his phrase. Here is a modern translation of the opening sentence that draws on explanations as we see them subsequently developed in *Sentiments*: However selfish we assume people to be, our capacity for mutual fellow feeling guides us in learning context-dependent rules of conduct that enable us to live in harmony with others.

Smith's most basic axiom in *Sentiments* is the Stoic principle of self-love, that each person is best qualified to be concerned with, and to manage, his own care (TMS, Second.II.II, p. 119; Seventh.II.II, p. 402; Seventh.II.III, p. 445). This axiom, known as non-satiated preferences in modern choice theory, did not lead Smith to base individual actions on some version of utility maximization. How did Smith avoid the seemingly obvious neoclassical implication of non-satiation à la Jeremy Bentham, William Stanley Jevons, Paul Samuelson, and modern game theory? Why did he not model human decisions as choosing actions to maximize utility? From our study of *Sentiments* we infer that in Smith's vision, common knowledge of self-love is what enables each person to judge from the context whether, and for

---

[15] Our notation for citing TMS is "Part.Section.Chapter, p. page(s)," for the Part, Section, and Chapters explicitly numbered in the text. Sections or chapters that are implied but not explicitly numbered as such in TMS are denoted in parentheses, e.g. Third.(I).VI, p. 250.

[16] To be precise, *altruism* entered the English language in 1852. Thomas Dixon (2008) offers a brilliant detailed study of how the word entered the English lexicon and how the concept has been evolving ever since.

whom, an action is beneficial or hurtful. An action is beneficial if it awards more of a resource (money, goods, or services) to another, and an action is hurtful if it provides less of a resource for another. The context of an action is essential because the resulting outcomes can only acquire meaning relative to the available decision alternatives defined by the context. For a person who is concerned only with maximizing her own reward, information concerning what benefits or hurts others is entirely irrelevant, and the context of an action has no significance as a signal sent by the decision-maker or to be read by other persons like themselves. In contrast, Smith's idea is that each of us, tacitly knowing that everyone strictly prefers more, and strictly dis-prefers less, is in a position thereby to judge the beneficial or hurtful intent of a person's action relative to alternatives that might be chosen. Consequently, actions are messages, part of a conversation, to be read as signals, responded to as signals, and in Smith such exchanges constitute the foundations of human sociability.

In this model, context or circumstances is a core feature of interactive decisions. Retrospectively, this is highly significant because in the 1980s and 1990s when experimental economists and cognitive psychologists observed widespread and replicable deviations from self-interested choices in two-person games like the ultimatum game, their explorations designed to find out why these had occurred soon established that context mattered greatly.[17] Indeed, varying context seems to have a far bigger and more diverse impact on observed decisions than varying payoff levels. These results were consistent with the model in *Sentiments*, but Smith's framework was not part of our mode of thinking. The mechanism in *Sentiments* that causes context to matter, that tempers and modifies the decision not to blindly follow one's own utility maximization, is social. Each person adaptively learns to respond in ways that "humble the arrogance of his self-love, and bring it down to something which other men can go along with" (TMS, Second.II.II, p. 120). Social maturation involves learning to follow rules that satisfy fitness norms or conventions that control the inconsiderate pursuit of one's self-interest. Conducting one's self in an other-regarding manner is the result of exerting the "self-command" necessary to build, service, and maintain social capital. Such learning is internalized as ethical, self-governing action.

Smith's socializing uses the common knowledge that everyone is self-loving to judge the propriety of conduct that is socially fit, and thereby

---

[17] For example, Smith's (2008b) chapter 10 is entitled "The Effect of Context on Behavior," but the theme derives from experimental findings not from theory and not from *Sentiments*.

pursuing his own interest. For Smith there is no unresolved observed contradiction between people pursuing their own interest, say in money, and choosing actions that are other-regarding. One's own interest includes living harmoniously and ethically with others, and choosing socially fit actions. *Sentiments* provides a framework that well prepares us to examine and study context, to understand social process, and that directs us away from a focus only on outcomes and their payoffs whose social meaning can only be derived from the context. Although the intellectual route has been much different, such a focus on the consequences of actions describes much of the recent history of piecemeal learning in experimental economics. *Sentiments*, we contend, integrates our modern relearning into a consistent whole. Smith's model is consistent with the modern findings in experimental economics and does not require modification in the light of evidence. *Sentiments* does, however, require a contemporary interpretation in its applications to modern findings.

The core message we develop from *Sentiments* is that humans are other-regarding in their personal interactions because we learn to follow rules of conduct that permit us to live in the company of our fellow human beings.[18] Such rules are situation-sensitive to the effect of our actions on the benefits and hurts of others, as well as to our own self. The human capacity for fellow feeling, in particular for mutual fellow feeling, is the primary mechanism through which we are socialized creatures. Without such innate capabilities, honed as practiced skills, there would be no human sociality in Smith's world. We are not other-regarding because we reductively prefer to be social, but through human empathy we come, as Robert Burns puts it, to "see oursels as ithers see us." In plain and unmistakably clear language Smith says: "Though it may be true ... that every individual, in his own breast, naturally prefers himself to all mankind, yet he dares not look mankind in the face, and avow that he acts according to this principle" (TMS, Second.II.II, p.120).

Here is the logic of Smith's system in *Sentiments*, as we interpret, develop, and apply it in this book: People have common knowledge that all are self-interested and are locally non-satiated – more is always better, less is always worse from any reference state. Otherwise, we cannot be socially competent rule-followers because we cannot be sensitive to who benefits or who is hurt by our actions, and to properly balance concern for

---

[18] Smith's model allows for diverse cultural adaptations since how others see us is subject to cultural variation even within Western European societies and their global extension, but this theme is beyond the scope of systematic exploration in this work.

ourselves and concern for others. Our rule-following judgments are highly
context dependent. The situation, and the pattern of benefits or hurts,
together effect the action chosen. What enables such sociability is our
capacity for mutual fellow-feeling; we cannot reach maturity without
being shaped to a highly variable extent by our experience of others and
the mark they leave on our development. Our desire for praise and
praiseworthiness, and to avoid blame and blameworthiness emerges from
this maturation. Smith's model leads to key propositions on intentional
acts of beneficence and injustice that invoke corresponding thoughts and
feelings of gratitude and resentment.

HUME, SMITH, AND UTILITARIANISM

In an important passage, Smith cites Hume's appeal to utility (usefulness)
as a principal cause of human sentiments. Smith, however, disavows utility
as the source of conscious individual motivation, though it may have the
effect of utilitarian efficiency (TMS, Fourth.(I).II, pp. 270–71, our italics):

> The same ingenious and agreeable author [David Hume] who first explained why
> utility pleases, has been so struck with this view of things, as to resolve our whole
> approbation of virtue into a perception of this species of beauty which results from
> the appearance of utility. No qualities of the mind he observes, are approved of as
> virtuous, but such as are useful or agreeable either to the person himself or to
> others; and no qualities are disapproved of as vicious but such as have a contrary
> tendency. And Nature, indeed, seems to have so happily adjusted our sentiments of
> approbation and disapprobation, to the conveniency both of the individual and of
> the society, that after the strictest examination it will be found, I believe, that this is
> universally the case.[19] *But still I [Adam Smith] affirm, that it is not the view of this*
> *utility or hurtfulness which is either the first or principal source of our approbation*
> *and disapprobation.* These sentiments are no doubt enhanced and enlivened by the
> perception of the beauty or deformity which results from this utility or hurtfulness.
> But still, I say, they are originally and essentially different from this perception.

Smith's explanation of conduct is always rooted in mutual fellow feeling.
Only after we understand how individuals experience each other should we
enquire after its efficacy for the individual and society. Hume was close to
the neoclassical utilitarian tradition; Smith was not. The philosopher

---

[19] Smith does not disagree with Hume, that human action will be efficient, will maximize
utilitarian welfare, but that does not explain why people choose the actions they do. Smith
wants carefully to distinguish the actions that people take based on how they see and
experience the world, from the larger ends their actions may achieve. It is a version of the
invisible hand metaphor. People achieve ecologically rational ends not part of their
intentions or prevision.

Samuel Alexander's clear-eyed but forgotten, early twentieth-century summary states what separated Hume and Smith, and that which we seek to develop in this book (1933, p. 249, our italics):

Like the utilitarians who came after him, ... [Hume] looked ultimately to the effects of action in the way of giving pleasure or pain. Adam Smith, with a surer eye, declared the sympathy which determines our approbation or disapprobation, not so much to be directed towards the effects of actions as to the impulses from which the action proceeds. *He considered our actions in their origin rather than in their outcome.*

THE CIVIL ORDER OF PROPERTY EVOLVED FROM THE SOCIAL ORDER OF PROPRIETY

Property in its modern use means ownership, or something that carries with it a right to exclude and have unrivaled access to for one's own individual or social purposes. More fundamentally "ownership" is derived from expectations established by consent. We commonly think of property as having its origin in the civil order of government. Strong cultural traditions, including trade, however, are far older than nations, and we must expect property to have ancient origins in social rules like "thou shalt not steal, bear false witness, or covet the possessions of thy neighbor." Stealing and lying are hurtful to others, and coveting corrupts our moral capacity for self-command. The origins of the social order of propriety were in human sentiment, and the practiced norms of the social order naturally underpinned the rules of property.

Concerning the origins of property, it is informative that in the century before Smith wrote, scholars used the words *propriety* and *property* interchangeably. *Propriety* and *property* are both descendants of the Anglo-Norman *propreté*, the Old French *propriété*, and the Latin *proprietas*. *Proprietas* itself is derivative of the ancient adverb *proprie*, meaning "exclusively, particularly, peculiarly, and properly."[20] Whereas John Locke used *propriety* in the early version of *Two Treatises of Government*, in many instances he changes to the use of *property* in later revisions.[21] In *Sentiments* the rules that apply to human conduct govern the propriety

---

[20] Prior to the time of Sir Edward Coke, English lawyers used *proprietas, propreté*, and *property* interchangeably in disputes about chattels. For detailed discussion and references, see Bart Wilson (2017).
[21] See Stephen Buckle (1991, pp. 172–73).

of individual actions (Part First of *Sentiments* is entitled "Of the Propriety of Action"), and conduct is expressed in actions governed by consensus. Smith always refers explicitly to the propriety or impropriety of intentional action. The laws of justice, including property, in the civil order of government evolve directly from the conventions governing the propriety of everyday action. The impropriety of hurtful actions is met with resentment, and the resentment brings measured punishment responses in retaliation: "As the greater and more irreparable the evil that is done, the resentment of the sufferer runs naturally the higher" (TMS, Second.II.II, p. 121).

Hence, in the civil order, justice is attained through sanctions aimed at punishing the perpetrator, and thereby avenging the natural resentment of the victim, wherever the laws of justice are breached.[22] Prevent or avenge intentionally hurtful acts of injustice, and you achieve justice. For Smith the "laws of justice" are negative. They specify actions that are unjust and subject to resentful retaliation if infractions occur. People have wide liberty to take any action that is not unjust. Imagine society as a large playing field within which people are free to pursue their own aspirations, careers, and business plans as they choose but governed always by rules that prohibit and recompense foul play. Any outcome of action – mediocrity, success, failure, riches, admiration – is acceptable so long as no fouls are committed. The individual is free to excel, as in a race, but not to cheat or lie or jostle others in the race.

PROPERTY, THE PROPENSITY TO EXCHANGE, AND WEALTH CREATION

Smith develops the foundation for understanding economic development in *Sentiments*. Property – the universal human custom of mutually recognizing what is mine and thine – is necessary but not sufficient, and in *Wealth* he adds a key axiom: The human "propensity to truck, barter and exchange." Just as disinterested commerce underlies the social order, Smith's axiom is simply an extension of human sociability to interested

---

[22] Note that the punishment response to acts of injustice is not utilitarian, distinguishing Smith's jurisprudence from modern law and behavioral law and economics (Fabrizio Simon 2016). As in Alexander, quoted above, the origin of the hurtful act was an intentional violation of fair play; the resentment of the victim (the origin of what offends) must be recompensed. Smith says it is the resentment and the impulse to punish in return that is addressed by the rules we follow; relationships are about not committing fouls, achieving justice by fair play.

commerce; it is "commerce" all the way up, from neighborly social exchange to the extended order of impersonal markets.[23]

In the neoclassical tradition, the modern economic model begins with dispersed information on preferences, resources, and technology, then applies Max-U to deduce prices and allocations. In *Wealth* the primitives are not tastes, costs, and technology, but the observed human propensity to trade, a propensity founded on two people improving their own non-satiated condition by exchanging one thing for another in but another social and ethical interaction. An immediate consequence of trading is new information – prices that people experience, observe, or learn about through gossip. Price information allows individuals to make comparisons between what is and what might be. A price for corn and for hogs allows the individual producer, based on his local circumstances, to ask if he can benefit by producing more hogs and less corn. In principle, as in modern preference theory based on perfect complete-ordering information, he could make any such comparison without prices, but it would be cognitively far more complex without prices to ease the mental calculus of comparison. Do I get more corn by growing it or through pig-corn exchange, selling pigs and buying corn? The formation of prices enables him better to discover preferences and costs through experience, and to seek information that is relevant for decision and innovation. Across markets and nationally, such discovery leads to labor specialization – a fundamental source of wealth creation. Although people intend their own benefit, the laws of justice channel their actions to enable others and the nation to prosper.[24]

In both *Sentiments* and *Wealth* action is driven by discovery in a world of uncertainty and consequences that are unknown until attempted: through repeat social interactions and trade, people adapt their responses to better themselves as well as others through gains from exchange. Experimental economists observe such a process every time we conduct

---

[23] If you doubt the claim, consider the breadth of meanings of *commerce* listed in the dictionary, which in the Oxford English Dictionary include: (1a) exchange between men of the products of nature or art, buying and selling together; (2a) intercourse in the affairs of life, dealings; (2c) intercourse or converse with God, with spirits, passions, thoughts, etc.; and (3) intercourse of the sexes; *esp.* in a bad sense [which is proper British for "sex"].

[24] Bernard Mandeville, who irreverently founded economic decision-making on the vice of self-love in *The Fable of the Bees*, and whose satirical, tongue-in-cheek humor scandalized Smith, nevertheless still concluded: "So Vice is beneficial found, / When it is by Justice lopt and bound" (1705).

a market experiment.[25] What was already articulated in Smith's two books could be summarized elegantly by Hayek over two centuries later: "Rules alone can unite an extended order.... Neither all ends pursued, nor all means used, are known or need be known to anybody, in order for them to be taken account of within a spontaneous order. Such an order forms of itself" (1988, pp. 19–20).

References

Alexander, Samuel. 1968 [1933]. *Beauty and Other Forms of Value*. New York: Thomas Y. Crowell Company.

Buckle, Stephen. 1991. *Natural Law and the Theory of Property: Grotius to Hume*. New York: Oxford University Press.

Camerer, Colin F. 2003. *Behavioral Game Theory: Experiments in Strategic Interaction*. Princeton, NJ: Princeton University Press.

Davis, Douglas D. and Charles A. Holt. 1993. *Experimental Economics*. Princeton, NJ: Princeton University Press.

Dixon, Thomas. 2008. *The Invention of Altruism: Making Moral Meanings in Victorian Britain*. Oxford: Oxford University Press.

Falk, Armin, Ernst Fehr, Urs Fischbacher. 2008. "Testing Theories of Fairness – Intentions Matter," *Games and Economic Behavior* 62(1): 287–303.

Fleischacker, Samuel. 2004. *On Adam Smith's "Wealth of Nations": A Philosophical Companion*. Princeton, NJ: Princeton University Press.

Hanley, Ryan Patrick. 2009. *Adam Smith and the Character of Virtue*. New York: Cambridge University Press.

Hayek, F. A. 1945. "The Use of Knowledge in Society," *American Economic Review* 35 (4): 519–530.

Hayek, F. A. 1988. *The Fatal Conceit: The Errors of Socialism*. Chicago: University of Chicago Press.

Howey, Richard S. 1989. *The Rise of the Marginal Utility School, 1870–1889*. New York: Columbia University Press.

Hume, David. 2000 [1740]. *A Treatise of Human Nature*, David Fate Norton and Mary J. Norton (eds.). New York: Oxford University Press.

Jaworski, Taylor, Vernon L. Smith, and Bart J. Wilson. 2010. "Discovering Economics in the Classroom with Experimental Economics and the Scottish Enlightenment," *International Review of Economics Education* 9(2): 10–33.

Jevons, William Stanley. 1862. "Notice of a General Mathematical Theory of Political Economy," Abstract of paper read to the British Association for the Advancement of Science.

Jevons, William Stanley. 1888 [1871]. *The Theory of Political Economy*, 3rd edition. London: Macmillan.

Johnson, Samuel. 2005 [1755]. *A Dictionary of the English Language*. CD-ROM. Oakland, CA: Octavo.

---

[25] See, e.g., Taylor Jaworski, Vernon Smith, and Bart Wilson (2010).

Kahneman, Daniel and Cass R. Sunstein. 2005. "Cognitive Psychology of Moral Intuitions," in *Neurobiology of Human Values*, Jean-Pierre Changeux, Antonio R. Damasio, Wolf Singer, and Yves Christen (eds.) Berlin-Heidelberg: Springer Verlag, 91–105.

Locke, John. 1967 [1690]. *Two Treatises of Government*. Cambridge: Cambridge University Press.

Mandeville, Bernard. 1989 [1705]. *The Fable of the Bees: Or Private Vices, Publick Benefits*. New York: Penguin Classics.

McCabe, Kevin, Mary L. Rigdon, and Vernon L. Smith. 2003. "Positive Reciprocity and Intentions in Trust Games," *Journal of Economic Behavior and Organization* 52(2): 267–75.

McCloskey, Deirdre N. 2006. *The Bourgeois Virtues: Ethics for an Age of Commerce*. Chicago: University of Chicago Press.

McCloskey, Deirdre N. 2016. *Bourgeois Equality: How Ideas, Not Capital or Institutions, Enriched the World*. Chicago: University of Chicago Press.

Montes, Leonidas. 2003. "Das Adam Smith Problem: Its Origins, the Stages of the Current Debate, and One Implication for our Understanding of Sympathy," *Journal of the History of Economic Thought* 25 (1): 63–90.

Montes, Leonidas. 2004. *Adam Smith in Context A Critical Reassessment of Some Central Components of His Thought*. London: Palgraves Macmillan.

North, Douglass C. 1990. *Institutions, Institutional Change, and Economic Performance*. Cambridge: Cambridge University Press.

North, Douglass C. 2005. *Understanding the Process of Economic Change*. Princeton, NJ: Princeton University Press.

Piketty, Thomas. 2014. *Capital in the Twenty-First Century*. Cambridge, MA: Harvard University Press.

Simon, Fabrizio. 2016. "Adam Smith and the Law," in *The Oxford Handbook of Adam Smith*. Christopher J. Berry, Maria Pia Paganelli, and Craig Smith (eds.). New York: Oxford University Press.

Smith, Adam. 1853 [1759]. *The Theory of Moral Sentiments; or, An Essay towards an Analysis of the Principles by which Men naturally judge concerning the Conduct and Character, first of their Neighbours, and afterwards of themselves. To which is added, A Dissertation on the Origins of Languages. New Edition. With a biographical and critical Memoir of the Author, by Dugald Stewart.* London: Henry G. Bohn. Available online and in electronic formats at http://oll.libertyfund .org/titles/2620.

Smith, Adam. 1981 [1776]. *An Inquiry into the Nature and Causes of the Wealth of Nations. Vol. I & II.* Indianapolis: Liberty Fund.

Smith, Adam. 1976 [1790]. *The Theory of Moral Sentiments*. London: A.Millar. Liberty Fund edition authorized by Oxford University Press. Available online at http:// www.econlib.org/library/Smith/smMS0.html.

Smith, Vernon L. 1962. "An Experimental Study of Competitive Market Behavior," *Journal of Political Economy* 70(2): 111–37.

Smith, Vernon L. 1982. "Markets as Economizers of Information: Experimental Examination of the 'Hayek Hypothesis,'" *Economic Inquiry* 20(2): 165–79.

Smith, Vernon L. 2008a. *Discovery – A Memoir*. Bloomington, IN: AuthorHouse.

Smith, Vernon L. 2008b. *Rationality in Economics Constructionist and Ecological Forms.* New York: Cambridge University Press.

Smith, Vernon L. and Bart J. Wilson. 2014. "Fair and Impartial Spectators in Experimental Economic Behavior," *Review of Behavioral Economics* 1(1–2): 1–26.

Viner, Jacob. 1991. *Essays on the Intellectual History of Economics.* Princeton, NJ: Princeton University Press.

Wilson, Bart J. 2017. "The Meaning of Property in Things," Available at SSRN: https://ssrn.com/abstract=2867734 or http://dx.doi.org/10.2139/ssrn.2867734.

2

Words and Meaning in Adam Smith's World

The constant evolution of language poses a twofold challenge for reading 250-year-old texts. Some words may have fallen out of general use today, and so when putting Adam Smith's ideas into our own words, we face the challenge of finding modern substitutes that may not be equivalent. Even if a word consistently stays in use, meanings drift and pose the danger of reading twenty-first-century meaning into the same eighteenth-century word. A little amateur-as-one-who-loves-words philology is valuable then in enabling modern readers to discern Smith's way of thinking about and modeling the social world.

PASSIONS, EMOTIONS, SENTIMENTS, AND AFFECTIONS

Three hundred years ago English-language authors used the words *passions, sentiments*, and *affections* about as much as they do now, which is to say, not very much. But for the latter half of the eighteenth century, the use of these three words spiked, appearing seven to nine times more frequently from 1750–1825 than in either 1700 or 2008 (see Figure 2.1). By the mid-1850s their use was well on the wane, and by 1920 the indiscriminating word *emotions* had supplanted all of them to become the dominant psychological category for the feeling caused by the situation that you find yourself in. Today we rarely talk about people's passions, sentiments, and affections in daily conversations. People's emotions, though, we talk about a great deal.

To understand Smith's *Theory of Moral Sentiments* we must take care not to treat our twenty-first-century meaning of emotion as a catchall substitute for his numerous references to passions, affections, and sentiments. To understand Smith's thinking, we need to be sensitive to his precise diction. It is true, as the philosopher Amy Schmitter notes, that

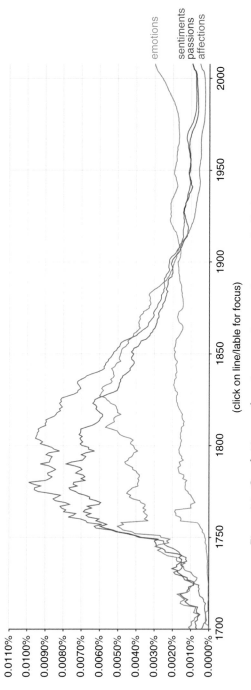

Figure 2.1. Google Ngram of *passions*, *emotions*, *sentiments*, and *affections*, 1700–2008
Source: Google Books Ngram Viewer (http://books.google.com/ngrams)

"Smith sometimes groups 'sentiment' with 'passions,' 'affections,' or 'feelings,'" but his book is not entitled *The Theory of Moral Passions, Affections, or Feelings* (Schmitter 2014, p. 206).[1] His book is about sentiments, and sentiments of a particular kind, namely the moral ones.[2] While he uses *emotions* some eighty times in *Sentiments*, including in the opening paragraph's second sentence, *sentiments* dwarfs it in comparison with 346 uses, or roughly once a page.

Sentiments, as the synonym discriminator Charles John Smith explains, "are things of the heart and mind" (1894, p. 595). Emotions in modern parlance may be of the heart, but they certainly are not of the mind. Emotions in the twentieth and twenty-first centuries are physiological, non-cognitive, involuntary feelings, which stand in dichotomous contrast to cognitive thoughts of the mind. We have emotions and an intellect, but the two do not overlap, and nothing really falls in between.[3] The corresponding poles in the eighteenth century were the passions and reason, but unlike the modern divide, Smith and his contemporaries bridged the two with sentiments and affections.[4] If intellect and reason are about thinking, and emotions and passions about feeling, sentiments and affections are about both thinking and feeling.[5] *The Theory of Moral Sentiments* explains the social world by combining moral feeling and moral thinking.

While Lord Kames specifies a sentiment as "every thought prompted by passion," Smith never outright defines the term (Kames 1762, p. 311). He leaves the exercise to the reader, which requires quite a little work for those of us unfamiliar with eighteenth-century diction and moral philosophy. After his famous opening sentence to the book, Smith continues (TMS, First.I.I, p. 3, our italics):

Of this kind is pity or compassion, the *emotion* which we *feel* for the misery of others, when we either see it, or are made to conceive it in a very lively manner. That we often derive sorrow from the sorrow of others, is a matter of fact too

---

[1] See, e.g., TMS (First.I.III, pp. 14–18).
[2] Another class of sentiments for Smith would be the philosophical/scientific sentiments of wonder, surprise, and admiration, which he uses to explain the history of astronomy. See Smith (1795).
[3] But see Antonio Damasio's 2005 book, *Descartes' Error*, which mounts an effort to change that mind set. Damasio returns to Smith's feelings-thinking integration theme, but as we have noted many times in this book, without reference to Smith, whose first book influenced neither contemporary psychology nor economics.
[4] Thomas Dixon (2003).
[5] The *Collins Cobuild English Language Dictionary*, known for its definitions via the use of the word in simple sentences, defines *sentiment* as, "A sentiment that people have is an attitude which is based on their thoughts and feelings."

obvious to require any instances to prove it; for this *sentiment*, like all the other original *passions* of human nature, is by no means confined to the virtuous and humane, though they perhaps may *feel* it with the most exquisite sensibility.

From this we can conclude that pity and compassion are emotions for Smith, and sorrow is a sentiment and like an original passion. On the following page he uses all three terms in the same sentence: "In every *passion* of which the mind of man is susceptible, the *emotions* of the by-stander always correspond to what, by bringing the case home to himself, he imagines should be the *sentiments* of the sufferer" (TMS, First.I.I, p. 5, our italics).

One could dismiss Smith's vocabulary choices as a mere matter of style, or as he would say, the sublime, but our contention is that he chose his words carefully. Smith published a review of Samuel Johnson's dictionary in 1755. "The merit of Mr Johnson's dictionary is so great," he begins with a classic British setup, "that it cannot detract from it to take notice of some defects" (Smith 1755, p. 232). The first defect is that Johnson's dictionary does not delineate the seven distinct senses of the common little word *but*. If a moral philosopher is willing to question a lexicographer and Britain's most distinguished man of letters as not being "sufficiently grammatical," wethinks Smith takes his word choice seriously.[6] Perhaps he did not deliberately choose each instance of *passions, sentiments, affections*, and *emotions* explicitly for the reasons we provide in the paragraphs to follow. Nevertheless, there is an order, we argue, that emerges in Smith's writing and that reflects and reveals his systematizing mind.[7] Nothing invites attention to the workings of that mind more than the ability of his key propositions to organize and enable understanding of the choices people make in the experiments we report in Chapters 8–10.

Consider first a counterfactual case. Why does Smith not switch the words around to say that "in every *sentiment* of which the mind of man is susceptible" and "he imagines should be the *passions* of the sufferer"? Because "the primary idea annexed to the word *passion*," Thomas Cogan explains in his *A Philosophical Treatise on the Passions* from 1800, "is that of *passiveness*, or being impulsively acted upon" (1800, p. 20, our italics). Smith is saying that passions are, as Cogan continues, "feelings to which the mind is subjected, when an object of importance, suddenly and

---

[6] Smith is also not shy to correct John Milton's diction in *Paradise Lost*: "The proper expression should have been *wonder'd*," not admir'd (1795, p. 33, original italics).
[7] The philosopher Eric Schliesser (2017) develops a rich account of Adam Smith's insights as a systems thinker.

imperiously, demands its attention" (p. 20). It is only the feeling part that Smith refers to when he says, "in every passion of which the mind of man is susceptible." The word *sentiments* does not work because our minds are not susceptible to thoughts. Our minds are susceptible to sudden and imperious demands of feeling on its attention. When we bring the case of a sufferer home to himself, however, we consider not only the passion of the sufferer, but the thinking and feeling of why the sufferer suffers, i.e., the sufferer's sentiments. Smith's model of human sociality delineates the mastering control of the feeling of a passion from the thinking and feeling of a sentiment.

Charles Smith also discriminates the meanings of emotion and passion in a way that neatly conforms to Adam Smith's use: "*Emotion* . . . is a strong excitement of feeling," whereas "*passion* . . . denotes the state when any feeling or emotion masters the mind" (1894, p. 429, original emphasis). Adam Smith is being Charles-Smithian precise when he writes about the *excitement* of feeling in the spectator upon observing a *state* of feeling in a sufferer: "Whatever is the *passion* which arises from any object in the person principally concerned, an analogous *emotion* springs up, at the thought of his situation, in the breast of every attentive spectator" (p. 5, our italics). Given the circumstances, we discern a state of feeling in someone, which has the effect of exciting feeling in ourselves. We do not discern an internal feeling in someone, but rather the state of a feeling, which from experience we would call, for example, love or gratitude or resentment. The excitement of feeling is what happens internally; the state of feeling that masters our mind is what others can externally sense from the situation, which importantly includes the physical and contextual manifestations of our internal feeling (knits in the forehead, smile on the face, hand in a fist, etc.).[8]

Such meaningful distinctions between passions, emotions, and sentiments explain why Smith principally refers to love, gratitude, and resentment as both passions and sentiments, but rarely as excited emotions.

- Love is an agreeable; resentment, a disagreeable *passion* (TMS, First.I. II, p. 12, our italics).
- But there are many other *passions* which we share in common with the brutes, such as resentment, natural affection, even gratitude, which do

---

[8] In the trust games we study in Chapters 8, 10, and 12 none of these face-to-face clues are available to allow the participants to read each other's feeling-thinking more precisely. Yet they coordinate well in violation of strictly self-interested independent action implying that a residue of practical knowledge has formed out of past feeling-thinking experiences.

not, upon that account, appear to be so brutal (TMS, First.II.I, p. 34, our italics).

- The *sentiment* which most immediately and directly prompts us to reward, is gratitude; that which most immediately and directly prompts us to punish, is resentment (TMS, Second.I.I, p. 94, our italics).
- The love of our own country seems not to be derived from the love of mankind. The former *sentiment* is altogether independent of the latter (TMS, Sixth.II.II, pp. 336–37, our italics).

When in such a state that love or resentment demand the attention of our minds, Smith says that "we are not half so anxious that our friends should adopt our friendships, as that they should enter into our resentments" (TMS, First.I.II, p. 12). It is not just a strong excitement of feeling that Smith evokes to contrast agreeable and disagreeable feelings, but the feelings to which our minds are subjected when the favors or injuries we have received demand our attention, and consequently the attention that we demand of our friends. The strong power with which resentment impulsively acts upon our minds is part and parcel of Smith's observation about how we expect our friends to respond to our resentment. Even though love may exert a strong power over our minds, we are not half so concerned that our friends respond to it as we are with our resentment. While love and resentment can be both an emotion and a passion, a passion's mastery over our mind more precisely makes Smith's point on the difference between love and resentment.

When Smith refers to love, gratitude, and resentment as sentiments, he means to combine thinking with feeling. Gratitude and resentment are central to Smith's observations on merit and demerit and the objects of moral reward and punishment. For a state of feeling does not prompt us to reward or punish without also prompting thoughts about the actions to be rewarded or punished. The linguist Anna Wierzbicka argues that there are three central components to the meaning of "X felt gratitude" (for Y having done Z): (1) Y did something good for X, (2) Y did not have to do Z, and (3) X wants to think good things about Y because of this (1999, pp. 104–5).[9] Moreover, Wierzbicka adds, when X thinks about (1)–(3), X feels something good. Gratitude is feeling something like all of this because X thought

---

[9] These elements are prominent in interpreting the role of context in enabling people in trust games to read the meaning in each other's actions and coordinate on cooperative outcomes.

something like this. *Thinking is as intricate to the sentiment of gratitude as feeling is.*

Resentment is the opposite sentiment to gratitude, evaluated in the domain of the bad. Replacing "good" with "bad," the three central components of gratitude sound like the core meaning of "*X* felt resentment" (for *Y* having done *Z*): (1) *Y* did something bad to *X*, (2) *Y* did not have to do *Z*, and (3) *X* wants to think bad things about *Y* because of this, and moreover, when *X* thinks about all of this, *X* feels something bad. Wierzbicka explains how the third part of "wanting to think bad [good] things about *Y* because of this" is important to the meaning of the resentment [gratitude]. If *Y* did something bad to me and I know he did not have to do it, I could still plausibly say under some circumstances that I am not resentful. But if I feel bad about what happened and I *want* to think bad things about *Y*, bystanders would not accept my claim that I do not resent *Y* for doing *Z*. They would say that that is what it means to be resentful.

As passions or emotions, gratitude and resentment cannot do the work that Smith needs them to do because he needs something that "most immediately and directly prompt us to reward and to punish" (TMS, Second.I.I, p. 96). Not only do I feel good or bad, and not only do I want to think good or bad things about *Y*, but the sentiments of gratitude and resentment prompt me to actually *do* good things for *Y* or *do* bad things to *Y*. *The thinking of a sentiment is the link between the feeling of a passion or emotion and the actions we are thus prompted to take for* Y *having done* Z.

Affections in the eighteenth century are much like sentiments, reasoned feelings or passion-ful thoughts, but are much more closely connected to classical Christian psychology, which hierarchically orders the soul. Passions are the lower sense appetites, and affections the higher intellectual appetites.[10] Love, for example, can be the base appetite for a mate or the transcendent commitment of one's heart to a savior.

Unlike the modern meaning of feelings of fondness or esteem, Smith uses affections the way his contemporary and the founder of geology James Hutton does, in the sense of a passive state of something being affected: "refraction is an affection of light" (Hutton 1794, p. 280). The first indication comes on the first page of *Sentiments* when Smith connects feeling with the verb *affect*, "As we have no immediate experience of what other men *feel*, we can form no idea of the manner in which they *are affected*, but by conceiving what we ourselves should *feel* in the like situation" (TMS,

---

[10] Dixon (2003).

p. 9, our italics). Note the passiveness of the past participle, of something that has happened to someone. Like any good writer, Smith is judiciously sparing with the passive sense of verbs, except with the verb *affect*, which he uses equally as much passively as actively. As part of its construction, the passive sense of affections implies a cause that happens to someone: "When we judge in this manner of any *affection*, as proportioned or disproportioned to the cause which excites it, it is scarce possible that we should make use of any other rule or canon but the correspondent *affection* in ourselves" (TMS, p. 18, our italics). Whereas a sentiment does not necessarily imply some cause in its network of meaning, nor the passivity of something that has happened *to* someone, an affection implies both and is important to Smith's observations because "philosophers have, as of late years, considered chiefly the tendency of affections, and have given little attention to the relation which they stand in *to the cause which excites them*" (TMS, p. 18, our italics). Whenever Smith refers to an affection, he means to refer to some cause that has excited it.[11] The same is not the case with sentiments.

Combining the active sense of sentiments with the passive sense of affections adds depth to the full quotation from above (TMS, p. 18, our italics):

> When we judge in this manner of any *affection*, as proportioned or disproportioned to the cause which excites it, it is scarce possible that we should make use of any other rule or canon but the correspondent *affection* in ourselves. If, upon bringing the case home to our own breast, we find that the *sentiments* which it gives occasion to, coincide and tally with our own, we necessarily approve of them as proportioned and suitable to their objects; if otherwise, we necessarily disapprove of them, as extravagant and out of proportion.

Part of judging an affection in someone else is judging how we ourselves would feel in the same state of being affected by something. How would a cause that excited someone else correspondingly serve as a cause to excite us? From the context of the situation, we would have to discern both how the other person is affected but also the cause of the affect. Then upon imagining having been similarly affected, we zero in on the sentiments, the thinking and feeling of the other person in this situation, and assess whether they "coincide and tally" with our thinking and feeling. We do not ponder the affection, the knits in the forehead or the smile on the face, as much as we do the sentiments of the other person.

---

[11] Schliesser (2017) provides a detailed account on the importance of triggering objects in his taxonomy of Smith's passions.

Onc aim of our book is to explain how Smith's more elaborate psychological and physiological framework of feeling informs how we think about insights in modern economics. Behavioral economics is an explicit modern attempt to reintegrate feeling into economic models. The goal of behavioral economics, as one of its chief proponents Colin Camerer explains, is "to find parsimonious utility functions, supported by utility psychological intuition, that are general enough to explain many phenomena in one fell swoop, and also make new predictions" (2003, p. 101). In econospeak, a utility function represents someone's preferences as a mapping of bundles of things into a real number. For example, if Evelyn the economist prefers ($40 for herself, $0 for her friend Frank) to ($25, $15) and both are feasible options for the economist to choose, a utility function represents ($40, $0) with a higher number than ($25, $15). Let's call Evelyn's utility function $U_E(\$e, \$f)$, where $\$e$ represents Evelyn's money and $\$f$ Frank's money such that $U_E(\$40, \$0)$ is greater than $U_E(\$25, \$15)$. This makes sense if the economist is only concerned with how much money she takes home.

Suppose, though, that Frank, if he were in the same position to choose, would be concerned that the difference in payoffs is too unequal and that he would feel better if he took less money home and Evelyn took home something greater than zero. How could a behavioral economist augment Evelyn's utility function to make sense of Frank's revealed preference for less money? The behavioral economist would add something to Evelyn's utility function that now makes Frank's utility function represent ($15 for Evelyn, $25 for Frank) with a higher number than ($0, $40). Let's call that added something Frank's inequality aversion function, or $I_F(\$e, \$f) > 0$, so that Frank's utility function would be $U_F(\$e, \$f) = U_E(\$e, \$f) + I_F(\$e, \$f)$. This preference for more equality over less, as the behavioral economist would call it, rationalizes why the friend does not strictly prefer more money to less. Our question is whether augmenting a utility function, parsimoniously or not, explains the friend's choice, or merely assumes that which is to be explained. We argue the latter and instead show how Smith's insights on moral sentiments, and how to model human social relationships, explain and generate testable predictions for why people do what they do.

SYMPATHY

The concept of sympathy is ancient and has been used to explain phenomena in such diverse settings as physiology, cosmology, and psychology.

Aristotle uses sympathy to explain the animalistic urge to urinate together.[12] In less androcentric times, he could have used the tendency for menstrual cycles to synchronize among women who live together. Plotinus describes the movements of the heavenly bodies and the events on Earth as moving in sympathy.[13] Following Hume, Smith begins his treatise on moral psychology with the two chapters on sympathy.

The philosopher Eric Schliesser astutely identifies five features common to all of the uses of sympathy throughout the ages (2015, pp. 7, 9):

- Sympathy explains action at a distance.
- Sympathy occurs among things that are alike.
- The cause of sympathy is invisible.
- The effect of sympathy can be instantaneous.
- Sympathy is bidirectional.

All five features are present in sympathy in *The Theory of Moral Sentiments*, which is one of the few key terms that Smith explicitly defines: "Sympathy, though its meaning was, perhaps, originally the same, may now, however, without much impropriety, be made use of to denote our fellow-feeling with any passion whatever" (TMS, First.I.I, p. 5). Sympathy explains why we in the audience of a tragic or romantic play would "enter into [the heroes'] gratitude towards those faithful friends who did not desert them in their difficulties; and we heartily go along with their resentment against those perfidious traitors who injured, abandoned, or deceived them" (TMS, First.I.I, p. 5). We see the protagonist as someone like us and sympathize with them. Note the details in Smith's diction. We do not fellow-feel with an emotion; we fellow-feel with their passion, the observable state of the feeling that has mastered our hero's mind. What we see and hear from them, though, imperceptibly causes us to take part in the state of their feeling. There is no observable material that causally connects the actor's passion to the fellow-feeling in us. It is a natural, self-evident phenomenon that invisibly connects two separate physical beings. We furthermore do not ponder what we have seen for a bit and then a wave of fellow feeling hits us. No, the fellow feeling happens instantaneously as the play unfolds on stage.[14]

And the sympathy goes in both directions. As Smith notes above in the second chapter entitled, "Of the Pleasure of Mutual Sympathy," when

---

[12] René Brouwer (2015).   [13] Eyjólfur Emilsson (2015).
[14] Compare the narrative of the homeless man reported in Chapter 6, and which resolves into feeling, thinking and knowing.

we take part in the resentful passion of a friend who has been hurt by someone else, our friend is anxious, through fellow feeling with us, that we enter into his resentment. There is a feedback loop in the invisible causal connection between us. We and our friend are co-affected through mutual sympathy. *That human beings fellow feel with other human beings is the first key axiom of Smith's theory of morality.* We cannot see or hear the sympathetic forces at work, but they are there. Human beings spontaneously and mutually sympathize. We just do.

THE SENSE OF PROPRIETY

Propriety is another late eighteenth-century word that is not used widely now, nor prior to 1750. The oldest example that The Oxford English Dictionary (OED) gives for sense 7 – "conformity to accepted standards of behaviour or morals" – is 1753. Sense 6 – "appropriateness to circumstances or conditions; suitability, aptness, fitness; conformity with what is required by a rule, principle, etc." – only goes back to 1612. Referring to Locke, Samuel Johnson swiftly defines *propriety* as accuracy and justness and then promptly moves on to the word *propt*. Smith's predecessors and contemporaries (Lord Shaftesbury, Bernard Mandeville, Francis Hutcheson, Bishop Joseph Butler, David Hume, and Adam Ferguson) do not use propriety as a core concept in their moral philosophies. Smith, however, relies critically on propriety and even more heavily, we would argue, on a *sense of* propriety, which readers must seize ownership of to comprehend Smith's theory of morality.

Anna Wierzbicka makes the bold claims that (1) the word *sense* is "one of the most common abstract nouns in the English language" and (2) "one of the most significant, though hidden, conceptual features of Anglo English as a whole" (Wierzbicka 2010, pp. 151, 155). For the past seventy-five years *sense* appears more often than *love* in Google's database of books, but it is the insights of her second claim that help us to understand Smith's key concept of propriety. Part First of *Sentiments* is entitled "Of the Propriety of Action" and opens with a section on "The Sense of Propriety," both of which since the 1960s sound rather quaint and more like the subject of Victorian-era literature than of a general theory of morality. Because a sense of propriety in *Sentiments* obviously means more than prudish sexual constraint and a strict social code of conduct, it is worth spending a little time to get comfortable with what it means for people to have a sense of propriety.

The core meaning of sense, as in the five senses, is rooted in the body. We smell, taste, touch, hear, and see with our bodies. In each sense, something is happening in the body right here, right now. The nose is smelling, the tongue is tasting, the fingers are touching, the ears are hearing, and the eyes are seeing. When our body is affected by something in our environment, our senses neurophysically convey knowledge about the world to our mind. Such knowledge is inherently experiential. As a young child we learned to recognize as smoke the particular collection of airborne particulates and gases emanating at this moment from the next room. Our senses are not just feelings in the body. They are bodily events that convey experiential knowledge about our current circumstances of time and place.

Wierzbicka argues that this core meaning of sense permeates the myriad of different ways the word *sense* is used as both a noun and a verb in English. We can sense someone's love for their children, but we cannot feel someone's love for their children. Though we cannot feel what they feel, we can take in the sights and the sounds of the situation which then convey to our mind experiential knowledge about what someone feels for their children. Something is indeed happening in our body because of what we are seeing and hearing, but the affection of our physical body is not the end of it. By experience we also know something about the situation.

In a similar way "the noun *sense*," Wierzbicka explains, "is frequently used in English to refer to something like experiential knowledge" (Wierzbicka 2010, p. 169). To say, "I have a sense that … " is not the same as to say, "I have a feeling that …" When we say, "I have a sense that she resents that questioner," we know something about the incident. We may have been in the room when the commenter questioned the speaker's integrity, or maybe we watched the presentation on YouTube. But if we were not present at the event and someone instead told us the story of what happened, we could not say, "I have a sense that she resents the questioner." We could however say, "I have a feeling that she resents the questioner." To have a sense is both to feel and to be in a position to know something about the situation. Other languages, like German and French, Wierzbicka notes, cannot make this distinction between "I have a feeling that" and "I have a sense that." This Anglo "habit of mind interprets quasi-bodily feelings that accompany some thoughts as a potential source of knowledge comparable to knowledge derived from the senses" (Wierzbicka 2010, p. 171).

A feeling can serve as a potential source of knowledge about a situation because the feeling is caused by what is happening right now in the environment. Because the sense, the feeling and knowing of a situation, is neurophysically imbodied and because people share the same biology, one person's sense of a situation is something that other people can also feel and thereby know. But while feeling and sense are both private and individual, it is only the sense of a situation that people can share. We cannot share the feeling. What I feel in my body is what I feel, and what you feel in your body is what you feel. In Smith's words, "we have no immediate experience of what other [people] feel" (TMS, First.I.I, p. 3), but I can share what I know and you can share what you know from the sense of a situation.

So whereas a feeling is subjective, a sense is intersubjective. The knowledge that we share from experience connects a sense to something in the external world, and we can use such intersubjectivity to determine something objective about the world, through agreement. The first person to smell smoke in a room is usually the first person to seek objective confirmation by asking, "Does anyone else smell smoke?" A sense, like the smell of smoke, is the foundation for a claim about something real in the world. Furthermore, as a claim of knowledge, a sense is subject to error. What I smell could be smoke from a fire or burnt toast.

Without much impropriety, we can say that Smith uses a sense of propriety to denote *the knowledge of what is the morally fit thing to do at this time and place and to know it not through mindful thinking but through bodily feelings.* A sense of propriety is not just an internal feeling; it connects a person to the external world because it is from other human beings that we know how to act in a morally fit way. Our sense of propriety uses feelings in the body, what we see and hear, to know from experience how to act. And like our other senses, our sense of propriety is intersubjective. We use our sense of propriety to determine something objective about the world and to lay a claim about something real in the world. Someone who senses something hurtful in what was just said seeks objective confirmation when whispering at the cocktail reception, "Did anyone else feel that remark was uncalled for?" Knowing from experience that the remark was hurtful is a claim that something real has happened in the world. The questioner did something to the speaker.

Feeling is at the heart of Smith's observations on morality. Sympathy, sentiments, and the sense of propriety all entail feeling. Sympathy is the spontaneous and mutual transmission of feeling from one person to another, and back again. Our feeling is not self-contained; we take part, we participate in the state of feeling in other people. We say, "Participate in the state of feeling," not simply, "Participate in the feeling," to stress that it is the observable (sens*ible*) condition of the person with which we sympathize, a circumstantial condition which manifests the internal feeling that has mastered the other person.

While feeling is at the heart of Smith's theory of morality, it would be a mistake to characterize it as an emotive theory. Sentiments and a sense of propriety are equally as important. *With sentiments Smith connects thinking to feeling, and with the sense of propriety he connects knowing to feeling.* Smith's observations on morality rest on feeling, thinking, and knowing. It is in the triad of these three (universal human) mental predicates that *Sentiments* offers insights into how we think about economics some 250 years after it was first published.[15] We will also show that the results from modern economic experiments can inform how this triad works in *Sentiments*.

References

Brouwer, René. 2015. "Stoic Sympathy," in *Sympathy: A History*. Eric Schliesser (ed.). New York, NY: Oxford University Press, 15–35.

Camerer, Colin F. 2003. *Behavioral Game Theory: Experiments in Strategic Interaction.* Princeton, NJ: Princeton University Press.

Cogan, Thomas. 1821 [1800]. *A Philosophical Treatise of the Passions.* Boston, MA: Wells and Lilly. (1821).

Collins Cobuild English Language Dictionary. Available at https://www.collinsdictionary .com/dictionary/english.

Damasio, Antonio. 2005. *Descartes' Error: Emotion, Reason, and the Human Brain.* New York, NY: Penguin Books.

Dixon, Thomas. 2003. *From Passions to Emotions: The Creation of a Secular Psychological Category.* Cambridge, UK: Cambridge University Press.

Emilsson, Eyjólfur. 2015. "Plotinus on *Sympatheia*," in *Sympathy: A History*. Eric Schliesser (ed.). New York, NY: Oxford University Press, 36–60.

Hutton, James. 1794. *Dissertations upon the Philosophy of Light, Heat, and Fire.* Edinburgh, UK: Cadell, Junior, and Davies.

Kames, Lord. 1855 [1762]. *Elements of Criticism.* New York, NY: F. J. Huntington, and Mason Brothers.

Schliesser, Eric. 2015. "Introduction: On Sympathy," in *Sympathy: A History*. Eric Schliesser (ed.). New York, NY: Oxford University Press, 3–14.

Schliesser, Eric. 2017. *Adam Smith: Systematic Philosopher and Public Thinker.* New York, NY: Oxford University Press.

---

[15] Three other mental predicates are deeply rooted in his observations. With moral sentiments like gratitude and resentment, we *want* to think good or bad things about someone, and with the sense of propriety, we come to feel and know something by seeing and hearing. Anna Wierzbicka (1996) defends that claim that all of these mental predicates – *feel, know, think, want, see,* and *hear* – are semantically atomic and universal to all human languages. They cannot be broken down and defined in terms of any other concepts, and every human being knows what they mean in every language ever spoken.

Schmitter, Amy M. 2014. "Passions, Affections, Sentiments: Taxonomy and Terminology," in *The Oxford Handbook of British Philosophy in the Eighteenth Century*, James A. Harris (ed.). New York, NY: Oxford University Press, 197–225.

Smith, Adam. 1982 [1755]. "Review of Johnson's *Dictionary*," in *Essays on Philosophical Subjects*. Indianapolis, IN: Liberty Fund, 232–41.

Smith, Adam. 1982 [1795]. "The History of Astronomy," in *Essays on Philosophical Subjects*. Indianapolis, IN: Liberty Fund, 33–105.

Smith, Charles John. 1894. *Synonyms Discriminated: A Dictionary of Synonymous Words in the English Language*. New York, NY: Henry Holt and Company.

Wierzbicka, Anna. 1996. *Semantics: Primes and Universals*. New York, NY: Oxford University Press.

Wierzbicka, Anna. 1999. *Emotions across Languages and Cultures: Diversity and Universals*. New York, NY: Cambridge University Press.

Wierzbicka, Anna. 2010. *Experience, Evidence, and Sense: The Hidden Cultural Legacy of English*. New York, NY: Oxford University Press.

3

Conduct in the Social Universe

Even more so than *sentiments* or *propriety*, the word *conduct* is a quintessentially late eighteenth-century word. Sure, we use it today when we talk to our middle schoolers about their report cards, or perhaps we hear it in news reports on such grave issues as presidential affairs in the Oval Office. But *conduct* is not the first word we go to, particularly in standard scientific analysis. The modern word of choice is *behavior*, as in behavioral chemistry, behavioral ecology, behavioral physics, behavioral political science, behavioral sociology, and yes, behavioral economics. Since the late nineteenth century, behavior can apply to any animate or inanimate thing, including ships, butterflies, water, stock markets, and chemical substances. The *Oxford English Dictionary* (*OED*) captures this meaning in definition 5: behavior is "the manner in which a thing acts under specified conditions or circumstances, or in relation to other things." Samuel Johnson's dictionary offers a total of six different meanings for behavior, not one of which reminds us of *OED*'s definition 5:

1. Manner of behaving one's self, whether good or bad. (Sidney)
2. External appearance. (I Samuel xxi)
3. Gesture; manner of action. (Hooker)
4. Elegance of manner; gracefulness. (Sidney)
5. Conduct; general practice; course of life. (Locke)
6. *To be upon one's behaviour.* A familiar phrase, noting such a state as requires great caution. (L'Estrange)

Every meaning of behavior in the eighteenth century is about people and how they interface with each other, especially the fifth one: conduct, general practice, and course of life. While Adam Smith uses *behaviour* some 80 times, *conduct* is his go-to choice 309 times, which is roughly on par with his usage of *sentiments*. *Conduct* appears twice in a chapter title and once in the title of the very important "Part Third" ("Of the Foundation of our Judgments concerning our own Sentiments and Conduct, and of the Sense of Duty"). *Behaviour* never appears in a title. The conjunction *X and behaviour* appears seventeen times where *X* is *conduct, character, sentiments,* or *countenance*; he also refers five times to *whole behaviour*. As he so often does, Charles Smith beautifully discriminates the synonyms for us (1894, p. 159, original emphasis):

> *Behaviour* refers to all those actions which are open to the observation of others as well as those which are specifically directed to others. As behavior refers more especially to actions, *demeanour* refers more directly to manners; or in other words *demeanor* regards one's self, *behavior* regards others.... As *behaviour* belongs to the minor morals of society, so *conduct* to the graver questions of personal life. But conduct may be intellectually tested as well as morally. A man behaves himself well or ill; he conducts himself well or ill, ably or inefficiently. Behavior should be seemly, conduct should be wise. We speak of a man's behaviour in the social circle, of his conduct in his family, as a citizen, or in life. Good conduct is meritorious and virtuous. Good behaviour may be natural or artificial. The conduct has relation to the station of men's lives, or the circumstances in which they are placed. Good conduct will include right behaviour as part of it, and a proper demeanour will flow necessarily out of it.

Notice that in the eighteenth century, "self-regarding behavior" is an oxymoron and "other-regarding behavior" a pleonasm. Someone's behavior is situated within a social group, observable by and directed toward other people. Behavior is not what you do when no one else is around. Behavior is how you naturally or artificially embed your actions in the rules that govern human intercourse. We sense behavior in ourselves and others to be seemly or unseemly, fitting or unfitting, appropriate or inappropriate, good or bad, and because we apply our sense of propriety to behavior, we feel something in our body and thereby know something about the situation we find ourselves in.

BEHAVIOR IN MODERN ECONOMICS

Since the ascent of positivism in the nineteenth century, behavior in the sciences is no longer about feeling something in our body. Behavior is something we interpret through reason and logic. Positivists mistrust the fuzzy feelings in our body. References to "touchy, feely things" are a put-down associated with unreliability. Feelings are unreliable for knowing something about the external world because they cannot be measured or compared. One benefit of purging bodily feeling from behavior is that our knowledge about behavior is no longer limited to our common human physiology. Our minds are free to apply behavior to nearly anything in the external world. Since the nineteenth century, behavior is not just about how humans act, but how ships, butterflies, water, stock markets, and chemical substances act under specified conditions or circumstances. In short, positivism de-anthropomorphized behavior and, in doing so, foreclosed the feeling-thinking-knowing theme in *Sentiments* as an accessible path to understanding human conduct.

Contemporary economists and cognitive psychologists maintain the positivist tradition, having merged it with Benthamite utilitarianism (but since Lionel Robbins, without the menacing considerations of normative ethics). Utility in economics is a measure which functionally relates an action to a desirable or undesirable outcome. Given a choice among alternatives, an individual is postulated to choose the action that maximizes her preference. Utilitarian preference functions perform heavy-duty work in modeling a vast range of human decisions: isolated individuals in psychophysical measurements, individuals choosing among uncertain probabilistic prospects, and individuals interacting through choices in two-person games or in small groups (public good and common property games). Since the late nineteenth-century marginal revolution of William Stanley Jevons, Carl Menger, and Léon Walras, the most expansive application of utility, as every economics major learns, has been to agents in supply-and-demand markets.

In his intermediate microeconomic text, Hal Varian defines the consumer's problem as follows: "If [a] consumer prefers one bundle to another, it means that he or she would choose one over the other, given the opportunity. Thus, the idea of preference is based upon [a] consumer's *behavior*" (2006, p. 34, original italics). Let's take a look at this concept of preferences. Examples of ordinary usage of the verb *prefer* include "to prefer beef to chicken" (Dictionary.com), "prefers coffee to tea" (American Heritage Dictionary), "prefers sports to reading" (Merriam-Webster), and "Some people prefer camping to staying in hotels; we prefer sleeping outside" (WordNet). One cannot help but notice the general form of the usage: "X prefers *a* to *b*." The contrasting difference between *a* and *b* is a difference of quality or kind. Beef and chicken are both kinds of meats from domesticated animals, but the taste of red meat differs in a qualitative way from white meat. Likewise, coffee and tea differ in their potable flavors; sports and reading are afternoon activities that stimulate the body and mind, respectively; and a night's rest beneath the stars differs in the comfort and view from slumbering on a mattress in a Hilton hotel.

How do economists use *prefer*? At prices of two dollars per apple and one dollar per orange, Evelyn prefers to purchase two apples and two oranges to one apple and four oranges. Why? Because as compared to the choice of one apple and four oranges on a budget of six dollars, Evelyn gets more utility per dollar spent from purchasing one more apple instead of the last two oranges. In econospeak, the marginal utility per dollar of apples is greater for Evelyn than the marginal utility per dollar of oranges. Notice that the difference between an economist's a and b is quantitative, not qualitative. Not only can we compare a and b, we can subtract $b = (1$ apple, 4 oranges) from $a = (2, 2)$ to define the difference between a and b as $a - b = (1, -2)$. Where's the flavor in that? Perhaps in the higher utility ranking of two apples and two oranges to one apple and four oranges, but that is not a difference in kind. In either case the consumer tastes apples and oranges. The fuzzy sensory perception of taste has been completely purged from the consumer's problem.

But taste was not the problem that a modern theory of value needed to solve. For all his genius, Adam Smith was befuddled by the Paradox of Value. Why would people at rather high prices buy diamonds, a product utterly useless for survival, and pay so little for water, something absolutely necessary for life? His resolution to the paradox was to posit that there must be two meanings of value: "The one may be called 'value in use;' the other, 'value in exchange.' The things which have the greatest value in use have frequently little or no value in exchange; and on the contrary, those which have the greatest value in exchange have frequently little or no value in use" (WN, p. 44).

Jevons, Menger, and Walras independently solved the Paradox of Value by inventing the concept of marginal utility and the subjective theory of value to support it. Looking past the distracting differences in the usefulness of different kinds of goods, the marginal revolution shifted the perspective from the value of the total amounts consumed to the marginal value of the next unit of a good. Henceforth, how did economists rationally reconstruct the observation that people buy different bundles of goods in response to changes in the prices of the goods? People have a consistent set of preferences defined on the goods, and a limited dollar budget to spend; if prices change, a person will Max-U by adjusting up or down their purchase of each individual good, until the marginal utility per dollar spent on each is the same. One critical assumption that economists make about preferences is that consumers are locally non-satiated; they always prefer more to less among neighboring items. Thus, three apples are preferred to two apples, and three oranges are preferred to two oranges. Utility is an internal individual currency that connects apples with oranges and anything else and defines a no-change equilibrium balance between the individual and external prices. The economist's problem is to explain the consistent manner in which people behave when subject to a given set of prices and a budget constraint.

The economist's problem is not to ask, "Why does Evelyn prefer a to b?" She just does. Nor would an economist ask why Frank prefers b to a. That's for someone in the marketing department to ponder. Frank simply has different preferences rationalized by a different utility function. For a given set of prices and budget, their behavior is their behavior. It does not matter what is going on in them internally. Well, it does not matter why Evelyn feels that two oranges and two apples taste better than one apple and four oranges even though the price of apples is twice that of oranges. But it does matter to the economist that Evelyn in general thinks that more apples are better than fewer apples, and more oranges are better than fewer oranges. For without that assumption we could not make sense of Evelyn's behavior. Behavior in economics is about choice, and choice expresses preference. To choose a over b is to prefer a over b. Choice necessarily reveals preference. Moreover, in expressing preferences through their choices, people are locally non-satiated.

Then, in the early 1990s researchers around the globe observed that people in laboratory experiments would regularly make choices that would result in lower cash payoffs for themselves when another available alternative would have made them materially better off. Sometimes, this lower payoff for themselves was coincident with a lower payoff for another person, and sometimes it was coincident with a higher payoff for another person.[1] Faced with a Paradox of Preferences, as revealed in choices, the economist's instinct was to posit – like Adam Smith did for the Paradox of Value – that there must be two meanings of *preferences*: preferences for the self and preferences for the social, where the latter was expressed as different choices than the former. Three prominent publications appeal to "social preferences" as the solution to the paradox:

---

[1] For a lower payoff for the other person, see, e.g., Werner Güth, Rolf Schmittberger, and Bernd Schwarze (1982); Robert Forsythe, Joel L. Horowitz, N. E. Savin, and Martin Sefton (1994); and Elizabeth Hoffman, Kevin McCabe, Keith Shachat, and Vernon Smith (1994); and for a higher payoff for the other person, see, e.g., Colin Camerer and Keith Weigelt (1988); Ernst Fehr, Georg Kirchsteiger, and Arno Riedl (1993); and Joyce Berg, John Dickhaut, and Kevin McCabe (1995).

- "social preference functions balance a person's desire to have more money with their desire to reciprocate those who have treated them fairly or unfairly, or to achieve equality" (Colin Camerer 2003, p. 11);
- "formal models of social preferences ... assume people are self-interested, but are also concerned about the payoffs of others" (Gary Charness and Matthew Rabin 2002, p. 817);
- "people exhibit social preferences, which means they are not solely motivated by material self-interest but also care positively or negatively for the material payoffs of relevant reference agents" (Ernst Fehr and Urs Fischbacher 2002, p. C1).

Why is the resolution to augment a utility function to distinguish between preferences for the self and preferences for the social? On the one hand, a robust 67 percent of people prefer ($25 for self, $15 for another) to ($40, $0), but we also have overwhelming evidence in another study that 97 percent of people prefer ($40, $0) to ($40 − m, m) for $0 < $m ≤ $40.[2] To make sense of this juxtaposition, economists assume that the axiom of local non-satiation applies without modification when people like Evelyn choose ($40, $0) instead of ($25, $15). Nothing new to be explained here. But what do economists do with the Franks of the world who prefer ($25, $15) to ($40, $0)? They appear to violate the axiom of local non-satiation for money. To rescue the Max-U paradigm we can assume, just like for different consumers of fruit, that Frank must have a different utility function with something extra, say, an inequality aversion function $I_F(\$e, \$f)$. But there is a key difference with this interpersonal situation. Unlike with consumers of fruit, we are precisely concerned about the deeply personal and social reasons going through the mind of someone who chooses ($25, $15) over ($40, $0). Frank's behavior is not just Frank's behavior. It matters what's going on in his head. By positing the existence of social preferences, economists are simultaneously asking (and answering), *why* does Frank prefer *b* to *a*?

A utility function that maps preferences into actions is a third-person analytical tool for organizing consumer behavior in markets. The nature of the question is tailor-made for the modern social scientific meaning of *behavior*, the manner in which a thing acts under specified conditions or circumstances. In this case the thing happens to be a person, and the

---

[2] For the former and latter, respectively, see Kevin McCabe and Vernon Smith (2000), the findings of which James Cox and Cary Deck (2005) replicate; and Todd Cherry, Peter Frykblom, and Jason Shogren (2002), the findings of which Robert Oxoby and John Spraggon (2008) replicate.

specified conditions or circumstances are that the consumer (1) knows her budget and the prices of oranges and apples and (2) thinks that more is better than less.[3] The economist is definitely not interested in what consumers of fruit feel that enables them to know what action to take in the situation they find themselves in.

Personal social interactions categorically differ from the consumer's general problem in our undergraduate and graduate textbooks. Social preferences like Frank's inequality aversion function are third-person analytics applied to the first-person problem of how Frank *feels*, a problem to which we in fact do not have access. The economist does not feel what Frank (or Evelyn) feels. The nature of the question about how Frank and Evelyn feel in social situations does not fit the analytical Max-U tool kit. Simply put, utility maximization, over outcomes only, is an inadequate and misapplied tool for the problem that Frank and Evelyn face in a personal social interaction.

EPICYCLES OR ORDERLY ORBITS?

Sometime prior to 1758, a year before *Sentiments* was published, Smith wrote an essay entitled, "The History of Astronomy," which was eventually published posthumously in 1795. We know it was written before 1758 from a note that Smith himself added regarding a comet that had been predicted to return in 1758.[4] In the footnote he updates his statement to say that the statement had been written earlier and that "the return of the comet had occurred agreeably to the prediction." Smith is referring to Halley's Comet that appears on schedule about every seventy-five to seventy-six years – a prediction whose confirmation was truly mind-bending for any remaining eighteenth-century skeptics of Newton. The return of Halley's comet in 1758 was the first time that any celestial body other than a planet had been shown to orbit the sun.

Comets were the original eccentric bodies of Hipparchic and Ptolemaic astronomy. The Earth was literally out of (*ec-*) the center of their orbs. When Copernican astronomy moved the center of planetary orbits to the sun, comets remained irregular and unpredictable. Only Newtonian

---

[3] The thing need not be a person as the work on rats by John Kagel, Raymond Battalio, Howard Rachlin, and Leonard Green (1981) and on pigeons by Battalio, Kagel, Rachlin, and Green (1981) demonstrates.

[4] Newton had a great impact on Smith's understanding of the observable world in terms of forces invisible to human perception, evident in one of his first manuscripts, a topic to which we will return in Chapter 7.

physics with its invisible forces of gravity could account for the movements of comets as regular and orderly around the sun. Clearly enamored by the ability of Newtonian theory to provide an orderly account of observations from the physical world, Smith sought to develop such a system for the social foundations of morality.[5]

Sentiments demonstrates the power of rule-governed systems that function beneath human sensible awareness to organize the orbits of people around each other. The individual is painted as inseparably connected from birth with overlapping social groupings based in family, extended family, friends and neighbors; these groupings in turn prepare and enable the individual to reach much beyond these narrow circles into daily life experiences. As Smith saw it, this is the world that first and originally defines the content and meaning of sociability, that defines the individual within their social context.

Smith and his intellectual cohorts in the Scottish enlightenment were astute observers of their respective worlds of primary interest as they searched for the hidden rules that ordered the complex phenomena they studied. Max-U applied to interactions among personal social interactions constitutes a fundamental departure from the intellectual modeling framework of *Sentiments*. Smith's observations on human sociality rest on conduct, which even if it could be converted into an adjective for the sense demanded, it could never modify chemistry, physics, or ecology. Conduct belongs to the weightier questions of *human* life. Animals like dogs and show cattle can behave themselves well or ill, but they do not conduct themselves well or ill. People conduct themselves well or ill. Smith's model eschews outcomes and their utility, including social preferences, and begins with actions as signals of rule-following conduct. It is a theory of human sociality devoted to understanding moral human action, the practice of life's duties.

No economist has ever published a paper dedicated to explaining why people like Evelyn choose ($40, 0) over ($25, $15). It is taken for granted that non-satiation explains their egocentric movements around people like Frank. Frank's orbit, however, is eccentric, at least to economists.[6] It is not centered about an "I" and therefore requires

---

[5] Ryan Hanley (2017) insightfully shows how Adam Smith was a synthetic thinker, whether the subject of his inquiry was astronomy or language, moral philosophy or political economy.

[6] This tells us something about how economists solve the puzzles they find in human action. But even more telling is what economists do when faced with something ordinary people would not find to be all too extraordinary. We make up a new connecting concept.

some explanation.[7] Something else internal to the individual needs to be locally non-satiated to explain his choice. Social preferences represented by an inequality aversion function appear to explain Frank's conduct, but as we shall see in the next chapter, that appearance is but a glamour of the natural scientific method. When pushed, economists cannot use social preferences to answer some rather basic questions. Under what circumstances will someone like Frank choose ($15, $25) over ($0, $40)? Or will Frank always choose ($15, $25)? Max-U is silent. In what situations is someone like Evelyn egocentric? Or should we assume that Evelyn is egocentric in whatever situation she finds herself in? Again Max-U is silent. Why? Because Ptolemaic Max-U treats Frank as an eccentric comet and Evelyn a predictable planet. There is no gravity to unify the movements of both planets and comets in the economist's solar system of preferences. Its representation by Max-U is devoid of the hidden forces of feeling that can explain both why Evelyns do what they do and Franks do what they do, but also why Evelyns often do what Franks do, and why Franks often do what Evelyns do. Social preferences are mere epicycles that jigger the observation of Frank's choice to fit the economist's deferent of local non-satiation. *Sentiments*, on the other hand, explains both Frank's and Evelyn's conduct with Smith's own groundbreaking theory of gravity.

FEELING PLUS THINKING PLUS KNOWING

The primary connecting principle in Smith's system of sociality is fellow feeling. Humans are not the only animal to sympathize. Highly social mammals like dogs, elephants, and primates of all kinds appear to fellow feel. The propensity to fellow feel seems, at best, less pronounced in gregarious mammals like cattle, meerkats, and kangaroos, which do not, if ever, routinely assist one another in need but which nevertheless feel ill at ease with solitude. More so than any other order of mammals, primates appear to take pleasure with being in each other's company.[8] How do we, and the eminent primatologist Frans de Waal, know that other primates fellow feel with each other and take pleasure with being in each other's company?[9] We sense it in their interactions with members of their own species; we fellow feel with the capuchin monkey and know something about its interactions from our own life experiences with members of our

---

[7] See also Maria Pia Paganelli (2017).   [8] Charles F. Hockett (1973).
[9] Frans de Waal (2009).

own primate species. The social impulse that fellow feeling supports is not rare among mammals, but it also is not the norm. Only 10–20 percent of all mammals cluster beyond seasonal mating and offspring nursing.[10]

Sympathy is the transmission mechanism that supports the impulse for sociality. It is the invisible means for carrying out the social impulse, but sympathy is not enough to explain the patterns of what individuals of a species do when relating to one another. Fellow feeling does not regularize and order the bulk of human interactions. After an aggressive conflict, a victorious chimpanzee will console the loser with a simple touch on the arm.[11] The act alleviates the distress of the loser and assures the loser that the prior social bond between the two is not irreparably broken. To explain this regular pattern of chimpanzee behavior is to explain how the social impulse is carried out: the victor participates in the loser's state of distress.

We perceive the chimpanzee's touch on the arm as we would perceive a fellow human's touch on the arm following such an event, an assurance that whatever discord there was between them, it is over. The issue is settled and the two are in concord again. There is, however, much more to the human scheduling pattern regarding an aggressive conflict than the primeval fellow feeling of the victor. *Human bystanders judge the propriety of the victor's and loser's sentiments and passions in their conflict.* To borrow the phrasing of Samuel Alexander, we contemplate sentiments and passions for their own sakes and superimpose a judgment of value on them.[12] In the course of fellow feeling, we contemplate other people's sentiments and passions not merely as they present themselves but for themselves.

We approve or disapprove of the victor's retaliatory rage, and we approve or disapprove of the loser's distress at the thought of being at odds with the victor. Approbation, Smith's word of choice for approving of sentiments and passions, is stronger and more positive than modern notions of approval. Likewise, disapprobation is stronger and more negative than the modern notion of disapproval. Approbation is not merely making something out to be good but a determination that it be positively so. It is both a feeling and a thought, or as Charles Smith explains, "approbation is the sentiment of which approval is the expression. We entertain approbation and express approval" (Smith 1894, p. 111).[13]

---

[10] Peter Jarman and Hans Kruuk (1996).   [11] de Waal (2009).
[12] Samuel Alexander (1933, p. 7).
[13] In the U.S. presidential election of 2016, many seem to have silently felt approbation for Donald Trump's declarations, but with no expression of approval when asked in polls.

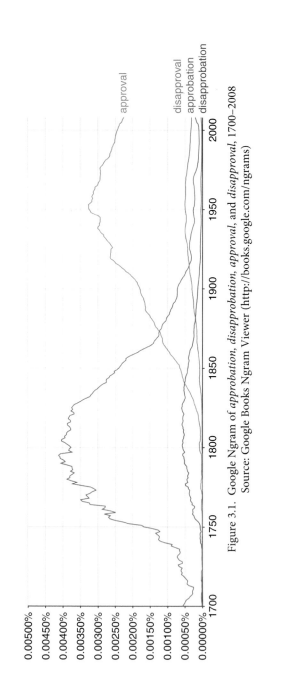

Figure 3.1. Google Ngram of *approbation*, *disapprobation*, *approval*, and *disapproval*, 1700–2008
Source: Google Books Ngram Viewer (http://books.google.com/ngrams)

Approbation and *disapprobation* are two more words peculiar to the late eighteenth century and central to Smith's theory of morality. As with the others, their use also peaked around 1800, when *approval* and *disapproval* are but barely a blip in a Google Ngram (see Figure 3.1 and compare its scale to Figure 2.1). Smith never once uses *approval* or *disapproval*, but *approbation* and *disapprobation* appear on average about once every other page. So we must familiarize ourselves with yet two more core concepts not in contemporary use and without precise modern equivalents.

Smith introduces approbation and disapprobation early in his book (TMS, First.I.III, p. 15):

> To approve or disapprove, therefore, of the opinions of others is acknowledged, by every body, to mean no more than to observe their agreement or disagreement with our own. But this is equally the case with regard to our approbation or disapprobation of the sentiments or passions of others.

To make someone's sentiment out to be suitable or fit, and determine it to be positively so, means to observe the agreement of that sentiment with our own thinking and feeling. The approbation of a sentiment is itself a composite sentiment, a sentiment of someone else's sentiment. We both feel that someone's sentiment is suitable or fit for the circumstances, and we think that the sentiment is positively so. And how do we know that someone's sentiment is suitable or fit for the circumstances? From our sense of propriety. By the feelings in our body we know from experience whether someone's sentiment is suitable or fit. When there is a correspondence between their sentiments and ours, we judge someone's sentiments to be suitable or fit. Fellow feeling is an invisible connection between us, but it is the feeling and thinking of approbation qua a sentiment and the feeling and knowing of our sense of propriety that forms the explanatory foundation for the scheduling pattern that is our morality. *That human beings judge the sentiments and passions of other human beings is the second axiom of Smith's theory of morality.* Human beings spontaneously judge the feelings and thoughts of others to be suitable or fit for the circumstances at hand. We may not say that we are judging your feelings and your thoughts. But it will happen. We will judge them. We just do.

GRAVITY OF THE SOCIAL UNIVERSE

The premise of Part First of *Sentiments* is that we judge the propriety of the "consequent action" by judging the propriety of the feelings and thoughts that attend the action (TMS, First.I.III, p. 17; Second.I.Intro, p. 93). Propriety or impropriety is one "quality ascribed to the actions and conduct of mankind" (TMS, Second.I.Intro, p. 93) and the object of one kind of approbation or disapprobation. A second distinct kind of approbation and disapprobation concerns another distinct quality of actions, their merit or demerit. Such is the topic of Part Second of *Sentiments*.

An action may be suitable or fit but still not deserve reward, and an action may be unsuitable or unfit but still not deserve punishment. Part Second of *Sentiments* explains what the good or ill desert of an action consists of, and it opens *with Smith's third axiom: "The sentiment which most immediately and directly prompts us to reward, is gratitude; that which most immediately and directly prompts us to punish, is resentment"* (TMS, Second.I.I, p. 94). Smith notes that there are many other passions "besides gratitude and resentment, which interest us in the happiness or misery of others," like love, esteem, hatred and dislike, but gratitude and resentment are the passions that "most directly excite us" (TMS, Second.I.I, p. 94–5). As states of feeling that master the mind, gratitude and resentment most directly excite us. But it is the thoughts prompted by the sudden and imperious demands on our attention that induce us to reward and punish. There is an excitement of feeling that masters the mind, *and* there are thoughts under the demand of our mind to do something, to return good for good and evil for evil.

Smith does not explain where the force of gratitude and resentment comes from. We just have them; they "seem to have been given us by nature" (TMS, Second.II.I, p. 113). As sentiments, gratitude and resentment are influences operating on a person so as to change the motion of a person, to produce an action. We do not see the force between a person in action and ourselves prompted thereby to act, but it is there like the gravity between the earth and the moon is there to explain their movements. Combine the sentiments of approbation and disapprobation with gratitude and resentment and we have the primary forces that Smith uses to explain the orderly orbits of human conduct. In his *Principia*, moral sentiments are the gravity of the social universe.

We have said that the primary connecting principle in Smith's system of sociality is fellow feeling. How can we be sure that this principle is not just another elaborately articulated form of internal representation of human motivation like social preferences that rationalizes the diversity expressed in human action across its many forms? Because internal fellow feeling alone is not predictive of context-specific actions. Our intersubjective sense of propriety – feeling plus knowing – is critical to tethering Smith's model to the external world. Together with other axioms and derived principles, *Sentiments* constitutes a system of sociality leading to propositions with empirical (predictive) content. That content includes the early ultimatum and trust game results that defied the predictions of Max-U, and led to post hoc "social preference" and "reciprocity" explanations that were not independent descriptions of the observations. They were explanations without a support framework of social theory, explanations by analogy with Max-U, where action implied outcome that yielded utility to the actor, or by analogy with gains from an exchange. Finally, Smith's propositions in *Sentiments* suggest new design variations on trust and ultimatum games with testable predictions, variations that were neither imaginable nor predictable by the post hoc attempts to explain the ultimatum and trust game results.

References

Alexander, Samuel. 1968 [1933]. *Beauty and Other Forms of Value*. New York, NY: Thomas Y. Crowell Company.

Battalio, Raymond C., John H. Kagel, Howard Rachlin, and Leonard Green. 1981. "Commodity Choice Behavior with Pigeons as Subjects," *Journal of Political Economy* 84: 116–51.

Berg, Joyce, John Dickhaut, and Kevin McCabe. 1995. "Trust, Reciprocity, and Social History," *Games and Economic Behavior* 10: 122–42.

Camerer, Colin F. 2003. *Behavioral Game Theory: Experiments in Strategic Interaction*. Princeton, NJ: Princeton University Press.

Camerer, Colin and Keith Weigelt. 1988. "Experimental Tests of a Sequential Equilibrium Reputation Model," *Econometrica* 56(1): 1–36.

Charness, Gary and Matthew Rabin. 2002. "Understanding Social Preferences with Simple Tests," *Quarterly Journal of Economics* 117(3): 817–69.

Cherry, Todd, Peter Frykblom, and Jason F. Shogren. 2002. "Hardnose the Dictator," *American Economic Review* 92(4): 1218–21.

Cox, James C. and Cary A. Deck. 2005. "On the Nature of Reciprocal Motives," *Economic Inquiry*, 43: 623–35.

de Waal, Frans. 2009. *The Age of Empathy: Nature's Lessons for a Kinder Society*. New York, NY: Crown Publishing.

Fehr, Ernst and Urs Fischbacher. 2002. "Why Social Preferences Matter: The Impact of Non-selfish Motives on Competition, Cooperation, and Incentives," *Economic Journal* 112: C1–C33.

Fehr, Ernst, Georg Kirchsteiger, and Arno Riedl. 1993. "Does Fairness Prevent Market Clearing? An Experimental Investigation," *Quarterly Journal of Economics* 108(2): 437–59.

Forsythe, Robert, Joel L. Horowitz, N. E. Savin, and Martin Sefton. 1994. "Fairness in Simple Bargaining Experiments," *Games and Economic Behavior* 6(3): 347–69.

Güth, Werner, Rolf Schmittberger, and Bernd Schwarze. 1982. "An Experimental Analysis of Ultimatum Bargaining," *Journal of Economic Behavior and Organization* 3(4): 367–88.

Hanley, Ryan Patrick. 2017. "Practicing PPE: The Case of Adam Smith," *Social Philosophy and Policy* 34(1): 277–95.

Hockett, Charles F. 1973. *Man's Place in Nature.* New York, NY: McGraw-Hill.

Hoffman, Elizabeth, Kevin McCabe, Keith Shachat, and Vernon L. Smith. 1994. "Preferences, Property Rights, and Anonymity in Bargaining Experiments," *Games and Economic Behavior* 7(3): 346–80.

Jarman, Peter J. and Hans Kruuk. 1996. "Phylogeny and Spatial Organization in Mammals," in *Comparison of Marsupial and Placental Behaviour*, David B. Croft and Udo Ganslosser (eds.). Fürth, Germany: Filander Verlag, 80–101.

Kagel, John H., Raymond C. Battalio, Howard Rachlin, and Leonard Green. 1981. "Demand Curves for Animal Consumers," *Quarterly Journal of Economics* 96(1): 1–16.

McCabe, Kevin and Vernon L. Smith. 2000. "A Comparison of Naïve and Sophisticated Subject Behavior with Game Theoretic Predictions," *Proceedings of the National Academy of Arts and Sciences* 97(7): 3777–81.

Oxoby, Robert and John Spraggon. 2008. "Mine and Yours: Property Rights in Dictator Games," *Journal of Economic Behavior and Organization* 66: 703–13.

Paganelli, Maria Pia. 2017. "We Are Not the Center of the Universe: The Role of Astronomy in the Moral Defense of Commerce in Adam Smith," *History of Political Economy* 49(3): 451–468.

Smith, Adam. 1853 [1759]. *The Theory of Moral Sentiments; or, An Essay towards an Analysis of the Principles by which Men naturally judge concerning the Conduct and Character, first of their Neighbours, and afterwards of themselves. To which is added, A Dissertation on the Origins of Languages. New Edition. With a biographical and critical Memoir of the Author, by Dugald Stewart.* London, UK: Henry G. Bohn. Available online and in electronic formats at http://oll .libertyfund.org/titles/2620.

Smith, Adam. 1981 [1776]. *An Inquiry into the Nature and Causes of the Wealth of Nations. Vol. I & II.* Indianapolis, IN: Liberty Fund.

Smith, Adam. 1982 [1795]. "The History of Astronomy," in *Essays on Philosophical Subjects.* Indianapolis, IN: Liberty Fund, 33–105.

Smith, Charles John. 1894. *Synonyms Discriminated: A Dictionary of Synonymous words in the English Language.* New York, NY: Henry Holt and Company.

Varian, Hal. 2006. *Intermediate Economics: A Modern Approach*, 7th ed. New York, NY: W. W. Norton & Company.

Wilson, Bart J. 2010. "Social Preferences are not Preferences," *Journal of Economic Behavior and Organization* 73(1): 77–82.

4

Frank Knight Preemptively Settles the Horse Race

Eighty years before there was such a thing called behavioral economics, Frank Knight pondered the limitations of the scientific treatment of human data. John Watson's methodological behaviorism was changing psychology in the 1910s and 1920s with its emphasis on measuring the observable, people's behavior and the external events involving them.[1] As a social philosopher – as well as an economic theorist, Knight was skeptical of the trend in social scientific thinking and in 1924 contributed an essay entitled, "The Limitations of Scientific Method in Economics," to *The Trend in Economics* edited by Rexford Tugwell. (Note what is definitive by where Knight places and does not place the definite article: "*The* Limitations of *Scientific Method* in Economics.")

Scientific method in economics, then and now, consists first of formulating a mathematical model of the individual's behavior as a utility maximization problem. To explain seemingly eccentric choices, modern economists construct models that incorporate other-regarding preferences, like inequality aversion, into an individual's utility function.[2] Others put perceptions of others' intentions in the utility function.[3] Still others mix in both intentions and other-regarding preferences.[4] Newer strands of research formalize behavior (never conduct) as a preference for reputation.[5] Or, alternatively, they model it as a preference for complying

---

[1] John Watson (1913).

[2] David Levine (1998), Ernst Fehr and Klaus Schmidt (1999), and Gary Bolton and Axel Ockenfels (2000).

[3] Matthew Rabin (1993) and Martin Dufwenberg and Georg Kirchsteiger (2004).

[4] Gary Charness and Matthew Rabin (2002), Armin Falk and Urs Fischbacher (2006), and James Cox, Daniel Friedman, and Steven Gjerstad (2007).

[5] Roland Bénabou and Jean Tirole (2006) and James Andreoni and B. Douglas Bernheim (2009).

with a norm.[6] The second step is to solve for what two or more individuals with these preferences would do when interacting with each other. Because what Evelyn does can affect Frank's utility and what Frank does can affect Evelyn's utility, the problem is to solve for an equilibrium in which neither Frank nor Evelyn will change what either does in response to the other while each maximizes their own utility. Suppose, for example, that if Frank does Z_{Frank}, Evelyn maximizes her utility by doing Z_{Evelyn}, and that if Evelyn does the same Z_{Evelyn}, Frank maximizes his utility by doing the same Z_{Frank}. In such a circumstance, Frank and Evelyn are said to be in equilibrium. Neither will change what they are doing because both are maximizing their own utility given what the other person is doing. Such is the insight of the beautiful mind of John Nash.

AN EXAMPLE OF BEHAVIORAL ECONOMICS METHOD

To explain the limits that Knight places on scientific method in economics, it will be useful to have a concrete example to refer to. We warn the reader with a metaphorical yellow triangular sign: MATH CROSSING AHEAD, but note that understanding the mathematical moves will not be necessary for the discussion that follows. In fact, we urge the reader to pay close attention to the motivation for the model and the verbs regarding the math. We also warn the reader that the theory contains jargony terms typical of economic modeling.

A Theory of Enviousness

We model enviousness as self-centered aversion to differences in outcomes. Aversion to differences in outcomes means people are willing to give up some material payoff to move in the direction of more equal outcomes. Aversion to differences in outcomes is self-centered if people do not care per se about enviousness that exists among other people but are only interested in the enviousness of their own material payoff relative to the payoff of others.

Because in the following we restrict attention to individual behavior in economic experiments, we will have to make some assumptions

---

[6] Alexander Cappelen, Astri Drange Hole, Erik Sorenson, and Bertil Tungodden (2007), Raúl López-Pérez (2008), Erin Krupka and Roberto Weber (2009, 2013), and Erik Kimbrough and Alexander Vostroknutov (2016).

(cont.)

about the groups of subjects and outcomes that are likely to prevail in this context. In the laboratory it is usually much simpler to define what is perceived as an unenvious allocation by the subjects. The subjects enter the laboratory as equals, they do not know anything about each other, and the experimenter allocates the different roles in the experiment at random. Thus, it is natural to assume that the subjects that enter the laboratory comprise their reference group and that an equal outcome is their reference point. More precisely, we assume the following. First, in addition to purely selfish subjects, there are subjects who dislike different outcomes. They experience envy if they are worse off in material terms than the other players in the experiment, and they also feel envy of others if they are better off.[7] Second, however, we assume that, in general, subjects suffer more from envy that is to their material disadvantage than from envy that is to their material advantage. Formally, consider two players indexed by $i \in \{1, 2\}$, and let $z = z_1, z_2$ denote the vector of monetary payoffs. The utility function of player $i \in \{1, 2\}$ is given by $U_i = z_i - \alpha_i \max |z_j - z_i, 0| - \beta_i \max |z_i - z_j, 0|$, for $i \neq j$ and where we assume $\beta_i \leq \alpha_i$ and $0 \leq \beta_i < 1$.

The second term in U_i measures the utility loss from disadvantageous envy, while the third term measures the loss from advantageous envy. Given their own monetary payoff z_i, player i's utility function obtains a maximum at $z_i = z_j$. The utility loss from disadvantageous envy ($z_j > z_i$) is larger than the utility loss if player i is better off than player j ($z_j < z_i$). Furthermore, the assumption $\alpha_i \geq \beta_i$ captures the idea that a player suffers more from enviousness that is to his disadvantage. Note that $\alpha_i \geq \beta_i$ essentially means that a subject is loss averse in social comparisons: negative deviations from the reference outcome count more than positive deviations. There is a large literature indicating the relevance of loss aversion in other domains.[8] Hence it seems natural that loss aversion also affects social comparisons.[9]

We also assume that $0 \leq \beta_i < 1$. $\beta_i > 0$ means that we rule out the existence of subjects who like to be better off than others. We impose this assumption here, although we believe that there are subjects with

---

[7] For numerous examples around the globe, see Helmut Schoeck (1966).

[8] See, e.g., Amos Tversky and Daniel Kahneman (1991).

[9] In *Sentiments* loss aversion is a prominent feature of human social experience and comparisons. See Chapter 5, *Principles 3* and *4*.

(cont.)

$\beta_i < 0$. The reason is that in the context of experiments we consider individuals with $\beta_i < 0$ have virtually no impact on equilibrium behavior. To interpret the restriction $\beta_i < 1$, suppose that player i has a higher monetary payoff than player j. In this case $\beta_i = 0.5$ implies that player i is just indifferent between keeping one dollar to himself and giving this dollar to player j. If $\beta_i = 1$, then player i is prepared to throw away one dollar in order to reduce their advantage relative to player i which seems very implausible. This is why we do not consider the case $\beta_i \geq 1$. On the other hand, there is no justification to put an upper bound on α_i. To see this, suppose that player i has a lower monetary payoff than player j. In this case player i is prepared to give up one dollar of their own monetary payoff if this reduces the payoff of their opponent by $(1 + \alpha_i)/\alpha_i$ dollars. For example, if $\alpha_i = 4$, then player i is willing to give up one dollar if this reduces the payoff of his opponent by 1.25 dollars.

Let's apply our model to a well-known simple bargaining game – the ultimatum game. A considerable body of experimental evidence indicates that in the ultimatum game the gains from the task are shared relatively equally. Our alternative to the standard self-interest model $(U_i = z_i)$ explains such "unenvious" outcomes. In an ultimatum game a proposer and a responder bargain about the distribution of a surplus of fixed size. Without loss of generality, we normalize the bargaining surplus to $10, allocable in $1 increments. The responder's amount received is denoted by m and the proposer's $10 − $m. The bargaining rules stipulate that the proposer offers amount $m \in \{$0, 1, \ldots, 9, $10\}$ to the responder. The responder can accept or reject $m. In case of acceptance the proposer receives a monetary payoff $z_1 = $10 − m, while the responder receives $z_2 = m. In case of rejection both players receive a monetary return of zero. The self-interest model predicts that the responder accepts any $m \in \{$1, \ldots, 9, $10\}$ and is indifferent between accepting and rejecting $m = $0. Therefore, there is a unique subgame perfect equilibrium in which proposer offers $m = $1, which is accepted by the responder.[10]

---

[10] A subgame perfect equilibrium is a refinement for a game with sequential play in which neither person will change what they are doing because both are maximizing their own utility given what the other person is doing *at every step of the game.*

(cont.)

There are numerous experimental studies from different countries with different stake sizes and different experimental procedures that clearly refute such a prediction.[11] The following regularities can be considered robust facts: (i) there are virtually no offers above $5; (ii) the vast majority of offers, roughly 60–80 percent, in almost any study are either $4 or $5; (iii) there are almost no offers below $2; (iv) low offers are frequently rejected, and the probability of rejection tends to decrease with $m, and (v) regularities (i) to (iv) continue to hold for rather high stake sizes.

To what extent is our model capable of accounting for the stylized facts of the ultimatum game? To answer this question, suppose that the proposer's preferences are represented by (α_1, β_1), while the responder's preferences are characterized by (α_2, β_2). The following proposition characterizes the equilibrium outcome as a function of these parameters.

PROPOSITION 1.   It is a dominant strategy for the responder to accept any offer $m > \$5$, to reject m if $m < \$m'(\alpha_2) \equiv 10 \cdot \alpha_2 / (1 + 2\alpha_2) < \$5$, and to accept $m > \$m'(\alpha_2)$.[12] If the proposer knows the preferences of the responder, they will offer

$$\$m^* \begin{cases} = \$5, & \beta_1 > 0.5 \\ \in \{\$m'(\alpha_2), \ldots, \$5\} & \beta_1 = 0.5 \\ = \$m'(\alpha_2) & \beta_1 < 0.5. \end{cases}$$

Proof: See Ernst Fehr and Klaus Schmidt (1999, p. 828).

Proposition 1 shows that there are no offers above $5, that offers of $5 are always accepted, and that very low offers are very likely to be rejected. In short, preferences for enviousness can explain the major facts of the ultimatum game.

---

[11] For overviews, see Alvin Roth (1995) and Colin Camerer (2003). In chapter 9 we use a proposition from *Sentiments* to reinterpret the ultimatum game as extortionist, run new versions based on voluntary play, and report a higher frequency of support for equilibrium play than is found in any of the extant literature. Smith models context; using it to study changes in context is more useful for understanding social relationships than fitting the right utility function to any particular context.

[12] A strategy (action) is said to be dominant when it maximizes someone's utility no matter how the other person may play. For this discrete game, $m'(\alpha_2)$ is rounded up to the nearest whole number.

If such a theory looks familiar, that is because the mathematics and its supporting verbs and general language are lifted from a 1999 article by Fehr and Schmidt in the *Quarterly Journal of Economics*. Their scientific aim is not to build a utility maximization model to describe or restate the robust facts of the ultimatum game that have been observed in laboratory experiments, but to present "a *simple common principle* that can explain this puzzling evidence" (Fehr and Schmidt 1999, p. 817, original italics). As Colin Camerer and George Loewenstein explain, such is the goal of behavioral economics more generally, to "increase the explanatory power of economics by providing it with more realistic psychological foundations" (Camerer and Loewenstein 2004, p. 3, original italics). "At the core of behavioral economics," they continue,

is the conviction that increasing the realism of the psychological underpinnings of economic analysis will improve the field of economics *on its own terms* – generating theoretical insights, making better predictions of field phenomena, and suggesting better policy. This conviction does not imply wholesale rejection of the neoclassical approach to economics based on utility maximization, equilibrium, and efficiency. The neoclassical approach is useful because ... it makes refutable predictions.

In the model we present above, the simple common principle is enviousness.[13] But where does this simple common principle come from? From us, given our prior knowledge of ultimatum game results. It is we, the social scientists, who import the principle from our own autobiographical experiences to explain the robust facts of the ultimatum game. It is we, the social scientists, who fellow feel something and thereby know something about the ultimatum game, and it is we, the social scientists, who apply the meaning of enviousness to the actions of the proposer and responder in the ultimatum game. The experiment is not speaking about the social meaning of enviousness. We, the social scientists, are.

Fehr and Schmidt import a different ex post principle, fairness, which they "model ... as self-centered inequity aversion" (1999, p. 819). They "assume" (their word) that which needs to be explained in the ultimatum game, namely that "people experience inequity if they are worse off," and it is they who import by assumption that "an equal outcome is their reference point" (Fehr and Schmidt 1999, p. 822).

When converted into the mathematics of utility maximization, both fairness and enviousness can be operationalized as disutility from unequal outcomes. Are fairness and enviousness the same thing? Far from it. Try

---

[13] We say "enviousness" and not "envy" to distinguish the state of envious feeling, the passion that masters the mind, from the sentiment of envy. See Chapter 2 for a discussion of the difference between passions and sentiments.

substituting enviousness for fairness and see how well that goes over. Let's see: progressive income taxes are a matter of enviousness. No … no, that does not work. How about substituting the other way in some Milton: Thus while he spake, each passion dimmed his face, / Thrice changed with pale – ire, fairness, and despair. Unless fairness is a characteristic of Satan, that does not work either.

So who is to say whose explanation of the ultimatum game, Fehr and Schmidt's or ours, is right? If it is the social scientist's choice, the principle explanation might not be simple or common. Or it might not be scientific explanation at all. Observe that in formulating a utility maximizing model, the theorist begins with a narrative description-explanation of player motivation and feeling, "fairness," but the mathematics, involving comparisons, is more general than the particular story. The model can fit other just-so narratives, in this case "enviousness."

A SMITHIAN RESPONSE TO TWENTIETH- AND TWENTY-FIRST-CENTURY BEHAVIORISM

Knight begins his essay on a pessimistic note. How much of human life is about "using given means to achieve given ends," that is, a maximization problem (Knight 1924, p. 97)? His answer: very little. The "first and most sweeping limitation" of the natural scientific method to economics is that life is about "exploring" and "discovering values" rather than producing and enjoying them "to the greatest possible extent" (Knight 1924, p. 97). The problem is not what choice maximizes some objective but an appreciation for exploring and discovering values of life, the three principles of which we would describe as what is good, what is true, and what is beautiful.

It is Knight's assumption that neither humankind nor its world "can be understood in terms of categories derived from the exigencies of adapting means to given ends" (Knight 1924, p. 101). In other words, we cannot understand the *values* of people and the world they live in, in the terms of a typical problem of maximizing an objective – call it preferences – subject to a set of constraints. It is precisely the assumption of behavioral economics, however, as evidenced by Camerer and Loewenstein and Fehr and Schmidt, that we can indeed understand the values of people – their feeling, thinking, and knowing about what is a good thing to do – in terms of a (single) choice that maximizes a utility function. The problem is that the assumption that Knight denies is not treated as an assumption in behavioral economics, as something to be interrogated and questioned in any model. Rather, utility maximization is a tool beyond question in behavioral economics. That is how we do economics: We calculate. Write down a maximization problem, solve, and repeat. This is the same tool that dominates neoclassical economic method, except that the form of the utility function differs in the two methodologies.

From a natural science perspective that attempts to be objective, the lives of human beings are a "mere matter of mechanics," by which Knight means the behavior of physical bodies subjected to forces or displacements, and the subsequent effects of the bodies on their environment (Knight 1924, p. 97). But it is impossible to discuss human life "in purely objective terms" (Knight 1924, p. 97). As the Goethean scholar of science Henri Bortoft eloquently explains (1996, p. 17, original italics):

Science believes itself to be objective, but is in essence subjective because the witness is compelled to answer questions *which the scientist himself has formulated.* Scientists never notice the circularity in this because they hear the voice of "nature" speaking, not realizing it is the transposed echo of their own voice.

For Knight, the transposed echo of the social scientist's own voice is the "common-sense notion of value as our starting point" (Knight 1924, p. 97). For some, it may or could be enviousness. For Fehr and Schmidt, it is fairness. The second limitation of scientific method to economics is that the scientific age is more about the results of the inquiry, the what-is-it-that-we-can-say-we-know-about-the-world, rather than the why-is-it-that-we-wish-to-understand-the-world. The why-is-it-that-we-wish-to-understand-the-world is a value, the search for what is true, and the scientific attitude, in Knight's words, "destroys the value" of the scientific process; "it emphasizes the quantitative aspect of the result" (Knight 1924, p. 99).

Behavioral economists, for example, focus on the quantitative results of the ultimatum game that "measur[e] how people feel about the allocations of money between themselves and others" (Camerer 2003, p. 9), not why they themselves wish to understand the world through the ultimatum game, nor why they wonder at the results or find them surprising or amazing. And we do not just mean why they wonder at results that reject the straw man of *Homo economicus*. We mean why they themselves wonder and interpret the actions of the participants *as they do*, as, for example, due to the notion of fairness or enviousness or inequality aversion. Behavioral economists treat the ultimatum game as a "simple game [that] test[s] game-theoretic principles in the clearest possible way" (Camerer 2003, p. 9). Is the ultimatum game actually simple, and how does a behavioral economist know that fairness or enviousness explains the results? Is this attribution of fairness or enviousness not the transposed echo of the behavioral economist himself?

When the eighteenth-century Scottish botanist Robert Brown discovered trapped particles moving through water inside a grain of pollen, his first thought was that the particles were alive.[14] His experience with the living world led him to attribute life to a particle that did not sink and appeared to be swimming. Brown was able to isolate the transposed echo of himself when he found a piece of quartz inside of which a drop of water had been trapped for millions of years. Such a specimen not subject to his own lived experience provided a nonliving alternative that could test his proposition that life explains the particles' movements. When he observed the same motion under the same conditions in inorganic as in organic substances, Brown could no longer postulate life as an explanation for Brownian motion. By the very nature of their work, behavioral economists do not have such nonhuman alternatives to isolate their own humanity and objectively test their theories. When studying ourselves, there is no escaping the transposed echoes of our own humanity.

Knight explains natural science as about predicting how "*like* things behave in the same way under the same conditions, or that what is true of one member of a class of similar is true of all" (Knight 1924, p. 104, original italics). He goes on to say that the conditions for prediction are the assimilability of things into classes, the objectivity of the classes, and the possibility of objective measurement. For example, particles in water trapped inside quartz and grains of pollen are assimilable into the objective class of particles suspended in a fluid, and they can be objectively measured with a microscope.

How well does the natural scientific method apply to personal social interactions of behavioral economics? Well, Knight asks, "are there objectively recognizable features in the situation which are uniformly associated with the different possible eventualities?" (1924, p. 115). For behavioral economics, Knight's and our answer is decidedly no. "There is much loose talk," Knight explains, "about the 'analysis' of mental phenomena, which . . . is largely a pernicious use of words; in general these cannot be taken apart or combined experimentally, and neither 'elements' nor 'compounds' have any general marks of identification" (1924, p. 107). There are no separable elements of fairness, enviousness, or inequality aversion that can be added mathematically or experimentally to a base desire that more is better than less, because these states of internal feeling do not have any

---

[14] See Deborah Mayo (1996), Chapter 7.

general marks that we can objectively identify. Sure, fairness and envious-ness as states of feeling have marks that are observable to us, like a smile on our face, a look askance, or an equal split of a windfall sum of money, but none of those general marks objectively pinpoint an internal state of feeling as fairness or enviousness.

What is inserted between the ultimatum game as stimulus and the participants' responses are feelings, doubly so: the participants' feeling of what is good about their task and the behavioral economists' feeling about the participants' feelings about their task. This feeling about what is good is what Knight means by the "common-sense notion of value" and what categorically separates quotidian "common-sense" prediction from natural-scientific prediction. Fairness and enviousness are com-mon sense notions of value. We feel something in our body and thereby know something that people commonly know from experience about value. Common-sense prediction does not treat human beings objec-tively, like things, like molecules in an Erlenmeyer flask. It "connects actions with feelings" as well as intentional states (Knight 1924, p. 111). And here's the kicker: we recognize motives, and we can articulate those motives, but we cannot articulate how we infer motives, "except most superficially" (Knight 1924, p. 112). Our conduct depends upon our autobiographical history and "imperceptible differences in the situation" (Knight 1924, p. 114).

We are taught and we learn how to read motives in others, but we are not taught and we do not learn objective, articulable summaries of people's motives, nor how we learn to recognize them as such. As Knight stresses, "it is possible for a good judge of human nature to form opinions with a high degree of validity as to what individuals or groups are likely to do under conditions present to observation. . . . But none of this is done by the methods of science" (1924, p. 117). He continues: "It may be possible . . . to show *afterwards* that what resulted in any case was what should have been expected from the 'forces' at work. But if these 'forces' cannot be identified and measured, simply, *in some other way other than by waiting for the effect which it is desired to predict*, it is obvious that there is no hope of predic-tion" (1924, p. 121, our italics). Behavioral economics, however, naively proceeds as if there is such a hope. It does so by invoking an invisible force like fairness that is posited to be both the cause for the action (its explana-tion) and the effect of it (its definition):[15]

---

[15] See, e.g., Bart Wilson (2012).

"Why did the proposer offer $5 to the responder?"
"Because that's fair."
"What is a fair outcome in the ultimatum game?"
"The proposer offers $5 to the responder."

Fairness, enviousness, and the like cannot, however, be identified and measured in any other way than by waiting for the effect which it is desired to predict. "The 'stimulus,' in most of the conduct which we need practically to predict, consists of 'reactions' [i.e., feelings, thoughts, and knowledge] of other persons, and is therefore equally unclassifiable and in large part unknowable" (Knight 1924, p. 123). What does Knight mean by unclassifiable and in large part unknowable?

F. A. Hayek explains that our ability to perceive a pattern in human conduct does not necessarily imply an ability to completely specify it.[16] Our sensory perceptions of patterns fall into three categories: (1) those that we can sense and can explicitly describe, (2) those that we cannot sense but can explicitly specify, and (3) those that we can sense but not explicitly specify. For example, in the first category we can sense a pentagon, like this one ⬠, and discursively describe it as such. The description fully describes the perception of a shape. But in the case of the second category, we cannot sense the 6-D pattern of the bee waggle dance, though the mathematician Barbara Shipman can completely specify it as a flag manifold projected onto a perceivable 2-D plane.[17]

Human conduct largely falls into the third category. We can obviously sense a pattern in conduct, but it is a non-specifiable pattern subject to error. We can recognize the actions and associated motivations of someone as being just, fair, or equitable, or beneficent, kind, or humane, but we cannot specify all of the perceptual elements that we treat as part of the same rule pattern (the sense of just as *just* but not *fair*, the sense of beneficent as *beneficent* but not *humane*). Our perception of conduct contains shades and subtleties of ethics and aesthetics that cannot be precisely specified by a set of x_i's and concomitant $U_i = (x_1, ..., x_n)$'s for $i = 1, ..., n$, which is why Knight in a 1922 article in the *Quarterly Journal of Economics* says "it is not enlightening to be told that conduct consists in choosing between possible alternatives."[18] Human conduct is not explicitly specifiable like a perceivable pentagon or a bee waggle dance in unperceivable six dimensions. It is an entirely different kind of sensible pattern. We cannot specify our *sense of* fairness or our *sense of* enviousness in what other people do because our sense of fairness and of enviousness are not

---

[16] F. A. Hayek (1963).   [17] Adam Frank (1997).   [18] Frank Knight (1922).

objective. Our sense of fairness and of enviousness are intersubjective. As social scientists it is important to avoid the error of seeing patterns of human conduct in subjects' actions that use our own perceptions of a one-to-one correspondence between action and preference as elements of a scientific explanation.

Denying that our own perceptions of conduct can be explicitly known as legitimate elements of scientific explanation, however, does not entail denying that our experimental subjects are perceiving non-specifiable patterns in each other's conduct and acting upon them. That our subjects do so must form a datum for analysis, and moreover, it is the foundation of *Sentiments*.

IT TAKES A MODEL TO BEAT A MODEL

Because it is generally sufficient for economists to "explain" human choices, particularly eccentric ones, by inserting something new ex post into a utility function, one rejoinder to Smithian-Knightian limitations on behavioral science is that we are neglecting the sizeable literature that already formalizes a preference for norm compliance. Let's take the work by Erin Krupka and Roberto Weber (2013) as an example.[19] How do they see their project? "We aim to put the horse (norm) before the cart (behavior), by introducing a novel incentivized method for identifying social norms separately from behavior. We use this method to measure social norms in several economic choice contexts, and then use these elicited norms to predict behavior a priori" (p. 496). Krupka and Weber have the right idea. It is too easy to label choices as a one-to-one preference for fairness or enviousness over payoffs. People bring their sense of propriety about social conduct with them into the laboratory where they learn the context of the experiment and then decide what they should do. But it is also too easy to assume that a norm is the explanatory cause of behavior and that it can be objectively measured. If someone is following a norm, the only (necessary but not sufficient) way we can recognize that the person is following the norm is to observe the action. The norm inside the head of an individual is not separately identifiable in the observable world.[20] Knight, in another article published in the *Quarterly Journal of Economics* in 1925,

---

[19] We choose their article because it is refreshingly transparent in explaining the authors' own thinking. The argument is the same for other examples like López-Pérez (2008) and Kimbrough and Vostroknutov (2016).

[20] See, e.g., Bart Wilson (2010).

hits the nail on the head: "A feeling [including that of following a norm], manifestly, is not an 'observed fact;' it is an inference from the behavior itself or at most what is 'reported,' which is to say that it is inferred from a report, which report itself is but an observed behavior fact" (1925, p. 375).

For example, we may say, "The lightning flashes," but the lightning is not the explanatory cause of a flash in the sky. Lightning *is* a flash. To call some observable phenomenon lightning it is necessary (but not sufficient) that we observe a flash of light, and just as there is no lightning without a flash of light, there is no norm without an action. The fact that one set of subjects in the Krupka and Weber experiment labels an action as "socially appropriate" or "socially inappropriate" does not mean that a specific norm is causing/predicting other people to act in such and such a way. Their report on the appropriateness of decisions is but a fact. Even when that scale, collected from one set of subjects, is converted into a number and put on the right-hand side of a regression to explain the actual decisions of another set of subjects, that's not causation/prediction. That's correlation. Such a regression is but a correlation of reported facts. The appearance of the procedures of the experiment combined with the grammar of the exercise force a story of explanatory cause and effect that is unfounded. This does not in any way detract from the facts that Krupka and Weber report, but their experiment itself does not provide support for a model of utility maximization as an explanation for why people do what they do in a laboratory experiment.

What then is the disconnection between a utilitarian model of behavior in the modern social science sense and Smithian human conduct? The difference lies in the unexamined modern assumptions that (1) actions map into outcomes and (2) norm following / other regarding behavior occurs *if and only if* preferences are norm following / other regarding. Rather, in *Sentiments* (1) the mapping is also from the social situation, including outcomes and payoffs as components, into action, and (2) there exists a non-utilitarian model of choice. Experimental economists discovered this when Max-U failed in experimental games; they explored why, and found that intentions mattered. Such considerations, however, were already at the core of *Sentiments*, which articulates principles and propositions for unpacking the meaning conveyed in the social context. In order to read the meaning of actions in their social context, individuals require common knowledge that more of a good (or less of a bad) is better for each, for then each knows which action is beneficial or hurtful to whom. In the absence of this common knowledge of individual non-satiation ("egocentrism"), no one can judge and select socially agreeable actions. Only by knowing that Frank is locally non-satiated does Evelyn know that Frank will reject an ultimatum offer of $m = $2 but not $m = $4. Her action already reflects its rule-governed social context, as well as our knowledge of each other's preferences (via our sense of propriety).

That Frank's action can be "explained" by an appended preference function defined by his everyday experiences with splitting the last piece of pie, incoherently fails to provide insight into the principles that govern his rule-following conduct. *Sentiments* provides such a system. If it had been part of the tradition in economics in the 1980s and 1990s, the results from experimental games would have been anticipated, as well as the subsequent demonstrations that intentions and a sense of propriety matter. As we shall see, adding or subtracting nodes to a game changes actions because it changes what people feel about the possible actions and thereby know from experience; adding or subtracting nodes changes the meaning people read into actions. But individual preferences – more reward is better, less is worse – does not change. Such prescience, in Smith, also predating modern psychology, deserves a sympathetic retrospective hearing.

The methods of natural science do not articulate for us how we can infer and predict what somebody will do. Behavioral economics is in this respect not a science, but rather the art of being human. As Knight emphatically says, "often, indeed, the premises can be discovered and put into words *afterward*, but that again is ... not science" (1924, p. 119, original italics). We can say ex post facto that fairness or enviousness or following a norm is why a proposer offers $5 and a responder rejects $2, but that is not science. That is a human being speaking with the everyday experience of being a human being. "The practical problem of getting along with our fellow human beings," Knight concludes, "must be attacked in the main by a method very different from the technique of natural science, a different kind of development and refinement of common sense, which carries us rather into the fields of aesthetics" (1924, p. 139), which, Samuel Alexander argues, includes ethics and truth as limiting cases.

"The first step ... is to recognize that man's relations with his fellow man are on a totally different footing from his relations with objects of the physical nature and to give up, except within recognized and rather narrow limits, the naïve project of carrying over a technique which has been successful in the one set of problems and using it to solve another set of a categorically different kind" (Knight 1924, p. 139). Knight expresses concern over, as he puts it, the "needless confusion" of using the idea of a static equilibrium in economics, which has a precise meaning in mechanics, but which is anything but precise in human conduct (1924, p. 133). For though we can "explain" human conduct ex post facto, that is, we can recognize our own meanings in what fellow human beings do, we cannot predict ex ante what any specific individual (who is not personally known to us) will do in the laboratory like we can predict water wave mechanics in the laboratory. Humans respond to meaning. And meaning can only be "suggested rather than stated" (Knight 1924, p. 126). Meanings "cannot be taken apart and put together, and it is a misuse of the term 'analysis' to apply it to our thought concerning them, just as all the rest of the technique of natural science is misapplied in their sphere" (Knight 1924, p. 127). Why? Because we cannot point out, that is, articulate, the sense qualities wherein the resemblance, say to fairness or enviousness, exists.

The behavioral economist may say that the equality of the outcome is all the resemblance we need. Except that different situations, as in how the people get to the point of making the decisions, matter. Fairness, enviousness, and inequality aversion are meanings that depend upon what we know about the situation, whether people are voluntarily playing the game, whether the roles are determined randomly or not, what the alternative to the equal outcome is, etc., etc. In other words, their meanings are anything but precise in human conduct.

Economics, it is said, is the study of choice. What is lacking in a choice-based preference for other people's payoffs or intentions or following norms is simply – or rather not so simply – the human being. In personal social situations the variegated mental predicates of human feeling, thinking, and knowing cannot be boiled down to and meaningfully and scientifically interpreted, ex post facto, by the mere choice of $m = \$5$. The assumption that human action unidirectionally maps into outcomes is untenable once one humbly accepts that human feeling, thinking, and knowing about what a good action is also map outcomes into action.[21] Economists are reluctant, to put it mildly, to give up their Max-U theorizing of social situations. The positivist credo in economics is "It takes a model to beat a model." With its own axioms and propositions *Sentiments* is such a model of bidirectional human social life. *Sentiments* is a model of *human*omics.

---

[21] The equivalent problem in econometrics is using ordinary least squares (OLS) to estimate structural parameters in a system of equations with endogenous variables. The unidirectional OLS estimates are inconsistent.

Neither Knight's critique nor our applications of it to ultimatum and trust games are contradicted by the predictive successes of supply and demand theory in laboratory experiments. That success concerns models of the aggregate market economic outcomes achieved, not models of the feeling, thinking, and choosing of the individual, and do not predict at that micro level of an individual's action.[22] Emotions, however, have been usefully, if not predictively, studied in laboratory settings. Kip Smith and John Dickhaut report an empirical investigation of "emotions and choice behavior" in a within-subjects comparison of English and Dutch clock auctions in which the heart rate of individuals is recorded as a physiological proxy for the measurement of an individual's emotional state. Thus to say that emotions relate to action here means that there is a correlation between the heart rate and decision responses. They find that choice by "individuals in the English-clock auction is less mediated by emotional factors than it is in the Dutch-clock auction" (2005, p. 332).

References

Andreoni, James and B. Douglas Bernheim. 2009. "Social Image and the 50–50 Norm: A Theoretical and Experimental Analysis of Audience Effects," *Econometrica* 77 (5): 1607–36.

Bénabou, Roland and Jean Tirole. 2006. "Incentives and Prosocial Behavior," *American Economic Review* 96(5): 1652–78.

Bolton, Gary E. and Axel Ockenfels. 2000. "ERC: A Theory of Equity, Reciprocity, and Competition," *American Economic Review* 90(1): 166–93.

Bortoft, Henri. 1996. *The Wholeness of Nature: Goethe's Way of Science*. Glasgow, UK: Floris Books.

Camerer, Colin F. 2003. *Behavioral Game Theory: Experiments in Strategic Interaction*. Princeton, NJ: Princeton University Press.

Camerer, Colin F. and George Loewenstein. 2004. "Behavioral Economics: Past, Present, Future," in *Advances in Behavioral Economics*, Colin Camerer, George Loewenstein, and Matthew Rabin (eds.). New York, NY: Princeton University Press.

Cappelen, Alexander, Astri Drange Hole, Erik Sørenson, and Bertil Tungodden. 2007. "The Pluralism of Fairness Ideas: An Experimental Approach," *American Economic Review* 97(3): 818–27.

Charness, Gary and Matthew Rabin. 2002. "Understanding Social Preferences with Simple Tests," *Quarterly Journal of Economics* 117(3): 817–69.

[22] In Chapter 1 we noted Adam Smith's critique of David Hume's confusion in identifying the outcome efficiency of human action with the reason for the action.

Cox, James C., Daniel Friedman, and Steven Gjerstad. 2007. "A Tractable Model of Reciprocity and Fairness," *Games and Economic Behavior* 59: 17–45.

Dufwenberg, Martin and Georg Kirchsteiger. 2004. "A Theory of Sequential Reciprocity," *Games and Economic Behavior* 47(2): 268–98.

Falk, Armin and Urs Fischbacher. 2006. "A Theory of Reciprocity," *Games and Economic Behavior* 54, 293–315.

Fehr, Ernst and Klaus M. Schmidt. 1999. "A Theory of Fairness, Competition, and Cooperation," *Quarterly Journal of Economics* 114(3): 817–68.

Frank, Adam. 1997. "Quantum Honeybees," *Discover Magazine*. Available online: http://discovermagazine.com/1997/nov/quantumhoneybees1263#.UXA6f0raix0.

Hayek, F. A. 1963. "Rules, Perception and Intelligibility," *Proceedings of the British Academy* 48: 321–44.

Kimbrough, Erik O. and Alexander Vostroknutov. 2016. "Norms Make Preferences Social," *Journal of the European Econonomic Association* 14(3): 608–38.

Knight, Frank H. 1922. "Ethics and the Economics Interpretation," *Quarterly Journal of Economics* 36(3): 454–81.

Knight, Frank H. 1997 [1924]. "The Limitations of Scientific Method in Economics," reprinted in *The Ethics of Competition*. New Brunswick, NJ: Transaction Publishers.

Knight, Frank H. 1925. "Economic Psychology and the Value Problem," *Quarterly Journal of Economics* 39: 372–409.

Krupka, Erin and Roberto A. Weber. 2009. "The Focusing and Informational Effects of Norms on Pro-social Behavior," *Journal of Economic Psychology* 30(3): 307–20.

Krupka, Erin and Roberto A. Weber. 2013. "Identifying Social Norms Using Coordination Games: Why Does Dictator Game Sharing Vary?" *Journal of the European Economic Association* 11(3): 495–524.

Levine, David K. 1998. "Modeling Altruism and Spitefulness in Experiments," *Review of Economic Dynamics* 1(3): 595–622.

López-Pérez, Raúl. 2008. "Aversion to Norm-breaking: A Model," *Games and Economic Behavior* 64(1): 237–67.

Mayo, Deborah G. 1996. *Error and the Growth of Experimental Knowledge*. Chicago: University of Chicago Press.

Rabin, Matthew. 1993. "Incorporating Fairness into Game Theory and Economics," *American Economic Review* 83(5): 1281–1302.

Roth, Alvin E. 1995. "Bargaining Experiments," in *The Handbook of Experimental Economis*, John Kagel and Alvin Roth (eds.). Princeton, NJ: Princeton University Press, 253–91.

Schoeck, Helmut. 1987 [1966]. *Envy: A Theory of Social Behaviour*. Indianapolis, IN: Liberty Fund.

Smith, Kip and John Dickhaut. 2005. "Economics and emotion: Institutions matter," *Games and Economic Behavior* 52: 316–35.

Tversky, Amos and Daniel Kahneman. 1991. "Loss Aversion in Riskless Choice: A Reference-Dependent Model," *Quarterly Journal of Economics* 106(4): 1039–61.

Watson, John B. 1913. "Psychology as the Behaviorist Views It," *Psychological Review* 20: 158–77.

Wilson, Bart J. 2010. "Social Preferences Are Not Preferences," *Journal of Economic Behavior and Organization* 73(1): 77–82.

Wilson, Bart J. 2012. "Contra Private Fairness," *American Journal of Economics and Sociology* 71(2): 407–35.

5

Axioms and Principles for Understanding Human Conduct

We offer a summary of Adam Smith's conception of the conditions that define the rules that govern human conduct as expressed in the choices of action by an individual. Today economists and psychologists call it decision-making or decision theory, and model it much more narrowly than did Smith for whom the individual was an inseparable part of a social system.

His discussion of the particular issues we select for examination are not conveniently collected in any one place in *Sentiments*, but his rigor is not thereby compromised. His concern is to convey a coherent and persuasive narrative form of his model with many examples and illustrations that the reader of his time could likely identify with. For Smith, moral theory is about the rules we follow and the theory must provide a coherent account of everyday observations from human social activity.

For Smith and David Hume before him, "experiments" are observations – cases, examples, illustrations – that constitute the evidence with which a system of reasoning must be consistent.[1] Thus, Hume argues that a science of human sociality must build on experiments that we have selected through careful observation of people's behavior in the context of their ordinary official or pleasurable day-to-day interactions in the company of others. From such cases "judiciously collected and compared," his intention is to contribute to a useful science.[2]

---

[1] That Hume and Smith might be interpreted as having gone too far, and, along with Isaac Newton, slipped into thinking or believing that they inferred their results (hypotheses) directly from observations, will not distract us from the importance of their recognition of the role of observations in disciplining the systematic treatment of social theory. See Vernon Smith (2008, chapter 13).

[2] Hume (1740, p. 6)

Hume and Smith see experiments as important generally to discipline our systematic, but abstract, reconstructions of sociality. Equally important – on the other side of that coin – experiments provided the specific forms of experience that shape and govern the fitness of the gradually emergent rules that people live by in their social groupings.

Smith strongly emphasizes that it is a fallacy to believe that our original moral perceptions of conduct are based on reason, even in those cases where general rules grow directly out of our experience and become an emergent order. These perceptions and the experience on which rules are founded are a consequence of our minds but not of reasoned thoughts:

> It is by finding in a vast variety of instances that one tenor of conduct constantly pleases in a certain manner, and that another constantly displeases the mind, that we form the general rules of morality. But reason cannot render any particular object either agreeable or disagreeable to the mind for its own sake. (TMS, Seventh. III.II, p. 470)

Let's unpack what Smith means by this. Part of conduct being pleasing or displeasing to the mind is that the meaning of it feels good or bad to us. What we feel about someone's conduct may be purely private, but what we know about it is not. Someone's conduct has value insofar as we sense the act to be likewise known by others to be good or bad because they, as a fellow human being, feel like we feel. Someone's conduct is not agreeable or disagreeable because it pleases the mind, but, to borrow a phrase from Hume, the conduct pleases "after . . . a particular manner."[3] The good or bad feelings of someone's conduct happen to a mind that knows other minds that likewise hold the same conduct to the same value standard, either good or bad. Smith is asserting that we do not logically think ourselves into making out any act to be agreeable or disagreeable; reasoned thoughts cannot make the mind feel the pleasure or displeasure of someone's good or bad conduct.

AXIOMS

The axioms we attribute to Smith are identified as such because they are elementary statements that, as we interpret Smith, he relies and builds on in developing certain higher level or derived principles and propositions that constitute his model of human sociality. The statements are also

---

[3] Hume (1740, p. 303): "We do not infer a character to be virtuous, because it pleases: But in feeling that it pleases after such a particular manner, we in effect feel that it is virtuous."

axioms in the sense that they are elementary self-evident commonly experienced truths.

Axiom 0: Human beings are non-satiated (Stoic self-love).

According to Smith, man is naturally self-loving. Stated in modern terms, the most fundamental axiom underlying his systematic treatment of action is common knowledge of non-satiation; that for each person more of a valued item (money or fungible goods) is better, and less of it is worse. It does not follow, however, as in neoclassical economics and in traditional game theory, that in our human associations our actions are concerned only to increase our own gain or to avoid our own loss. From our birth, we are shaped into social creatures, but we are also instruments of that shaping. To be social is to be other-regarding, to take into account the feelings of gratitude or resentment in others in response to an action we choose, within multilateral consensus. Perhaps because he thought it was transparently obvious, nowhere does Smith seem to state the incisive work this axiom does in understanding human sociability. However, Smith's use of the axiom of self-love, and common knowledge thereof is everywhere implicit in his examples and propositions. His statement of the axiom is quite explicit.

- Every man is, no doubt, by nature, first and principally recommended to his own care; and as he is fitter to take care of himself than of any other person, it is fit and right that it should be so. (TMS, Second.II.II, p. 119)
- Every animal was by nature ... endowed with the principle of self-love ... (TMS, Seventh.II.II, p. 402).

And, wryly but more expansively, we are informed that:

We are not ready to suspect any person of being defective in selfishness. This is by no means the weak side of human nature, or the failing of which we are apt to be suspicious ... Carelessness and want of economy are universally disapproved of, not, however, as proceeding from a want of benevolence, but from a want of the proper attention to the objects of self-interest. (TMS, Seventh.II.III, p. 446)

But why does his model demand Axiom 0? Without common knowledge that all are self-interested, Smith's actors would not know, given the particular circumstances and opportunities to act, whether and to whom the specific outcome of an action is beneficial or hurtful relative to an action, or actions, that could have been taken. Yet his whole system derives from judgments concerning how a person, whose action affects another person, either benefits or suffers hurt by the action relative to an available alternative action. You cannot speak of individuals having a common sense of what is beneficial or hurtful without such an axiom. An action hurts me but benefits you, whereas the context allows another action that benefitted us both. Hence, common knowledge that for each person affected more is desirable and less is undesirable is an integral part of making the judgments necessary for us to implement the fellow-feeling basis of our sociality. Universal self-love is an input to the formation of the other-regarding rules that make us social.

Modern behavioral theorists are located firmly in the neoclassical utilitarian tradition in the sense that it assumed that action yields an outcome yields utility, and vice versa: Action *if and only if* the outcome increases utility.[4] Hence, social preferences are about other-regarding action *if and only if* other-regarding utility $U_{self}(x_{self}, x_{other})$. I give up more for myself in accepting your offer to cooperate because I derive utility value from your receiving more; i.e., implicitly I believe you prefer more. But if you harbor other-regarding utility, this may conflict with your preferences. The exchange of gifts and favors makes sense in an environment of socialized self-lovers who feel gratitude for such actions but creates potential inconsistencies otherwise.

Trade and markets for goods and services are extensions of human sociality in which we make an immediate or contractually pledged payment in compensation for the items provided to us by others, and in like manner, we expect compensation from others for what we provide and deliver to them. Being voluntary, the result (in the absence of fraud, misunderstanding, misrepresentation, and false labeling) is unhurtful, and does not depend on gratitude carried over into the future, as in reciprocity exchanges across time. All such trades in economics are exchanges of gifts, in the sense that each has to give in order to receive. Thus:

Give me that which I want, and you shall have this which you want, is the meaning of every such offer; and it is in this manner that we obtain from one another the far greater part of those good offices which we stand in need of Smith. (WN, p. 26)

---

[4] For example in Ernst Fehr and Urs Fischbacher (2002, p. C1): "A substantial number of people exhibit social preferences, which means they are not solely motivated by material self-interest but also care positively or negatively for the material payoffs of relevant reference agents." Also in Colin Camerer (2003, p. 43): "The data falsify the assumption that players maximize their own payoffs as clearly as experimental data can ... (and) is a crisp way of measuring social preferences rather than a deep test of strategic thinking."

Market exchange extends sociality to people we do not, and never may know, so that the response to goods given is immediate recompense in goods or money, not the universally expressed and recognized, "I owe you one," as with a friend's or neighbor's favor. There, exchanges are across time, and memory markers brightened by feelings of gratitude help to sustain reciprocity. Trade with strangers facilitated by externally enforced property right rules, substitute for trust in helping to guard us against fraud. Consequently, we need not rely entirely upon the rules and conventions in our close-knit communities to enjoy an orderly means of benefiting from much larger networks of people. In this sense, Smith's Axiom 0 underlies the creation of both social and economic betterment in which our self-interest is governed by rules of conduct that avoid harming others and that encourage beneficence toward others.

Although civil rule-of-law property rights substitute for trust and trustworthiness to help facilitate impersonal markets, enforcement costs would reduce and might destroy the gains from exchange if every trade required the watchful eye of police enforcement. Hence, the importance of Smith's principle of self-command in providing some element of endogenous support where transactions can easily escape external monitoring. We are reminded of the roadside vegetable stands sprinkled through rural America, often unattended but with a cash box where you can leave your money in payment for items taken.

We merely restate the next three axioms from Chapters 2 and 3:

Axiom 1: Human beings fellow feel with each other.

Axiom 2: Human beings judge the sentiments and passions of each other.

Axiom 3: Gratitude and resentment, respectively, are the sentiments that most immediately and directly prompt human beings to reward and to punish each other.

To which we add one assumption:

Assumption 1: If action Z^ε for $\varepsilon \in \{good, bad\}$ is the object of sentiment $\sigma(\varepsilon) \in \{gratitude, resentment\}$, then X doing Z^ε is the object of $\sigma(\varepsilon)$.

In short, we assume that we judge the moral stance of people by the actions they take. As Goethe and Wittgenstein say: In the beginning was the deed. Smith nowhere makes this assumption explicit, though he regularly maps back and forth between the action and the person being the object of gratitude and resentment. We will also need the following definition:

Definition 1: We say that Z^ε appears to deserve action $\alpha(\varepsilon) \in \{reward, punish\}$ if Z^ε is the proper and approved object of $\sigma(\varepsilon)$.

Smith uses these four axioms in Part Second to establish a lemma on desert, though he does not call it that (TMS, Second.I.I, p. 96). We will find the lemma useful in presenting Smith's major propositions in Part Second.II.I:

Desert Lemma: If X does Z^ε and Z^ε is the object of $\sigma(\varepsilon)$, Z^ε appears to deserve $\alpha(\varepsilon)$.

Proof: By Assumption 1 if Z^ε being the object of $\sigma(\varepsilon)$, X is the object of $\sigma(\varepsilon)$. By Axiom 1 we fellow feel with X's sentiments for doing Z^ε, and by Axiom 2 we use our sense of propriety to judge the fellow-felt sentiments of X doing Z^ε.

Case 1: If, when judging X's sentiments, we think that X did not have to do Z^{good}, i.e., we think that the sentiments of X are proper; and if, when judging X's sentiments, we want to think *good* things about X because of this, i.e., we approve of the sentiments of X; and if, when judging X's sentiments, we feel something *good* when we think about all of this, then by the definition in Chapter 2 we feel gratitude towards X.

Case 2: If, when judging X's sentiments, we think that X did not have to do Z^{bad}, i.e., we think that the sentiments of X are improper; and if, when judging X's sentiments, we want to think *bad* things about X because of this, i.e., we disapprove of the sentiments of X; and if, when judging X's sentiments, we feel something *bad* when we think about all of this, then by the definition in Chapter 2 we feel resentment towards X.

By Axiom 0 we know that X is made better off with $\alpha(good)$, and that X is made worse off with $\alpha(bad)$. By Axiom 3 we are prompted immediately and directly either to reward Z^{good} by doing $\alpha(good)$ in Case 1 and or to punish Z^{bad} by doing $\alpha(bad)$ in Case 2. In both cases by Definition 1 Z^ε appears to deserve action $\alpha(\varepsilon) \in \{reward, punish\}$. ∎

Is this lemma belabored? Most definitely, it is, and probably philosophically incomplete in all sorts of details. But the three points from the lemma worth belaboring and envisaging are: (1) every Axiom 0–3 is critical to the human sense of merit and demerit, (2) Smith's account of desert is both formal and capable of formalization, and (3) the lemma explicates why modern behavioral economics has spun its wheels in trying to give coherence to economists' intuitions about desert.

Before we can decide to act, thinking, feeling, and knowing must be an integral part of why someone appears to deserve reward or punishment. We cannot take apart the feeling, thinking, and knowing in regard to someone's act or combine such mental predicates experimentally or even identify their general marks on how it appears to our minds that someone deserves reward or punishment. Nevertheless, the minds of our experimental participants do indeed think, feel, and know something about each other's appearance of desert. Sussing out such mental predicates by waiting for the effect to manifest itself in a subsequent action is not scientific explanation, but that does not make the behavioral economists' experiments any less interesting. They are part of the evidence that Smith's theory can handle.

A fourth axiom is essential to understanding how Smith interprets an individual's choice of an action in the light of how others see the action. As we will show, this axiom ultimately underlies Smith's theory of justice (and of property) and his theory of beneficence in all human relationships.

Axiom 4: As compared to a normal baseline condition, human beings experience an asymmetrical change between feeling something good (e.g., joy) and feeling something bad (e.g., sorrow).

Because we experience love as an agreeable, resentment as a disagreeable, passion, Smith argues that we are much more concerned that our friends sympathize with our resentments than with our favors. Although our friends need not be friends to our friends, we can hardly tolerate them if they cannot be enemies of our enemies. "The agreeable passions of love and joy can satisfy and support the heart without any auxiliary pleasure. The bitter and painful emotions of grief and resentment more strongly require the healing consolation of sympathy" (TMS, First.I. II, p. 12–3).

These attitudes arise from a fundamental asymmetry between our joy and our sorrow, not as an isolated property of the individual, but as a social creature. For someone in a reasonably comfortable position – or as Smith puts it, "who is out of debt, and has a clear conscience" – little can be added to his state of well-being. But much can be taken from that state. Our experience of anything that can be added is small in comparison with the social psychological depths to which we can fall in adversity. Hence, the latter can potentially depress the mind much further below its natural state than more increments of good fortune can raise him above it (TMS, First. III.I, p. 62–3).

PRINCIPLES

Human sociality is ancient. Except for orangutans and small nocturnal prosimians (e.g., galagos and mouse lemurs), primates spend their lives in large social communities. Sometime in history (anywhere from 250 thousand years ago (kya) to as late as 70–100 kya) when *Homo sapiens* became fully symbolic, we started judging the abstract qualities of the things we do.[5] Killing a conspecific in ones' community became not merely the physical movement of taking a life, of bashing in a head with a stone, but murder, a complex action superimposed with moral qualities. Our bare physical movements at some point became *actions*, primarily moral and only secondarily physical. And when our actions themselves became important, that is, when we came to contemplate our actions *for the sake of contemplating them*, beneficent, prudent, and unjust actions became weightier *acts* of beneficence, prudence, and injustice. Such contemplation did not stop with individual moral or immoral acts. We contemplated our acts as a collection, as a whole, and in doing so the individual things we did became our *deeds*, graver and more prominent. Our deeds came to mean something about who we are as individuals and to say something about us to the rest of our community. As Samuel Alexander says, we learned to know the "I" through our daily experience with the "We." Human sociality may be primeval, but only one precocious primate came to possess a self-contemplating character, a sense of duty socialized to and accountable for living a life with a large number of other members of its kind.

The principles we attribute to Smith are general truths that Smith explains, and which, along with key axioms above, serve as bases for more extensive statements. In the next chapter, we further identify such statements as propositions with rich predictive content.

Principle 1: Out of a desire to satisfy our social impulse, human beings self-examine their own sentiments, impartially judge their own conduct, and exercise self-command in resonance with the judgment of others.

In judging the sentiments and passions of others (Axiom 2), "we soon learn, that other people are equally frank with regard to our own" (TMS, Third.(I).I, p. 164). Our sympathetic sensitivity to how others experience and react to us leads us to become sensitive to the image we project to others and thus to exercise self-command in our personal conduct. Each

---

[5] For example, William Rendua et al. (2014) find evidence that early peoples began burying their dead.

person attunes their own willed ends to intersubjectively satisfy the impulse of sociality (TMS, Third.(I).I, p. 162):

We endeavour to examine our own conduct as we imagine any other fair and impartial spectator would examine it. If, upon placing ourselves in his situation, we thoroughly enter into all the passions and motives which influenced it, we approve of it, by sympathy with the approbation of this supposed equitable judge. If otherwise, we enter into his disapprobation, and condemn it.

Part of the process of judging our own conduct is self-examining our own sentiments. Even though "we can never survey our own sentiments and motives," we can "endeavour to view them as at a certain distance from us. But we can do this in no other way than by endeavoring to view them with the eyes of other people, or as other people are likely to view them" (TMS, Third.(I).I, p. 161). "This is the only looking-glass by which we can, in some measure, with the eyes of other people, scrutinize the propriety of our own conduct" (TMS, Third.(I).I, p. 164).

As fallible beings we either meet the intersubjective standard and exercise self-command when acting, or we fail to meet the standard and fail to exercise self-command. In either case we take part in the state of the disinterested spectator's feeling. If we fellow feel with the approbation of the judge in the looking-glass, we approve of our own conduct. The feeling of making out our conduct to be good, and the thinking that it is positively so, pleases our mind because the conduct satisfies our social impulse. But if we sympathize with the disapprobation of the judge in the looking-glass, we disapprove of our own conduct. The disapprobation of our bad conduct displeases our mind because the conduct runs counter to our social impulse.

From Axiom 4, Smith derives his important second principle:

Principle 2: Human beings experience asymmetrically gains and losses from our own and other's actions.

"We suffer more . . . when we fall from a better to a worse situation, than we ever enjoy when we rise from a worse to a better" (TMS, Sixth.I, p. 311). Prudence first requires us to seek security. To avoid exposing "our health, our fortune, our rank, or reputation" to loss. We are anxious to protect the advantages we have attained, and we seek to avoid risking loss in the acquisition of more advantages.

In their study of decision-making, cognitive psychologists recognized this asymmetry in their independent discovery of "loss aversion" as it surfaced beginning in the 1970s, and in a great many experimental studies of individual choice involving gambles defined on the domain of monetary loss as compared with choice defined on the gain domain. For any initial reference state, most people were willing to pay a premium to avoid a risk of loss, but they would pay a premium to accept a risk of gain. The expected utility implication was that individual utility functions were defined over deviations in wealth (income), whatever might be the initial reference level of wealth. For positive increments utility was increasing and concave; for negative increments utility was decreasing, but convex.[6]

This formalization corresponds to Adam Smith's conception, except that for Smith gain and loss to the individual had extensive social dimensions – reputation, status and esteem – as well as individual health and fortune (chance or probability) in outcomes. He modeled the social person, not the individual. However, we know of no recognition of similar elements of motivation, let alone citations of *Sentiments,* in the early psychology literature. Smith's contributions were never discovered, and could not influence their modern independent discovery.

Because Smith derived Principle 2 from a more elementary examination of human joy and sorrow, he was able to extract additional testable fine-tuned results beyond simple gain-loss asymmetry as we find it in the modern literature. Thus, Smith recognizes some important differences between what we might call a person's natural asymmetric experience of joy and sorrow, and the sympathy that is felt toward the joy or sorrow of another, which can be summarized as a third principle:

> *Principle 3: Human beings sympathize more readily with a friend who moderately feels good or deeply feels bad than the reverse: Envy easily attenuates our participation in the good feelings of another; whereas our participation in the bad feelings of another is more strongly felt.*

Let chance lift a person immediately to levels of gain far in excess of any previously experienced. Smith assures us that the congratulations forthcoming from even one's best friends will not be perfectly sincere for all of them. Such is the universal human sentiment of envy. If the person has good judgment and is sensible of this, he will play down the joy and avoid the elation as the situation naturally tends to inspire in order to avoid being offensively jubilant (TMS, First.II.V, pp. 55–56).

In opposite measure we may struggle to contain our sympathy with the sorrow of another. We make effort to suppress it, but not always

---

[6] See Daniel Kahneman and Amos Tversky (1979).

successfully. We feel no similar opposition with our sympathy with joy. "We often feel a sympathy with sorrow when we would wish to be rid of it; and we often miss that with joy when we would be glad to have it" (TMS, First.III.I, p. 62). We may express our elation with our neighbor's success while inwardly feeling the regrets of envy even though we are ashamed of that envy.

The strong gain-loss asymmetry stated in Principle 3, affects Smith's approach to motivation, and thence to the understanding of human conduct as expressed in action. We capture this strong bifurcation by stating separately his motivational principles in the domain of gain on the one hand, and in the domain of loss on the other.

Principle 4 (a): Human motivation for action arises from wanting praise and to be praiseworthy (the gain domain).

Another consequence of our impulse for sociality is that people naturally seek to be loved but also genuinely to be deserving of that love. Therefore, they desire honest praise and praiseworthiness, as social indicators or markers of the affection they seek. Even if one's conduct does not invoke praise, one desires to be worthy of praise, to be "the natural and proper object of praise" (TMS, Third.(I).II, p. 166). Praise and praiseworthiness are connected, though our love of praiseworthiness does not derive from our desire for praise; the two are distinct and independent of one another.

Principle 4 (b): Human motivation for action also arises from not wanting blame and to not be blameworthy (the loss domain).

People naturally dread to be hated, and to be hateful; they dread to be the object of hatred. And accordingly people desire to conduct themselves so as to assiduously avoid both blame and blameworthiness (TMS, Third.(I).II, p. 166).

Of these two motivations, however, the avoidance of blame and blameworthiness is far more compelling than the desire to be the object of praise and to feel an attendant sense of praise-worthiness. Thus: "A wise man may frequently neglect praise, even when he has best deserved it; but, in all matters of serious consequence, he will most carefully endeavour so to regulate his conduct as to avoid, not only blameworthiness, but, as much as possible, every probable imputation of blame" (TMS, Third.(I).II, p. 184).

When humans participate in the state of feeling with each other, we use our physical senses to comprehend the manifestations of someone's internal feeling, which includes not just what we see and hear regarding the person, but the entire set of circumstances or context in which the person is acting. We see their tears and hear the frustration in their voice, but we also know that they chose to take out an adjustable rate mortgage to buy a house rather than to rent one. Our sense of the propriety of an action accounts for the circumstances of time and place in which the action was taken.

> *Principle 5: Human actions are signals shaped by their propriety or impropriety, given the circumstances or context of the action.*

We can sense what another feels only "by conceiving what we ourselves would feel in a like situation" (TMS, First.I.I, p. 3). Fellow-feeling therefore arises from the situation, the circumstances, the context in which we act and observe others acting, and which excites that sympathy (TMS, First.I.I, pp. 4–8). Otherwise, drawing on our social experience, we are not able to judge the propriety or impropriety of another's action, nor can others judge our action except from the context in which we choose one action and not an alternative that is available, each with a distinct pattern of outcomes. "In the suitableness or unsuitableness, in the proportion or disproportion which the affection seems to bear to the cause or object which excites it, consists the propriety or impropriety . . . of the consequent action" (TMS, First.I.III, p. 17).

> *Principle 6: The circumstances or context of an action acquires importance because it enables human beings to read intentions and find meaning in each other's actions.*

Any praise or blame consequent to an action depends on the intentions perceived in the action (TMS, Second.I.III, p. 100; Second.III.Intro, p. 133). "To the intention or affection of the heart, therefore, to the propriety or impropriety, to the beneficence or hurtfulness of the design, all praise or blame, all approbation or disapprobation, of any kind, which can justly be bestowed upon any action, must ultimately belong" (TMS, Second.III. Intro, p. 134).

> *Principle 7: An equilibrium concept, if it can be said to exist, is based on mutual fellow-feeling and lives in rule space.*

In a section entitled "Of the Pleasures of Mutual Sympathy" (TMS, First. I.II), Smith explains that whatever might be the source of our sympathetic emotions, or the circumstances that evoke our sympathy, we are naturally pleased to observe in others the same fellow-feeling we experience in ourselves. Observing the contrary causes us to feel discordance, which is painful for us. For example, you hold the door open for a stranger; instead of a "thank you," your action is ignored.

Smith notes that some have argued that our actions in response to these common experiences of pleasure or of pain are derivable from "certain refinements of self-love." "Man, say they, conscious of his own weakness, and of the need which he has for the assistance of others, rejoices whenever he observes that they adopt his own passions, because he is then assured of that assistance; and grieves whenever he observes the contrary, because he is then assured of their opposition" (TMS, First.I.II, p. 10). Smith could be describing one (among many) of the modern utilitarians who is alert to identifying subjective elements of pleasure or pain that enter postulated social utility functions defined over actions that yield individual sense experiences. He rejects any such approach: "But both the pleasure and the pain are always felt so instantaneously, and often upon such frivolous occasions, that it seems evident that neither of them can be derived from any such self-interested consideration" (TMS, First.I.II, p. 10).

Why does Smith say that because such pleasure or pain is felt "instantaneously" it cannot be attributable to "refinements" of self-love? Because, as we interpret him, common knowledge of self-love allows us to sense or read the pattern of hurts and benefits in our action or that of another, and "insensibly" (without conscious forethought and contemplation) to invoke a rule-governed response from our long experience with the circumstances defined by the given context. The cultural fixity of rule-following responses are acquired by a slow progression and are subject to errors and inconsistencies because of shortcomings in our self-command, our vulnerability to the temptations of the moment and to the ambiguity and error in reading the circumstances of action. Thus (TMS, Third.(I).IV, p. 224):

Our continual observations upon the conduct of others, insensibly lead us to form to ourselves certain general rules concerning what is fit and proper either to be done or to be avoided.... It is thus that the general rules of morality are formed. They are ultimately founded upon experience of what, in particular instances ... our natural sense of merit and propriety, approve, or disapprove of. We do not originally approve or condemn particular actions; because, upon examination, they appear to be agreeable or inconsistent with a certain general rule. The general rule, on the contrary, is formed, by finding from experience, that all actions of a certain kind, or circumstanced in a certain manner, are approved or disapproved of.

The rules we acquire are fashioned through the marks made upon us by our experience in interacting with others, embracing acts of praise/praiseworthiness, and avoiding acts of blame/blameworthiness. Echoing

Hume, they serve us well by diminishing the set of greater inconveniences we would otherwise endure.

References

Camerer, Colin F. 2003. *Behavioral Game Theory: Experiments in Strategic Interaction.* Princeton, NJ: Princeton University Press.

Fehr, Ernst and Urs Fischbacher. 2002. "Why Social Preferences Matter: The Impact of Non-selfish Motives on Competition, Cooperation, and Incentives," *Economic Journal* 112: C1–C33.

Hume, David. 2000 [1740]. *A Treatise of Human Nature*, David Fate Norton and Mary J. Norton (eds.). New York, NY: Oxford University Press.

Kahneman, Daniel and Amos Tversky. 1979. "Prospect Theory: An Analysis of Decision under Risk," *Econometrica* 47(2): 263–91.

Rendua, William, Cédric Beauval, Isabelle Crevecoeur, Priscilla Bayle, Antoine Balzeau, Thierry Bismuth, Laurence Bourguignon, Géraldine Delfour, Jean-Philippe Faivre, François Lacrampe-Cuyaubère, Carlotta Tavormina, Dominique Todisco, Alain Turq, and Bruno Maureille. 2014. "Evidence Supporting an Intentional Neandertal Burial at La Chapelle-aux-Saints," *Proceedings of the National Academy of Sciences* 111(1): 81–6.

Smith, Adam. 1853 [1759]. *The Theory of Moral Sentiments; or, An Essay towards an Analysis of the Principles by which Men naturally judge concerning the Conduct and Character, first of their Neighbours, and afterwards of themselves. To which is added, A Dissertation on the Origins of Languages. New Edition. With a biographical and critical Memoir of the Author*, by Dugald Stewart. London, UK: Henry G. Bohn. Available online and in electronic formats at http://oll.libertyfund.org/titles/2620.

Smith, Adam. 1981 [1776]. *An Inquiry into the Nature and Causes of the Wealth of Nations*. Vol. 1 & 2. Indianapolis, IN: Liberty Fund.

Smith, Vernon L. 2008. *Rationality in Economics*. Cambridge, UK: Cambridge University Press.

6

Propositions Predicting Context-Specific Action

Less evident from *Sentiments* are the mechanisms whereby rules emerge as conventions; i.e., become fixed by some form of mutual interaction in society, and which renders one society different from another. The example below illustrates Smith's model.

EXAMPLE OF A RULE, ADAPTATION TO THE RULE, AND EQUILIBRIUM HARMONY IN RULE SPACE

In a first-person narrative here is a personal one-on-one experience of Vernon that illustrates how the fine-grained context of actions, in this case the action taken and the alternative action not taken (but corrected), together give mutual meaning (mutual fellow-feeling) to the propriety of a rule. Also illustrated is the adaptation whereby the failure of one party to follow the right rule is greeted with disapproval and the error corrected to yield "equilibrium" in rule space (agreement). Moreover, the monetary stakes are small, but the consequences in terms of praise/praiseworthiness and blame/blameworthiness are large to the participants, and this is what motivates change. Vernon picks up the story from here:

> In Tucson, Arizona, homeless people commonly occupy islands at major traffic intersections. In the suburbs, individuals equip their island stations with an inventory of newspapers. The same familiar individuals appear regularly on particular traffic islands for extended periods – property rights governed by mutual consent seem clearly to be functioning in this community with no official external enforcement. I sometimes buy a newspaper at one island, although the internet has weened me away from the regular

(cont.)

reading of print media. Arriving in the left turn lane by the island near my home, I saw the familiar figure of the past two to three years at his post as I stopped behind several waiting cars. I rolled down the window, and he walked within reach. As I reached out my right hand to give him five dollars, he started to accept it with his left hand while his right hand held out a copy of the folded newspaper for me to take. Insensibly, on autopilot, I said, "That's ok, you can keep the paper." He immediately withdrew both hands, and replied quite simply and informatively, "I only sell newspapers." Fortunately, I got the message immediately. (Feeling, then thinking?) I rescued him and myself from our embarrassment, recovered, and said, "I will take it." I did, he took the bill, and we looked into each other's eyes and smiled.

In this encounter, I saw myself as volunteering generosity twice over, paying him and allowing him to sell the paper to another person. However, I was badly misreading him. He was a self-sufficient businessman; he was delivering value in return for payment. If he had accepted my bill and allowed me to decline the newspaper, it would have corrupted the meaning he intended and was concerned to convey. There was a critical disharmony between the rules that each of us followed. A rule maps the circumstances, including payoffs (who gives and who receives how much) into an action, as determined by its propriety. He corrected the impropriety – the source of disharmony – in a way that enriched the mapping from circumstances into action for both of us. From my perspective, the correction was not to be forgotten. In terms of the understanding we seek in this book, it was a lesson in how rules adapt through shared experiences among strictly self-interested individuals. It is entirely acceptable for me to give him a generous tip; that simply signals that I am especially grateful for his services. But there is no way that I can refuse his product and part with my five dollars. He has integrity. He is not corrupt, and he is not going to let me be the instrument of his corruption, of his failure to be true to himself. The transaction was not just about a sale; it was also about the perceived self-dignity of the seller, and the recognition of that state by the buyer. If he were to make an exception, he starts down a slippery slope; he does not.

(cont.)

A second encounter, months later, confirmed and elaborated this image. It also demonstrates my rule modification in the light of experience – the prominent theme in *Sentiments* is that rules emerge from experience, in particular, repeat experience. My wife Candace and I were in the coffee-snack seating area of the local supermarket near his island. It was midafternoon. He was across the room talking with some local high school students, both he and they having finished for the day. My wife spoke to me, saying, "He does not look very good. I am going to give him five dollars." I said, "Do not. Ask him if he has a newspaper." She did, and he was pleased. He insisted that we wait while he went to get one, although Candace indicated that we were soon to leave any way and could come out to get the paper. But he had this service orientation, and soon returned with the paper. As the transaction was being completed, he volunteered: "Some of my customers ask if I have any of yesterday's newspapers, so I always keep a few for the next day." A window on his range of services.

We have not seen him for a year, and his station has passed to another person. The operant property rights do not permit waste. There are rules of propriety in maintaining possession. There are rules for orderly customer relations. We may suppose there are rules of succession.

Observe that understanding the actions taken in our transaction has nothing to do with utilitarian social preferences. In this narrative, I (Vernon) had not the slightest doubt that he preferred more money, and surely, he doubts not that I preferred more. Sociability is about fellow feeling, propriety, and following mutually approved protocols, not a neoclassical error in failing to specify the right utility function.

BENEFICENCE AND JUSTICE AS VIRTUES

In Part Second, Section II of *Sentiments* Smith applies the sense of merit and demerit to the exercise of two primary virtues, beneficence and justice. A virtue is a practiced and persisting goodness. The philosopher Julia Annas defines a virtue, taking its goodness for granted, as "a lasting feature of a person, a tendency for the person to be a certain way. It is not merely a lasting feature, however, one that just sits there undisturbed. It is *active*: to have it is to be disposed to act in certain ways. And it *develops* through selective response to circumstances" (2011, p. 8, original italics). Notice that virtue is a tendency, not a certainty, for a person to act in a certain way. While "virtue only," in Smith's words, "is regularly and orderly," humans are nevertheless fallible (TMS, Sixth.II.I, p. 330). We can on occasion ill fall short of exercising our skills of virtuousness.

While the indispensable virtue of justice may be a familiar concept to the reader, the word *beneficence* has an archaic ring to it, sounding more like an eighteenth-century word than a twenty-first century one (when did you last use the word in conversation?).[1] *Beneficence* is, literally from Latin, "well doing," and according to the *OED* only entered the lexicon in the sixteenth century. Its older Latin relation, *benevolence*, is used by Chaucer (that would be in 1384). Benevolence is, literally, "well willing." Thus, *benevolence* consists of the intention to do good for another, *beneficence* the action that does good for another. A niggardly, selfish, or mischievous man, as determined by the circumstances, cannot be beneficent even if what he does is good. Thus, beneficence always presupposes benevolence; specific beneficent actions signal intent, but both sender and receiver of the signal require the whole context or circumstances to interpret the action.

Charles Smith distinguishes *benevolence* from *benignity* (another eighteenth-century-sounding word), *humanity*, and *kindness* (1894, pp. 165–66):

> Benignity is, as it were, dormant, or passive benevolence. It is a matter more of temperament than will.... As benevolence is inherent, so benignity may be shown on special occasions only.... Humanity expresses an impulse rather than a quality ... [and] is not so much a virtue when exhibited as something the absence of which is positively disgraceful and evil.... Kindness is very like benevolence, but is rather a social than a moral virtue. It applies to minor acts of courtesy and good will, for which benevolence would be too serious a term.

The conceptual distinction between kind intentions as applicable to minor acts and benevolence as applicable to more serious, and hence beneficent, acts, reinforces Adam Smith's claim that the general rules of conduct are "loose, vague and indeterminate, and present us rather with a general idea

---

[1] "Society ... cannot subsist among those who are at all times ready to hurt and injure one another. The moment that injury begins, the moment that mutual resentment and animosity take place, all the bands of it are broke asunder.... Beneficence, therefore, is less essential to the existence of society than justice. Society may subsist, though not in the most comfortable state, without beneficence; but the prevalence of injustice must utterly destroy it" (TMS, Second.II.III, pp. 124–25).

of the perfection we ought to aim at, than afford us any certain and infallible directions for acquiring it" (TMS, Third.(I).VI, p. 250). In other words, as a non-specifiable pattern there is room for disagreement within general rules of conduct for interpreting an act in context as connoting minor or major intentions of doing good.[2] "Disagreement" implies disequilibrium and impels change; individuals must either adapt the rules they follow, or the normative rules of propriety must adapt. The latter is a long-run adaptation: if individuals continue to resist compliance with the *norma agendi*, the ancient Roman concept of "the standard which is to be acted," then the standard adapts to the popular will.

Although Smith's language is eminently the King's English in the eighteenth century, his thinking and modeling logic are freshly relevant to understanding human sociality in the twenty-first century. Astonishingly, it leads to testable propositions that have predictive consequences, many of which were discovered independently in the last fifty years. As the first extensive work in social psychology, *Sentiments* also makes evident the proposition that there is no individual psychology distinct and separable from human social experience as it emerges from our unique experiences of fellow feeling.

Smith compares how we apply our sense of merit and demerit in the first chapter of Part Second, Section II. The first two paragraphs, each being a single sentence, read as two relational propositions, though he does not call them that. With a much less obvious presentation, we find two other propositions in the chapter, each corresponding to extensions of the first two.

PROPOSITIONS ON BENEFICENCE

We begin with Smith's own words, followed by our restatement and proof: "Actions of a beneficent tendency, which proceed from proper motives, seem alone to require reward; because such alone are the approved objects of gratitude, or excite the sympathetic gratitude of the spectator" (TMS, Second.II.I, p. 112).

> *Beneficence Proposition 1: If X does something good (Z^{good}) for Y because she wants to do something good for Y, Z^{good} appears, with nothing further needed, to deserve reward by Y.*

---

[2] Where in modern game theory is the assumption of agreement on the interpretation of the act? Hidden obscurely in the assumption that every individual *j* always chooses the largest possible pot of utilitarian pleasure.

Proof: By Principle 1, Y self-examines his own sentiments after X does Z^{good} for Y because X wanted to do something good for Y. By the Desert Lemma, Z^{good} appears to deserve reward. By Principle 4, Y wants to be praiseworthy and does not want to be blameworthy, i.e., Z^{good} appears, with nothing further needed, to deserve reward by Y. ∎

First, notice that the beneficent act is all that is needed for someone to deserve reward. Secondly, Smith's proposition regarding the response to a virtuous act is, like virtue itself, a tendency. The proposition suggests, rather than states exactly, how someone will respond to a beneficent act. When dealing with human beings, we must get comfortable with the imprecision of our humanity. In our inquiries, our science, we cannot predict human conduct like we are able to predict water wave mechanics.

Corollary: Human beings reciprocate beneficence.

If Y's are disposed to respond to X's beneficence with their own acts of beneficence, then Beneficence Proposition 1 becomes a virtuous circle. Reciprocity is not a postulate in *Sentiments*. Rather, it is more systematically a corollary derived from the sentiment of gratitude on the part of the beneficiary in response to the intentional act of another. "Of all the persons . . . whom nature points out for our peculiar beneficence, there are none to whom it seems more properly directed than to those whose beneficence we have ourselves already experienced" (TMS, Sixth.II.I, p. 331).

Much of the research on ultimatum and dictator games was motivated by a reciprocity interpretation of the results and the costly punishment and reward strategies that characterized subject behavior. Joyce Berg, John Dickhaut, and Kevin McCabe summarize it this way in their seminal paper (1995, pp. 138–39):

In conclusion, experiments on ultimatum game, repeated prisoners' dilemma games, and other extensive form games provide strong evidence that people do punish inappropriate behavior even though this is personally costly. Furthermore, subjects take this into account when they make their decisions. The investment game provides evidence that people are also willing to reward appropriate behavior and this too is taken into account. Taken together these results suggest that both positive and negative forms of reciprocity exist and must be taken into account in order to explain the development of institutional forms which reinforce the propensity to reciprocate.[3]

The reciprocity narrative as an explanation of trust/trustworthiness derived much of its weight from concepts in evolutionary theory and in particular the developing field of evolutionary psychology theory that involved social exchange algorithms for "mind reading," "intentionality," and "cheater detection."[4] Following upon Berg, Dickhaut, and McCabe, many experiments established that intentions ("appropriate behavior") mattered; moreover, experimenters found treatments that manipulated intentions or context had a greater impact on choices than treatments that varied payoffs.[5] The concept of reciprocity, however, is not elemental like Axioms 0–3 and Principles 1 and 4, and as such does not explain beneficence like *Sentiments* does.

Smith's second proposition on beneficence is, in his own words (TMS, Second.II.I, p. 112):

Beneficence is always free, it cannot be extorted by force, the mere want of it exposes to no punishment; because the mere want of beneficence tends to do no real positive evil. It may disappoint of the good which might reasonably have been expected, and upon that account it may justly excite dislike and disapprobation: it cannot, however, provoke any resentment which mankind will go along with.

We will need one further assumption before stating the proposition:

Assumption 2: If something deserves punishment (reward) by Y, then that something appears to deserve punishment (reward) by Y.

Deserving reward and punishment is something that other people sense to be the case if it is indeed the case.

---

[3] Before his death, John Dickhaut helped to instigate an extension of these original experiments to the study of three-person trust games in which person A could transfer money which was tripled, to person B, who could transfer money that was tripled again to person C. Person C could then return money to B, and B could return money to A. The original qualitative patterns of trust and trustworthiness continued to be represented in the three-person case. See Thomas Rietz, Roman Sheremeta, Timothy Shields, and Vernon Smith (2013).

[4] See Elizabeth Hoffman, Kevin McCabe, and Vernon Smith (1998). Herbert Gintis and Dirk Helbing (2015) model human sociality based on social context-dependent preference functions defined over actions, payoffs, and beliefs as inputs. They conclude that high levels of cooperation can be achieved as an equilibrium if a minority of agents (all others are self-interested) follow the "altruistic" norm of "strong reciprocity" by unconditionally cooperating and always punishing defectors. Unlike *Sentiments*, preference functions implicitly do much of the work in explaining this conclusion.

[5] For discussions of stakes and context, see Colin Camerer (2003, pp. 60–61) and Vernon Smith (2008, Chapter 10); for intentions, see Kevin McCabe, Vernon Smith, and Mike LePore (2000) and Ernst Fehr and Bettina Rockenbach (2003).

Beneficence Proposition 2: If X does not do something good (Z^{good}) for Y because she does not want to do something good for Y, the lack of Z^{good} does not, solely by itself, deserve punishment by Y.

Proof (by contradiction): Suppose the lack of Z^{good}, solely by itself, deserves punishment by Y. By Assumption 2, the lack of Z^{good}, solely by itself, also appears to deserve punishment by Y. By Definition 1, the lack of Z^{good}, solely by itself, is the proper and approved object of resentment. A central component of the meaning of "Y felt resentment for X having not done Z^{good}" is that X did something bad to Y by having not done Z^{good}. But this, solely by itself, is a contradiction, for "not doing Z^{good} for Y" is not actually "doing something bad to Y" because nothing at all has been done to Y. ∎

The noun phrase *mere want* is important for understanding Smith's second proposition on beneficence. Today, we predominantly use the adjective *mere* to emphasize how insignificant or inadequate something may be. Smith, however, is using "mere" in the older sense derived directly from the Latin *merus*, meaning "pure" or, as Samuel Johnson defines it, "this only." The phrase "want of X" also sounds archaic, for we chiefly use the synonym *lack*. A little something is lost, though, in moving from the "want of X" to the "lack of X." Whereas the "lack of X" connotes a simple factual state of affairs, the web of meaning surrounding the "want of X" includes, in addition to the factual lacking of something, an element of desire from the verb *want*. This is not unimportant to Smith's proposition, for we, out of self-love, would really like all sorts of X's to do all sorts of good things for us. But Smith assures us that beneficence is an act of free choice. We cannot use force to extort beneficence, which is what punishment would be, the following through on an extortive threat for not having done something good for us.

PROPOSITIONS ON INJUSTICE

Smith's first proposition on injustice is symmetrical with respect to his first proposition on beneficence: "Actions of a hurtful tendency, which proceed from improper motives, seem alone to deserve punishment; because such alone are the approved objects of resentment, or excite the sympathetic resentment of the spectator" (TMS, Second.II.I, p. 112). Our restatement is likewise symmetrical to Beneficence Proposition 1:

Injustice Proposition 1: If X does something bad (Z^{bad}) to Y because he wants to do something bad to Y, Z^{bad} appears, with nothing further needed, to deserve punishment by Y.

Proof: See analogous proof for Beneficence Proposition 1. ∎

The opposite side of beneficence, which stems from proper motives and tends to do real and positive good, are actions that stem from improper motives and tend to do real and positive harm. The careful reader will notice an elision in our restatements as Beneficence Proposition 1 and Injustice Proposition 1. Smith's diction includes an asymmetrical difference in one word: An act of beneficence seems alone to require reward, but an act of injustice seems alone to deserve punishment. Because humans can and do err in their interpretations of actions as beneficent and hurtful, Principle 2 on the asymmetry of gains and losses would caution us from stating both propositions as requiring both reward and punishment. An error in interpreting an act as beneficent or attributable to X would not make X worse off if Y indeed did reward her. The requirement to reward X arises from a problem in the opposite direction, for failing to reward X's action may lead X to think that Y is ungrateful, which, according to Hume is no small thing: "Of all crimes that human creatures are capable of committing, the most horrid and unnatural is ingratitude" (1740, p. 300).

An error, however, in interpreting an act as hurtful or attributable to X would make X worse if Y indeed did punish her. Furthermore, unlike a requirement, desert for hurtful actions leaves open the possibility for mercy and forgiveness when there is no error in interpretation of facts. Such a weaker condition is not necessary in the domain of gains, which may account for Smith's stronger statement for acts of beneficence. The substance of Smith's thinking – one to which we are not accustomed, and our education ill prepares us – is revealed in his careful diction.

Better to show gratitude where none is required than fail to show gratitude where it is. We feel dismay for the error that a guilty person go unpunished, but we recoil at any prospect that an innocent person be punished for a crime that he did not commit. Our feelings are not symmetric with respect to error in reading acts of beneficence, or in reading acts of injustice, and there is no symmetry in these asymmetries. Smith's sagacity in recognizing gain/loss asymmetry and probing its deeper roots of meaning has far-reaching implications for who we are as social creatures.

Finally, we consider the fourth proposition, which in Smith's own words is: "Though the breach of justice ... exposes to punishment, the observance of the rules of that virtue seems scarce to deserve any reward" (TMS, Second.II.I, p. 117).

> *Injustice Proposition 2: If X does not do something bad (Z^{bad}) to Y because she does not want to do something bad to Y, the lack of Z^{bad} does not, solely by itself, deserve reward by Y.*

> *Proof (by contradiction):* See analogous proof for Beneficence Proposition 2. ∎

The violation of justice calls for punishment, but law-abiding conduct does not deserve reward. Although it merits our respectful approval and we may dutifully and respectfully avoid hurting our neighbor, such action is not entitled to the rewards of gratitude. Commonly we can obey the laws of justice by simply not acting, as when we avoid disturbing our neighbor. Alternatively, we act in accordance with the laws of justice by stopping at a red light, but in neither case do we expect a reward for thus doing our duty (TMS, Second.II.I, p. 117).

These two propositions are the core of Smith's concept of justice. Why do they imply justice, given that they concern hurt and punishment? Smith defines justice negatively, as the absence of injustice. Thus: "Mere [pure] justice is, upon most occasions, but a negative virtue, and only hinders us from hurting our neighbour" (TMS, Second.II.I, p. 117). In his *Lectures on Jurisprudence* he succinctly puts it this way: "The end of justice is to secure from injury" (Smith 1766, p. 399). We return to this important topic later.

THE GENERALITY AND SYMMETRY OF ADAM SMITH'S MORAL UNIVERSE

It is curious, and we think informative, to note that the foundation of Smith's theory of morality is not built upon the notion of right and wrong. He does not mention *right and wrong* until Part Third, chapter IV and then only once. The phrase only appears twice in Part Fifth, chapter II, and not until the lately added Part Sixth does it finally appear a dozen times. Smith's core moral terms are a sense of propriety and impropriety, and approbation and disapprobation in Part First, good and ill desert, and merit and demerit in Part Second, and self-approbation and self–disapprobation, and duty in Part Third, chapters I–III. Anna Wierzbicka argues that "'right' and 'wrong' are not universal human concepts but English words without equivalents in other European languages, let alone in languages of more remote cultures and societies" (2006, p. 65). She continues:

I hasten to emphasize that in saying this I am not taking the position of a cultural, moral, or linguistic relativist. On the contrary: colleagues and I have tried to document ... the existence of linguistic universals, and we have argued, on the basis of empirical cross-linguistic research, that these universals include the concepts good and bad. We have also argued that while good and bad can be used across a wide range of domains and are by no means restricted to moral discourse, they can occur in all languages in combinations like "I (you, someone, this person) did something bad/good" or "it is good/bad if someone does something like this."

Anglophones may translate classic Greek and Roman writers with "right" and "wrong," but the semantic equivalents of *bonum* and *malum*, particularly in other European languages, are more closely and contextually translated as "good" and "bad," *das Gute* and *das Böse, il bene* and *il male, el bien* and *el mal, le bien* and *le mal* (Wierzbicka 2006, p. 66).[6] The English words *right* and *wrong* additionally connote a rational justification of actions, or a lack thereof. If we say that somebody did something wrong, we are not just saying they did something bad. We are also saying that the person cannot rationally justify why they did something bad. Doing the wrong thing connotes a rationalized assessment of the means by which the thing was done. Doing a bad thing purely connotes an evaluation of the thing done, namely, that it was bad.

To the cultural and moral relativist who wants to dismiss Smith's theory of morality as a system limited to his times and place, we politely beg to differ. *Sentiments* does not rely on the comparatively modern Anglo notions of right and wrong, as so many modern moral philosophies do. Smith's system relies on the universal human ideas of "doing something good for someone because you want to do something good for them" and "doing something bad to someone because you want to do something bad to them." One aim in restating Smith's propositions as we do is to spell out the simplicity and universality with which he can be read (in any language).

The second aim in our restatements is to clearly demonstrate that Smith's comparison of beneficence and justice are systematic and symmetrical. His comparison is systematic in that his observations simultaneously account for our moral responses to both good and bad deeds done to us with both proper and improper motives, and it is symmetrical in that he

---

[6] Or perhaps, "good" and "evil," with the latter emphasizing a wanting to do bad things to other people.

observes a regularity and an order to how humans reward, punish, do not reward, and do not punish each other. Succinctly put, *we reward beneficence and do not punish its want; we punish injustice, but do not reward its want.* We reward doing something good, which includes intending to do something good, because it does real and positive good, and we do not punish the want of doing and intending to do something good because it does no real or positive harm. And we punish doing something bad, which includes intending to do something bad, because it does real and positive harm, and we do not reward the want of doing and intending to do something bad because it does no real and positive good.

CHANCE AND THE SENSE OF MERIT AND DEMERIT

Lest we overweight the critical role of intentions, Smith hastens to observe that where actions are affected by independent external events, the impact of the consequences of an action can have a biasing effect on how we actually perceive its merit or demerit. Although we all acknowledge the abstract principle that intentions should be the sole determinant of judgments concerning the actor's merit or demerit, our sentiments are not entirely determined by it due to the irregular effect of "fortune"; i.e., the effect of uncontrolled no-fault chance events on the action. Smith refers to this as an "irregularity of sentiment" (TMS, Second.III.Intro, p. 135). The irregularity that he addresses arises from the conjunction of action with chance, or the occurrence of events over which we have no control, though our own action is entirely well intended. Smith proceeds to explain why this is so with elaborate care, but pursuing it in detail, especially when he gets to negligence, would divert us too far from our main theme (TMS, Second.III).[7] Because of its importance and its potential predictive power, however, we will state the propositions that follow from his examination of the effect of the conjunction of action with chance on our sense of deserved merit or demerit, which in turn affect the motivation to reward or punish the action.

Smith's two propositions that apply to these circumstances are as follows (TMS, Second.III.II, p. 141): If the conjunction of chance ("fortune") and our intentional (praisable or blamable) action fails to produce the results expected of the action, then it diminishes the sense of merit or demerit due to the action. Smith's example – where a friend solicits an office on your

---

[7] Keith Hankins (2016) explores the complexities of Smith's treatment of the problem of the "irregularity of sentiments."

behalf – implies that the category concerns cases in which the outcome (a fixed prize, that either you get or you do not), whether expected to be bad or good is not itself effected by the random event. That is, the friend takes a soliciting action, and then chance selects the outcome. In these cases, the effect on the principal's judgment of merit or demerit is to decrease both; i.e., if an intentionally beneficent act fails, the sense of its merit decreases; similarly, if an intentionally hurtful act fails, the sense of its demerit decreases. The desire to reward the action in the first case, and the urge to punish the action in the latter would both decline. In this proposition, the effect of the action on the judgment of merit or demerit is similar to reducing the probability of the fixed good or bad outcome occurring – the sense of gain (good) is smaller, and the sense of loss (bad) is smaller.

In Smith's second proposition, if the conjunction of chance and the actor's intention gives occasion to extraordinary pleasure or pain relative to the results expected of the action, then it increases our sense of the merit or demerit of the action. The effect of the action is to "throw a shadow of merit or demerit upon the agent, though in his intention there was nothing that deserved either praise or blame" (TMS, Second.III.II, p. 147). Hence, where the outcome, a gain or loss, is enhanced – made better or worse than expected – and is quite unintended by the action, then the sense of its merit or demerit is increased. Your desire, given the option, would be to increase the reward of the actor when the outcome is good, and to increase his punishment if the outcome is bad. Imagine – using Smith's illustration of a friend soliciting an office for you – that the outcome, expected to be fixed, is variable. The solicitation reveals the unexpected prospect that an even better office will result; the consequence is to increase your sense of merit for your friend's action, though it was no part of his intentions.[8]

References

Annas, Julia. 2011. *Intelligent Virtue*. New York, NY: Oxford University Press.

Berg, Joyce, John Dickhaut, and Kevin McCabe. 1995. "Trust, Reciprocity, and Social History," *Games and Economic Behavior* 10: 122-42.

Fehr, Ernst and Bettina Rockenbach. 2003. "Detrimental Effects of Sanctions on Human Altruism," *Nature* 422: 137–40.

Gintis, Herbert and Dirk Helbing. 2015. "*Homo Socialis*: An Analytical Core for Sociological Theory," *Review of Behavioral Economics* 2: 1–59.

---

[8] In the loss domain, the example might be that your friend intervenes to prevent your salary from being reduced, and you are dismissed. Your sense of your friend's demerit, however unintended the outcome, is worsened.

Hankins, Keith. 2016. "Adam Smith's Intriguing Solution to the Problem of Moral Luck," *Ethics* 126(3): 711–46.

Hoffman, Elizabeth, Kevin A. McCabe, and Vernon L. Smith. 1998. "Behavioral Foundations of Reciprocity: Experimental Economics and Evolutionary Psychology," *Economic Inquiry* 36(3): 335–52.

Hume, David. 2000 [1740]. *A Treatise of Human Nature*, David Fate Norton and Mary J. Norton (eds.). New York, NY: Oxford University Press.

McCabe, Kevin, Vernon L. Smith, and Michael LePore. 2000. "Intentionality Detection and 'Mindreading': Why Does Game Form Matter," *Proceedings of the National Academy of Sciences* 97(8): 4404–9.

Rietz, Thomas A., Roman M. Sheremeta, Timothy W. Shields, and Vernon L. Smith. 2013. "Transparency, Efficiency and the Distribution of Economic Welfare in Pass-Through Investment Trust Games," *Journal of Economic Behavior and Organization* 94: 257–67.

Smith, Adam. 1853 [1759]. *The Theory of Moral Sentiments; or, An Essay towards an Analysis of the Principles by which Men naturally judge concerning the Conduct and Character, first of their Neighbours, and afterwards of themselves. To which is added, A Dissertation on the Origins of Languages. New Edition. With a biographical and critical Memoir of the Author, by Dugald Stewart.* London, UK: Henry G. Bohn. Available online and in electronic formats at http://oll .libertyfund.org/titles/2620.

Smith, Adam. 1982 [1766]. *Lectures on Jurisprudence*. Indianapolis, IN: Liberty Fund.

Smith, Vernon L. 2008. *Rationality in Economics Constructionist and Ecological Forms.* New York: Cambridge University Press.

Wierzbicka, Anna. 2006. *English: Meaning and Culture.* New York, NY: Oxford University Press.

7

Propriety and Sympathy in a Rule-Governed Order

Non ex regular ius summatur, sed ex iure quod est regula fiat.

What is right is not derived from the rule, but the rule arises from our knowledge of what is right.

Julius Paulus, quoted in F. A. Hayek (1973, p. 162)

Reflecting more discursively on the formal structure of the model in *Sentiments*, we continue to engage many of the same issues but speak to the origin, purpose, and value of the model in understanding social order. More specifically, we discuss Smith's insightful metaphor of the impartial spectator for understanding the roots of self-command, the mechanism whereby a decentralized social order can exist and thrive. In the process we learn more about Smith's way of thinking, an essential part of understanding the power and usefulness of *Sentiments*. To apply the model, it helps to be practiced in thinking in the same way.

UNCOVERING THE SOCIAL FOUNDATIONS
OF THE RULES WE FOLLOW

Influenced by Newton and astronomy, Smith understood the enormous power of rule-governed systems to organize observations while functioning beneath human sensible awareness.[1] Newton's program had been about precise articulation of the hidden forces governing the natural motion of bodies, and integrating the laws governing earthly and heavenly motion into a coherent unity. Similarly, Smith's program is about discovering what it means to be social while simultaneously uncovering the

---

[1] Adam Smith (1795).

hidden forces that determine the rules that governed human conduct. His project in *Sentiments* is to address how moral conduct emerges out of human interactive experience to form a system of general rules that wisely orders society (TMS, Seventh.III.II, p. 469). In *Wealth* he extends that system into markets and national economy to enable a better understanding of the sources and evolution of the economic order evident to the careful observer of eighteenth-century life in Northern Europe.

ORIGINS OF ORDER ARE NOT IN CONSCIOUS HUMAN REASON

Smith is sensitive to important differences between rules governing the natural physical order and those emerging in socioeconomic life. He warns that maxims in the latter arise "by experience and induction" and we should never confuse their functional efficiency with their cause; i.e., the general rules we follow emerge out of inductive experience and are not the consequence of applying reason or deliberate human design. Everywhere in the universe we find means precisely adjusted to the ends that result. The wheels of a watch follow mechanical principles that ensure the accuracy of its time-keeping, but in achieving its end they are not endowed with any such intention; that is provided by the watchmaker. When we account for operations in the mind in human affairs (TMS, Second.II.III, p. 126):

We are very apt to confound these two different things with one another. When by natural principles we are led to advance those ends, which a refined and enlightened reason would recommend to us, we are very apt to impute to that reason, as to their efficient cause, the sentiments and actions by which we advance those ends.

Smith is in broad agreement with his friend Hume, who argued that the rules of justice and of property acquire its social and economic efficacy in a very slow and gradual evolutionary process driven "by our repeated experience of the inconveniences of transgressing it" (Hume 1740, p. 315). While Hume's characterization is correct, Smith's project is to work through the process whereby the dynamics of human sentiment operated to reduce those inconveniencies and increase human social and economic betterment.

Thus, as Smith and his intellectual contemporaries appreciate, "Man [both the individual and the species] is made for society" and the peace of that society depends upon morality (Ferguson 1792, p. 199). Moreover, the rules of morality, as Hume explains, "are not *arbitrary*" (Hume 1740, p. 311, original italics), and from Smith: "Vice is always capricious: virtue only is regular and orderly" (TMS, Sixth.II.I, p. 330). In the language of F. A. Hayek, the leading twentieth-century scholar, the core of whose work continues in this Scottish tradition, we are speaking of a spontaneous order directed and mediated by the community-grown rules of interaction in small familial-like groups.[2]

Smith's careful and incisive distinction between the functional efficiency of the rules of order in society (and economy in his second book), and how these rules evolve and do work in social economy through the actions of people, have important parallels in economic methodology today.

Theorists, experimental and behavioral economists alike, tend to think about economic agents in the economy and the laboratory in terms of their models of the rational or social behavior of individuals. We tend not to model agent/subject actions from the participant's perspective within the economic environment *as they might experience and see it.* Herbert Simon distinguishes between subjective rationality, based on how the subject perceives and evaluates her situation, and the objective rationality of the experimenter/theorist: "To predict how economic man will behave we need to know not only that he is rational but how he perceives the world – what alternatives he sees and what consequences he attaches to them" (Simon 1956, pp. 271–72). In *Sentiments*, Smith models the "subjectively rational" individual who selects actions in his social or economic exchange environment. Once the neoclassical tradition became dominant, our models defined our conversation about agent/subject action. Smith, if not Hume, sees the difference, and warns us not to confuse efficiency – which may well be achieved by the rules we follow – with the feelings that propel human discovery of the governing rules. Smith reaches first for a model of the social then the economic person, only then asking about its interpretation in terms of fitness or optimality as a system. Thus, behavioral economists model action as satisfying a social preference function – the utilitarian solution to why people exhibit other-regarding behavior. The theorist and the experimentalist describe observations in terms of incremental outcomes, and equilibrium properties derived from their models.

One consequence is that laboratory (and field) data sometimes confirm, sometimes falsify, the models. Why the difference? To answer that question requires models of both the agent/subject and of social welfare. We apply *Sentiments* to interpreting/modeling the actions of the agent/subject (Chapters 8–10) and use the earnings of individual subjects and the

---

[2] F. A. Hayek (1988).

efficiencies achieved in their dyadic relationships to evaluate performance (Chapter 13).

ORIGINS ARE IN HUMAN SENTIMENT: PROPRIETY
AND THE EMERGENCE OF RULES

In *Sentiments* we judge and evaluate the actions of others according as they benefit or hurt us and are judged to be intentional, and hence relational. To make such a judgment requires us to know the circumstances of action well enough to assess the intentions of the actor-agent. We naturally feel gratitude for intentional actions tending to benefit us, and feel resentment in response to intentionally hurtful actions. Because of these prominent features of our persona, and our awareness of like mental-emotional phenomena in others, our actions are subject to a disciplined form of self-command that aligns them with what other people, the impartial spectator, humankind, and so on can or cannot "go along with." The affective actions of others on us, and our learning to take account of our like actions on others, lead us to judge and evaluate human actions according to their propriety; i.e., ability to inspire the approbation or provoke the disapprobation of others. From that common sense of propriety, together we forge rules that help us to live in harmony.

There are two closely linked classes of rules: (1) The standards of good and bad conduct that prevail in our communities and reflect the operations of a social consensus on actions that are proper and fitting; (2) the rules we follow as individuals, the propriety and fitness of which are judged in terms of their alignment with the community norms.

How do we as individuals come to be followers of rules that conform appropriately to our community norms? The proposed mechanism of adjustment is clear in *Sentiments*: rules arise out of our desire for praise and praiseworthiness, and our desire to avoid blame and blameworthiness (Principles 4a and 4b in Chapter 5). Approved actions are encouraged by vocal and bodily expressions of gratitude, and are subject to the likelihood of in-kind or monetary reward; disapproved actions are discouraged by vocal and bodily expressions of resentment, and are subject to in-kind or monetary loss as punishment proportioned to the resentment felt. However, our sense of the precise rule to follow is always tempered by uncertainty – uncertainty about how well the shape of our rule fits the standard (rule acceptance by others), and uncertainty as to how accurately we are reading the circumstances that condition our choice of action.

The encounter with the homeless man reported in the previous chapter demonstrates Smith's point about "vocal and bodily expressions." The man's disapproval of the buyer's interpretation of the transaction was registered spontaneously, via the withdrawal of the hand poised to accept the money, and of the hand offering the newspaper. These actions, coupled with a verbal declaration signaled his revulsive disapproval of the implications of transferring money while not accepting the merchandise. The meaning implicit in the transaction was at stake, independent of the personal identities of the transactors. Each could have been a different person subject to the same motivation. It was about the propriety of a rule in the circumstances described and about the need to modify that rule to achieve resonance in mutual fellow feeling between self-loving social transactors. Interactions are about feeling, thinking, and knowing (Chapter 2).

In Chapter 8 we summarize results from a variety of earlier-reported two-person laboratory experiments that failed to confirm game-theoretic predictions under conditions thought to be particularly favorable to those predictions. Using Smith's model, we interpret people's actions as expressions of rule-governed standards of good and bad conduct conditioned by the context defined by the game tree and its payoff outcomes; i.e., we look at the participants as if they peopled the world modeled in *Sentiments*. In this personal relational environment, the propriety of conduct is the mediator of action. Each game is an opportunity for people to interact under the conventions that have shaped each player's history. We postulate that Smith's propositions are statements that govern the general rules of propriety that people live by. How well do his propositions, à la Bruno Latour, postdict outcomes in these games?[3]

In Chapters 9 and 10 we report new experimental designs and results made possible by Smith's propositions. How well do particular propositions predict outcomes in this new generation of games? Equally important, how well do the propositions taken together prepare us, the observers, to better understand how the subjects see each game, to read each other's actions, and to respond? The failure of the traditional Max-U model in these games left us only with conjectures involving notions of fairness, inequity aversion, reciprocity-as-exchange, anger, intentions – names consistent with our conjectures about the empirical findings, but without a new theoretical rudder to navigate the highly replicable body of new evidence.

---

[3] Bruno Latour (1999).

The arguments that follow make use of our interpretation of Adam Smith's theory of the mental and emotional states that serve to mediate the individual actions that excite those states; accordingly, we provide an overview of these principles of action, relating it where appropriate to the more formal statements in Chapter 6.

MERIT AND DEMERIT IN JUDGMENTS

According to Smith, our judgment of the actions and conduct of people rests on a social sense of merit or the quality of deserving reward, and its opposite, a sense of demerit or of deserving punishment. Gratitude is the sentiment that directly prompts us to reward actions that are beneficial to us, while resentment is the sentiment that invokes a punishment response for actions that are hurtful to us. "To reward, is to recompense, to remunerate, to return good for good received. To punish, too, is to recompense, to remunerate, though in a different manner; it is to return evil for evil that has been done" (TMS, Second.I.I, p. 94). In modern language Smith is saying that positive reciprocity arises from a sense of gratitude, negative reciprocity from feelings of resentment; the former explain the tendency to reward, the latter to punish. He elaborates by adding that our desire to reward a close associate is not satisfied if that person comes into good fortune for reasons that have nothing to do with an action we take, although we are happy for him. Pleased as we are, our gratitude is not satisfied unless we are the instrument of an action that makes him better off. Otherwise, our sense of obligation to him is not satisfied: if I owe you one, only I can deliver on the obligation. Similarly, if we have been the object of a hurtful action, our resentment is not satisfied, except we take a reciprocal action of punishment: "Resentment would prompt us to desire, not only that he should be punished, but that he should be punished by our means, and upon account of that particular injury which he had done to us" (TMS, Second.I.I, p. 96).[4]

A guiding principle in Smith's system is the idea that the arrogant forms of self-love must at all times be humbled to serve the pursuit of actions that conform to the judgments of one's impartial spectator (TMS, Second.II.II, pp. 119–120; Seventh.II.II, p. 389). Moreover, this mechanism does not

---

[4] Smith here anticipates his subsequent argument that the rules-as-norms that form out of experience in our small groups are the basis for the rule of law in the civil order: "The natural gratification of this passion tends, of its own accord, to produce all the political ends of punishment; the correction of the criminal, and the example to the public" (TMS, Second.I.I, p. 96).

reduce simply to a form of constrained utility maximization but arises out of a relationship. Outcomes are important in these judgments, but only because they are part of the context of interaction and do not become one-dimensional determinants of the actions we take.

THE IMPARTIAL SPECTATOR

Our actions are subject to a discipline of self-command by principles that operate through the metaphor of the "fair and impartial spectator," or simply the impartial spectator (TMS, Third.(I).I, p. 162):

> We endeavour to examine our own conduct as we imagine any other fair and impartial spectator would examine it. If, upon placing ourselves in his situation, we thoroughly enter into all the passions and motives which influenced it, we approve of it, by sympathy with the approbation of this supposed equitable judge. If otherwise, we enter into his disapprobation, and condemn it.

The words "fair," "impartial," and "equitable" were chosen, we argue, quite deliberately by Smith to represent judgment by a neutral referee as to whether an action was fair or foul under the applicable rules of interaction given the circumstances. Within Smith's metaphor of the impartial spectator is a second sports metaphor of judgment under the rules of the game.[5] Smith repeatedly makes reference to actions that "other people" or "mankind," or the "impartial spectator," "can go along with" (or not). The impartial spectator constitutes an internalization of what is approved or not approved by others. We are encouraged to take actions that others can go along with, and deterred from actions that they find objectionable. What makes rule-following a powerful, flexible, decentralized force of change is self-command; we come to discipline each other as equals among equals, and thereby increase human social betterment.

Implicit in Smith's metaphor of the impartial spectator is the social-psychological foundations of his model of action within human relationships. This is most evident in the mental experiment Smith uses to

---

[5] For a discussion on the word *fair* as playing within the rules of social practice, see Bart Wilson (2012), particularly footnote 7, which discusses the eighteenth-century meaning of the word. Adam Smith's usage of *fair,* never *fairness,* stands in sharp contrast to the interpretation and discussion in Nava Ashraf, Colin Camerer, and George Loewenstein (2005, pp. 136–137). Also see Ernst Fehr and Klaus Schmidt (1999) and Armin Falk, Ernst Fehr, and Urs Fischbacher (2008) where experimental behavior is interpreted in terms of fairness – equality of outcomes. Vernon Smith (2008, pp. 161–65) discusses and gives examples of some of the many (and slippery) senses in which "fairness" is used in experimental contexts.

explicate the social maturation in every individual, Smith's *sozial gedanke-nexperimente*. He asks us to imagine a human being growing up entirely isolated from any communication with others. Such a person could not have any idea of what it means to have a deformed mind, of the merit or demerit of his conduct' nor even of the beauty or deformity of his own face. None of these things is part of his perception because he has no mirror allowing him to view them. If, however, he is brought up in society, he is provided with that mirror. It is represented in the form of the "countenance and behaviour" of all those that he encounters in space and time who are quick to mark their approval or disapproval of his sentiments (TMS, Third.(I).I, p. 162).

Our conception of personal beauty or deformity is intersubjectively drawn from our experience of others and not subjectively from our experience of ourselves. However, we soon become aware that others are subject to the same image shaping; hence, we are concerned to know how they view our appearance. Our concern for our own appearance arises because of its effect on others. If we were a stranger to society, we would be indifferent in all such matters. Similarly, with respect to our moral behavior, we first are aware of how the conduct of others affects us, but we soon learn how we come across to others. This mirror enables us in some measure to view our own conduct through the eyes of others (TMS, Third.(I).I).

Smith uses these ideas to construct his "impartial spectator." Thus, in screening and passing sentence on my conduct, approving or condemning it,

I divide myself, as it were, into two persons.. . . I, the examiner and judge, represent a different character from that other I, the person whose conduct is examined into and judged of. The first is the spectator, whose sentiments with regard to my own conduct I endeavour to enter into, by placing myself in his situation, and by considering how it would appear to me, when seen from that particular point of view. The second is the agent, the person whom I properly call myself, and of whose conduct, under the character of a spectator, I was endeavouring to form some opinion. The first is the judge; the second the person judged of: But that the judge should, in every respect, be the same with the person judged of, is as impossible, as that the cause should, in every respect, be the same with the effect (TMS, Third.(I).I, p. 164–5).

Smith is articulating the essential operant elements whereby we become "empathetic," or as he puts it, whereby we come to possess the sentiments of "fellow-feeling." Consequently, he asserts:

To be amiable and to be meritorious; that is, to deserve love and to deserve reward, are the great characters of virtue; and to be odious and punishable, of vice. But all these characters have an immediate reference to the sentiments of others. Virtue is not said to be amiable, or to be meritorious, because it is the object of its own love, or of its own gratitude; but because it excites those sentiments in other men. [6] (TMS, Third.(I).I, p. 165)

This characterization of human sociality serves to mediate human action, however imperfectly. As a social-psychological process it emerges as rules, first in our families, extended families, and friendship enclaves, but ultimately influences the form of law codified by civil society (TMS, Second.II. II; Sixth.II.I).

AVOIDING THE ERRORS OF SELF-DECEIT

Why does Smith see the impartial spectator as a neutral referee? It is because self-perception is subject to biased error. Without a capacity to judge our own conduct with the eyes of a neutral referee, we are at risk of corrupting our social fitness via the vain pursuit of praise by shameless self-promotion and even self-deceit.

The foolish liar, who endeavours to excite the admiration of the company by the relation of adventures which never had any existence; the important coxcomb, who gives himself airs of rank and distinction which he well knows he has no just pretensions to; are both of them, no doubt, pleased with the applause which they fancy they meet with. But their vanity arises from so gross an illusion of the imagination, that it is difficult to conceive how any rational creature should be imposed upon by it. When they place themselves in the situation of those whom they fancy they have deceived, they are struck with the highest admiration for their own persons. They look upon themselves, not in that light in which, they know, they ought to appear to their companions, but in that in which they believe their companions actually look upon them. (TMS, Third.(I).II, p. 168)

Concerning the sources of partiality to which we are vulnerable, Smith devotes a chapter to a remarkably astute treatment of "self-deceit" (TMS, Third.(I).IV). His purpose is to explore the sources of corruption of our judgments of our own conduct, both in the heat of the moment and in later reflection, wherein the expressions of our self-interest can be excessive. These deficiencies in homegrown sources of self-discipline, however, are in part overcome by what we learn from observing others, the effect of which become incorporated into general rules.

---

[6] For Smith one's own love is not a utilitarian object.

NATURE RESCUES WHERE REASON ALONE WOULD FAIL

There are two occasions when we have an opportunity to be attentive in considering and evaluating our conduct: (1) At the time of action, and (2) afterward, looking back at our decision. At neither time are we likely to be impartial. At the time of action, the passions of the moment combined with our self-loving nature too easily trump the prospect of viewing our action from the perspective of others. Cooler reflection is possible after our action when we can examine our conduct in the light of the impartial spectator. "The man of today is no longer agitated by the same passions as the man of yesterday" (TMS, Third.(I).III, p. 222). Now, however, our conduct seems of less importance, no longer enlivened by the context experienced. To view our behavior with candor, to remove the "veil of self-delusion," is a challenge not easily breeched.

Indeed, self-deceit is humankind's fatal weakness, leading to "half the disorders of human life" (TMS, Third.(I).III, p. 223). To fully see ourselves as others see us would surely produce a reformation because we would be unable to tolerate the sight.

However, due to the importance of this human weakness, nature has not left us entirely to our own inner devices, "the delusions of self-love," in providing us with a solution. We constantly experience and observe the conduct of others who leave an indelible mark upon us. Without sensible awareness we tend to absorb general rules as to what is approved and to be done, or is disapproved and not to be done. Some actions are outrageous to us and to all who observe them, serving to confirm and reinforce our sense of their inappropriateness. Inwardly we commit to avoiding such actions in the contexts wherein they are relevant. In contrast, other actions are met with acclaims of approval from all and our sense of their rightness is reinforced. Consequently, we come to absorb "fit and proper" rules to be followed. They emerge out of our experience and become our natural sense of merit and propriety, of demerit and impropriety. Our approval or disapproval of circumstantial actions is not the consequence of our making mindful comparisons between the actions and certain general rules and engaging in conscious learning. Rather, the rules are formed out of our encounter with experiences in which we discover that actions of a certain kind and manner are liked or disliked. Once, however, such general rules become "fixed in our mind by habitual reflection," they become very useful in thinking through how to correct any errors or "misrepresentations" in more conscious reflective moments (TMS, Third.(I).IV, pp. 223–28).

Hence, the instantaneous response occasioned when a homeless man refuses payment unless his newspaper is accepted. Smith is saying that some experiences are jarring and that we resort to reason to sort out the incongruences, but that is not nature's normal means of habit formation.

BENEFICENCE AND JUSTICE CONCERN JUDGMENTS OF OTHERS

The impartial spectator enters in two ways: Our judgments of the actions of others and our judgments of, and actions by, ourselves. Propositions that grow out of our judgments of the actions of others include the propositions on beneficence and injustice stated in the previous chapter, to wit (TMS, Second.II.I, pp. 112–13):

- Properly motivated beneficent actions alone require reward. Why? Because it is these actions alone that inspire our gratitude.
- Improperly motivated hurtful actions alone deserve punishment. Why? Because these actions alone provoke our resentment.
- The want of beneficence cannot provoke resentment. Why? Because beneficence is always free – by definition voluntarily given – and cannot be exhorted by force. It does no intentional positive evil and it is not a proper object of punishment.
- Symmetrically with the last proposition, the want of injustice – justice – does not call for reward. Why? Because innocence is passive and not rewardable. And hence society does not provide rewards for not disturbing your neighbor, for dutifully stopping at a red light. Justice is a negative virtue; defined by all the actions left over after society agrees, based on previously experienced harm, what and how much such actions are punishable. *Justice is not about doing good things; it is about eliminating or diminishing bad things, based on well-trodden past experiences* on which it is easier to get agreement than on conjectured good things with an uncertain future.

In *Sentiments* the sentiment of resentment has a central role in expressing disapproval and emerges in human social interactions, providing common experience and a consensual foundation for rights to take action in social groupings. Thus, resentment safeguards justice by provoking the punishment of an injustice already done to another, while protecting against injustice by deterring others who fear punishment if they commit a like offence (TMS, Second.II.I, pp. 113–14). Retaliation is a law of Nature that requires the violator of the laws of justice to feel that evil done to another;

he who simply observes and does not violate the laws of justice merits no reward, but only respect for his innocence (TMS, Second.II.I, p. 117).

LIMITS ON THE SET OF ACTIONS BY THE AGENT WHO IS HIMSELF THE PERSON JUDGED

For Smith, the scope of our action, which is disciplined by our judgment of ourselves and therefore encompasses our self-command, is circumscribed by the operation of natural motivational forces. Keep in mind that he sees such discipline as arising from local experience, where we can influence and be influenced by our neighbors. Smith examines this issue in a perceptive and well-known thought experiment. We are asked to consider how a European "who had no sort of connection" with China (TMS, Third.(I).III, p. 192) would respond to hearing that a dreadful earthquake had struck this remote land. Nava Ashraf, Colin Camerer, and George Loewenstein, for example, use this section of *Sentiments* to discuss how, as they say, "Smith argued that natural sympathy often falls short of what is morally justified by mass misery" (2005, p. 134). The error here is in thinking that in Part Third of *Sentiments* Smith is discussing the moral justification of our actions. He is not. Rather, he is evaluating "the Foundation of our Judgments concerning our own Sentiments and Conduct, and of the Sense of Duty" (TMS, Third.(I), p. 159). This is confirmed four pages later when Smith carefully explains that "all men, even those at the greatest distance, are no doubt entitled to our good wishes, and our good wishes we naturally give them. But if, notwithstanding, they should be unfortunate, to give ourselves any anxiety upon that account, seems to be no part of our duty. That we should be but little interested, therefore, in the fortune of those *whom we can neither serve nor hurt, and who are in every respect so very remote from us, seems wisely ordered by Nature*" (TMS, Third.(I).III, p. 197, our italics).

Smith is modeling the conduct expressed in our actions, not our more abstract sense of humanity. In that model we are disciplined by judgments that focus our attention on issues where our actions can make a difference – serve or hurt – through our choices. Nature does not dissipate our energy by importuning us to be concerned with issues that we cannot in some measure influence. Obviously, technology may change the scope of conditions that we can do something about, but Smith could neither anticipate nor be held accountable for innovations that alter the domain on which his principles were defined.

In *Sentiments* Smith goes far beyond our project of developing designs for experiment and predicting and explaining the actions people take. *Sentiments* enjoyed and has continued to enjoy a following in philosophy and ethics and explorations in secular and religious concepts of the virtuous person.

ASYMMETRY IN GAINS AND LOSSES, POSITIVE VERSUS NEGATIVE RECIPROCITY AND ESCALATION

In *Sentiments* the asymmetry between gains and losses (Principle 2) enables us to locate in our own and mutual feelings why positive reciprocity does not escalate out of control, whereas negative reciprocity does. These phenomena are reinforced by others, whose sympathy with the joy of their friends is muted, but with their sorrow sympathy is strong (Principle 3). The manic in us restrains, but the depressive reigns; societal violence escalates, whereas peace is always uneasy; economic prosperity builds, depressions crash; stock markets rise gradually, uncertainly and hesitantly, but declines are abrupt, decisive. In law (Smith's central use of Principle 2), the penalty for robbery and theft (which dispossesses) is greater than for violation of contract (reducing only the expectation of gain). The former is thus more urgently in need of escalation control.

References

Ashraf, Nava, Colin F. Camerer, and George Loewenstein. 2005. "Adam Smith, Behavioral Economist," *Journal of Economic Perspectives* 19(3): 131–45.

Falk, Armin, Ernst Fehr, Urs Fischbacher. 2008. "Testing Theories of Fairness – Intentions Matter," *Games and Economic Behavior* 62(1): 287–303.

Fehr, Ernst and Klaus M. Schmidt. 1999. "A Theory of Fairness, Competition, and Cooperation," *Quarterly Journal of Economics* 114: 817–68.

Ferguson, Adam. 1792 [2005]. "Of Man's Progressive Nature," in *Selections from the Scottish Philosophy of Common Sense*, George A. Johnston (ed.). Chicago, IL: The Open Court Publishing Company.

Hayek, F. A. 1973. *Law, Legislation and Liberty, Volume 1: Rules and Order*. Chicago, IL: University of Chicago Press.

Hayek, F. A. 1988. *The Fatal Conceit: The Errors of Socialism*. Chicago, IL: University of Chicago Press.

Hume, David. 2000 [1740]. *A Treatise of Human Nature*, David Fate Norton and Mary J. Norton (eds.). New York, NY: Oxford University Press.

Latour, Bruno. 1999. "Give Me a Laboratory and I Will Raise the World," in *The Science Studies Reader*, M. Biagioli (ed.). New York, NY: Routledge.

Simon, Herbert A. 1956. "A Comparison of Game Theory and Learning Theory," *Psychometrika* 3: 267–72.

Smith, Adam. 1853 [1759]. *The Theory of Moral Sentiments; or, An Essay towards an Analysis of the Principles by which Men naturally judge concerning the Conduct and Character, first of their Neighbours, and afterwards of themselves. To which is added, A Dissertation on the Origins of Languages. New Edition. With a biographical and critical Memoir of the Author*, by Dugald Stewart. London, UK: Henry G. Bohn. Available online and in electronic formats at http://oll .libertyfund.org/titles/2620.

Smith, Adam. 1982 [1795]. "The History of Astronomy," in *Essays on Philosophical Subjects*. Indianapolis, IN: Liberty Fund, 33–105.

Smith, Vernon L. 2008. *Rationality in Economics: Constructivist and Ecological Forms*. New York, NY: Cambridge University Press.

Wilson, Bart J. 2012. "Contra Private Fairness," *American Journal of Economics and Sociology* 71: 407–35.

8

Trust Game Discoveries

The widely cited paper by Joyce Berg, John Dickhaut, and Kevin Mccabe (hereafter, BDMc) provided the key methodology, and the unpredicted and unpredictable results that would change research directions and attitudes, and usher in a fundamental challenge to late twentieth-century thinking in the study of economic behavior.[1] Outpourings of subsequent studies sought to replicate and understand the elements driving the "bizarre" BDMc findings.[2]

In their complete information game, BDMc, recruited thirty-two pairs of participants distributed across three different sessions. In each session, they recruited half the individuals for room A, and half for room B. Each person receives ten $1 bills as an upfront payment for showing up on time, and in this limited sense was earned compensation, and no longer the experimenter's money. In room A, each individual is free to select from their payment any number from 0 to 10 of $1 bills to be sent to their anonymous and randomly paired counterpart in room B. En route, the amount sent is tripled before delivery to the counterpart in room B. BDMc implement a "double blind" or double anonymity protocol in which each pair is not only anonymous with respect to each other, but all are anonymous with respect to the experimenters who can never know whom sent who how much money.

Anonymity and double anonymity in one-time play protocols are levels-of-stringency test conditions designed to invite and encourage self-loving action by making it transparently evident that it is OK not to send money, and it is OK to keep any money received. If cooperation fails, we have

---

[1] Joyce Berg, John Dickhaut, and Kevin McCabe (1995).
[2] Noel Johnson and Alexandra Mislin (2011) collect data on 162 replications using over 23,000 subjects for their meta-analysis of the BDMc investment trust game.

evidence of the power of self-interested motivation, Max-U(*own payoff*), when the cloak of secrecy is thick enough. If cooperation is observed, we expand the range of conditions where the standard "strangers" model fails. In exploring the boundaries of that persistence, BDMc opened the door to the excitement of a great field of new learning. That exploration has not been disappointed.

For the equilibrium of the game (technically, subgame perfect equilibrium, SPE), it is sufficient that (1) all are strictly self-interested, (2) this is common knowledge, and (3) each chooses to maximize their own utilitarian outcome. Under such conditions individuals in room A send nothing, and those in room B return nothing if any money is sent.[3] This prediction does badly even under the supposed favorable condition where no one, not even the experimenter, can know the identity of any individual actor. Quite conclusively, it was a good idea for researchers to seek better ways of thinking about two-person connectedness. Massive prediction failure ought to motivate reevaluation and new learning on a similar scale. As we aim to show here, that failure was not newsworthy within the framework of *Sentiments.* Moreover, *Sentiments* expands the range of new experimental designs and predictions.

On average, individuals in room A sent $5.16. The average payback (amount returned) was $4.66. Only two sent nothing, while five sent all $10. Twenty-eight of the thirty-two people in room A sent more than $1.

Because sending money did not pay, on average, it seemed likely that people's beliefs about others in the game were seriously mistaken. Surely, the subjects would adapt and correct their error by cluing them in on some historical data. That rescue intuition, however, turned out to be as perversely wrong as the original equilibrium predictions. BDMc tested this highly plausible intuition by conducting a "social history" treatment a few days after running the first experiments. In this treatment twenty-eight new pairs of subjects are recruited, using the same parameters and protocol, but with one exception. Each subject is provided a complete report of the earlier experiment results in the instructions—number of persons sending each possible amount, the average returned for each amount sent and the net profit (loss) for each amount sent. The report shows that the only amounts sent that yield any net profits are $5 and $10.

---

[3] The game is a two-sided dictator game with gains from exchange. The gains feature is a key attribute of many of these games, that, when added, has significant impact on action. See, e.g., this effect on ultimatum games in Chapter 9.

In the social history treatment, the average amount sent increases slightly to $5.36, but the average payback increases to $6.46. The discovered-trust norm, "be generous in sending" does not deteriorate, and the trustworthy norm, "be generous in rewarding trust" is enhanced. Three of 28 now send nothing, half (14) of the people in room A send $5 or $10, but only one recipient in room B kept all the money.

In the large subsequent literature, skeptical scholars continued to find empirical defiance of Max-U rationality in choosing actions: In one example, Andreas Ortmann, John Fitzgerald, and Carl Boeing reexamine the BDMc experiments using treatments that they believed would change the findings. They "modify the way information is presented to participants and, through a questionnaire, prompt strategic reasoning" (Ortmann, Fitzgerald, and Boeing 2000, p. 81). However, they report: "To our surprise, none of our various treatments led to a reduction in the amount invested" (Ortmann, Fitzgerald, and Boeing 2000, p. 81). This robustness continued to challenge traditional theory and analysis in follow-on studies.

In the sections that follow, we analyze derivatives of the BDMc games. Our analysis, however, assumes that individuals are guided by the axioms, principles, propositions, and framework of thinking in *Sentiments*. The many variations on these experiments provide an opportunity to revisit the designs and the results, and to apply the model in *Sentiments* to reanalyze and postdict outcomes. Much as our modern minds articulate the rational reasoning of self-interested players who apply backward induction to the game, and implement Max-U(*own payoff*), we apply the argument in *Sentiments*.[4] Smith's model does not make specific predictions, but rather predictions conditional upon how the participants read the circumstances of each game and Smith's model guides us in how to read those circumstances.

Participants in these games routinely and deliberately depart from playing payoff dominant strategies. Our training in economics and game theory does not prepare us to think and navigate in a world of dominated choices (choosing less money instead of more money). Trust games force us to enter that world, but it is an error to enter it masked by presumed altruism or by preferences incoherently named "social." Choosing in accordance with the *Sentiments* model is not selfless. Rather it is an expression of human fellow feeling and self-command, disciplined by the fair and impartial spectator, and requiring strictly self-interested players to

---

[4] In Chapter 10, Table 10.1 we compare the traditional backward induction analysis with a Smithian representation of how the players themselves see the game.

know and agree on who potentially is hurt or benefits from alternative actions taken. We ask why this model's predictions outperform, and are richer than, the predictions provided by the neoclassical model while depending necessarily on Axiom 0, common knowledge of non-satiated actors.

TWO-CHOICE ALTERNATIVES IN SIMPLE SINGLE-PLAY TRUST GAMES

Kevin McCabe and Vernon Smith (2000) report an experiment on the two-person extensive form "trust" game shown in Figure 8.1. Inspired directly by BDMc, it was intended as a more "severe test" of the BDMc results.[5] Like Ortmann et al. (2000), McCabe and Smith (2000) thought they could uncover a crack in the persistence of cooperation; their approach was to allow only starkly contrasting outcomes. The first mover (in blue) chooses to either play right and end the interaction, sending each person on their way with an additional $10, or to play down, foregoing the sure $10 and turning the decision-making over to the second mover (in orange). If the first mover chooses to play down, then the second mover decides between playing right, with the experimenter paying her $25 and the first mover $15, or playing down, with the experimenter paying her $40 and leaving nothing for the first mover. Relating this design to the BDMc experiment, the payoff outcomes correspond to a person in room A either sending $0 to their paired counterpart in room B, yielding $10 for each, or sending $10, which is tripled to $30. The second mover then can split the $30 evenly, yielding $15 for the first mover and $25 total for the second mover, or keep all the money, $40 total. The authors thought that reducing choice to these stark alternatives in their "Invest $10 trust game," with the clear prospect of all the gains going to second movers, might greatly reduce cooperative choices. However, that was not to be.

If the first mover is fully aware of the choice that the second mover faces, and vice versa, how do we understand the actions of two anonymous people when faced with this situation? Adam Smith notes that unless the situation calls for the exactness of a rule of justice, "our conduct should rather be directed by a certain idea of propriety, by a certain taste for a

---

[5] See Deborah Mayo (1996, p. 177) for the definition of "severe test" as applied to the confirmation of a hypothesis. In the text we are thinking of a severe test as part of an exercise in exploring the boundaries of dis-confirmation of the hypothesis.

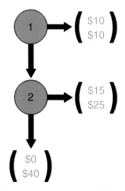

Figure 8.1. Two-person, invest $10, trust game

particular tenor of conduct, than by any regard to a precise maxim or rule" (TMS, Third.(I).VI, p. 249). If that sounds fairly "loose, vague, and indeterminate" (TMS, Third.(I).VI, p. 250), then that is because "there are no rules by knowledge of which we can infallibly be taught to act upon all occasions with prudence, with just magnanimity, or proper beneficence" (TMS, Third.(I).VI, p. 251). Consequently, Smith implicitly recognizes in these passages that the rule a particular individual might follow may vary with the circumstances that constitute particular "occasions."

Sentiments therefore excludes as being pertinent for all occasions the modern economist's very precise and accurate concept of subgame perfect equilibrium. This theory predicts that the first mover would immediately end the game and receive $10 because, if given the opportunity to make the decision, the second mover would choose $40 over $25 for herself, thereby leaving the first mover with nothing. Fortunately, "nature, … [has not] abandoned us entirely to the delusions of self-love. Our continual observations upon the conduct of others, insensibly lead us to form to ourselves certain general rules concerning what is fit and proper either to be done or to be avoided" (TMS, Third.(I).IV, p. 223–24).

What general rules of fit and proper behavior are applicable to this game and to the experiences of this community of participants? In addition, what would those rules predict? Let us first consider, as subgame perfection does, the second mover, but from the perspective in *Sentiments*. If given the opportunity to make a decision, the second mover would "endeavor to examine [her] own conduct as [she] imagines any other fair and impartial spectator would examine it. If, upon placing [herself] in his situation, [she] thoroughly enter[s] into all the passions and motives which influenced it, [she] approve[s] of it, by sympathy with the approbation of this supposed equitable judge. If, otherwise, [she] enter[s] into his disapprobation, and condemn[s] it" (TMS, Third.(I).I, p. 162).

In this game the question is whether, by sympathy with the impartial spectator, the second mover would approve or disapprove of choosing to play right and approve or disapprove of choosing to play down. Choosing to play right yields a higher payment from the experimenter to both individuals as the first mover forewent a sure $10 for both. A fair and impartial spectator could thus approve of playing right; both are better off because of the actions of both people. Moreover, by Beneficence Proposition 1 (Chapter 6) the first mover's action is properly motivated, and is likely to engender gratitude and invoke a reward response in the second mover. Choosing to play down, however, sends the first mover home with nothing after foregoing a sure $10. Thus, however anonymous the participants may be in this interaction, an impartial spectator could reasonably disapprove of playing down.

Now consider the first mover. From past experience with friends and classmates, he expects that "nature, which formed men for that mutual kindness, so necessary for their happiness, renders every man the peculiar object of kindness, to the person to whom he himself has been kind" (TMS, Sixth.II.I, p. 331, as in the Corollary in Chapter 6). In other words, experience has taught him that if he kindly passes play for a mutual gain for the both of them, a second mover might be expected to kindly reciprocate him, the person to whom he himself has just been kind.

But must the impartial spectator disapprove of the second mover playing down? Not necessarily, if our conduct is indeed directed by a certain idea of propriety and not a precise rule. Recall that the first mover has the choice between playing right or down, and if the first mover chooses down, the second mover has the choice of playing right or down. An impartial spectator could reason that in these circumstances, the experimenter specified the second mover rules. Everyone, including the first mover, with knowledge of the rules has agreed to participate in this experiment. Thus, if the first mover willingly chooses to play down, an impartial spectator could also approve of the second mover playing down, for if the experimenter did not wish to observe whether or not the second mover might actually choose to play down, the experimenter would not have given her the option. By this rationalization, it is okay to take all the money.

Sentiments thus informs the economist that the rules of interaction in the trust game simply "present us with a general idea of the perfection we ought to aim at, [rather] than afford us any certain and infallible directions for acquiring it" (TMS, Third.(I).VI, p.250). This general idea of perfection is founded upon our autobiographical experiences "of what, in particular instances, our moral faculties, our natural sense of merit and propriety, approve, or disapprove of" (TMS, Third.(I).IV, p. 224). Different people, either with different experiences, or different interpretations as to how their experience applies to the game in question, may converge on different responses in this one-shot choice, which provides no opportunity for each person to learn from repeat interaction more about their matched counterpart. Smith's propositions on beneficence and injustice, however, provide specific guidelines in interpreting how we can expect people to read each other in taking action in these games.

Here are the pooled results from three different laboratory studies of choice in Figure 8.1: there are a total of 98 first movers. Fifty-two choose to play right and 46 choose to play down. Of the 46 second movers who have the opportunity to make a decision, 31 (67 percent) choose to play right, and 15 (33 percent) choose to play down.[6] So, while the general propositions in *Sentiments* cautiously makes no specific prediction about what people will do in the trust game,[7] experimental economics can inform Smith's theory of the general principles with which impartial spectators approve and disapprove of playing right and playing down. By randomly assigning participants to conditions with systematic variations in the procedures, we can trace out some of the contextual principles that excite and mediate whether more impartial spectators approve or disapprove of playing right and playing down.

In a laboratory experiment, subjects typically make decisions anonymously with respect to each other, but the experimenter knows by name what each subject did in order to pay them (privately) what they earn. This is the protocol for the data reported above. In a second condition, James Cox and Cary Deck (2005), as did BDMc, implement an elaborate procedure to ensure that the subjects also make their decisions anonymously

---

[6] McCabe and Smith (2000), James Cox and Cary Deck (2005), and Anthony Gillies and Mary Rigdon (2017). Other results not included in this pooling are reported in Anna Gunnthorsdottir, Kevin McCabe and Vernon Smith (2000), who use first-year-only (freshman) subjects who had been administered the Machiavellian (Mach) test. For the 103 pairs scoring low or average on the test, 47 percent of first movers moved down; 54 percent of the second movers cooperated. The first movers with High Mach scores moved 50 percent down, but only 28 percent of the high Mach second movers chose to cooperate, with 72 percent choosing to take all the money (28 total subjects).

[7] The critic who asserts that a Smithian analysis of this game is unhelpful because it does not make a specific prediction has the burden of providing and demonstrating a set of rules for this interaction that are, in the words of Adam Smith, "precise, accurate, and indispensable" (TMS, Third.(I).VI, p. 250).

with respect to the experimenter. The experimenter cannot match decisions to specific individuals. Interestingly, this change in procedures asymmetrically effects the decisions of both people. First movers pass the play by
choosing to play down at the same rate in both conditions. However, 13 out
of 17 (76 percent) second movers choose to play down with double
anonymity, but only 5 out of 13 (38 percent), choose to play down with
single anonymity. It seems that increasing the privacy of the interaction is
an aspect of the context that compromises the sense of gratitude for a
beneficent action, and excites more to approve playing down by the second
movers. An unresolved question is why the first movers do not anticipate
that the second movers are more disposed to choosing down over right
with double anonymity.[8] Hence, empirical support for the Corollary on
reciprocal beneficence in Chapter 6 is stronger under single than double
anonymity; complete privacy encourages more actions that are self-
regarding.[9]

The contrast in conduct with single and double anonymity sheds light
on the motivation Principles 4a and 4b (in Chapter 5) in *Sentiments*, where
it is argued that people desire not only praise but to be worthy of the praise
(and avoid blame and blameworthiness). Where we modify anonymous
interaction by adding third parties—here, the experimenters—who can
never know the person's choice, people make more decisions that are
self-regarding. In *Sentiments* Smith suggests that the "wise man," meaning
the man whose impartial spectator governs his self-command with unusual
force, will be assiduous in avoiding any imputation of blame. The rules we
follow derive from mutual fellow-feeling, supported by self-command, and
it is the latter that we presume is weakened at the margin in achieving
cooperation when the experimenters cannot observe subjects' identity.

---

[8] The conduct of the second movers in choosing to play right, under double anonymity, may
be praiseless and only praiseworthy, and thus its motivation weakened compared with
single anonymity; similarly, the second mover's choice of playing down may be less
discouraged by being only blameworthy compared with single anonymity. Any such
second order effects may be more difficult for the first movers to anticipate in another
person. (Our formal representation in Chapter 11 includes this prospect among the rules
people follow, as a failure of self-command.)

[9] This correlates with a large literature in which subjects are found to "lie and cheat" using
deception protocols wherein people believe they are acting with complete privacy. See, for
example, Dan Ariely (2012). The use of deception by scientists in studies designed to show
that people deceptively lie and cheat illustrates the importance of Smith's emphasis on
context. It is OK to lie and cheat in the name of science! ["This self-deceit, this fatal
weakness of mankind, is the source of half the disorders of human life" (TMS, Third.(I).IV,
p. 223).]

Gillies and Rigdon (2017) consider how knowledge of the payoffs affects play in the trust game. In what they call a "Private Game," each person only knows their own payoffs associated with playing right and down. As shown in Figure 8.2, the first mover only knows that he receives $10 from choosing to play right and that if he passes the play, the second mover is choosing between $15 and $0 for him. The catch is that the first mover does not know what the second mover's payoffs are from choosing to play right or down, and the first mover knows that the second mover does not know what his payoffs are from choosing to play right or down. Likewise, the second mover does not know what the first mover's payoff is from choosing to play right, only that her payoff is $10 from the first mover choosing to play right. Neither participant, therefore, can know how their decision produces benefit or hurt. The strong implication is that people will choose in their strict self-interest.

Without knowledge about how his decision affects the second mover, the first mover is unable to conclude that the second mover will reciprocate his trusting action of playing down with a trustworthy one of her playing right, and that is what Gillies and Rigdon observe. Fifteen of 45 (33 percent) first movers play down in the private knowledge trust game as opposed to 21 of 50 (42 percent) first movers do in the full common knowledge game.

More dramatic is the response of the second mover's impartial spectators. Only 3 of 15 (20 percent) second movers play right in the private knowledge trust game in contrast to 14 of 21 (67 percent) who do so in the full common knowledge game. More impartial spectators approve of

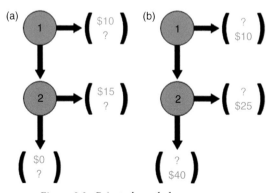

Figure 8.2. Private knowledge trust game

(a) The first mover's view

(b) The second mover's view

playing down, taking the higher payoff of $40, when they are unaware of what the first mover forewent in choosing to play down and unaware of what the first mover will receive ($0). Since neither player knows the payoff of the other, gratitude and the Corollary on reciprocal beneficence cannot enter into judging the propriety of each other's actions in the context of this interaction (Principles 5 and 6 in Chapter 5; Chapter 6); hence their self-love cannot be "humbled" by the impartial spectator and is necessarily more important under such game circumstances.

In the complete knowledge version of the game in Figure 8.1, Gillies and Rigdon also consider in a separate treatment condition how the second movers behave when they are asked to make their decision conditional on the first mover having chosen to play down. The second movers, however, are paid based upon those decisions only if the first mover actually chooses to play down. The second mover's choice is not implemented if the first mover chooses to play right. In this treatment, the impartial spectators are hypothetically invoked as opposed to being explicitly excited with the first mover's actual choice of playing down. Whereas 14 of 21 (67 percent) second movers choose to play right when the first mover has actually chosen to play down, only 20 of 43 (47 percent) the second movers choose to play right when asked to assume the first mover has chosen to play down.[10] The distinction made in these experiments correspond to games played in extensive versus normal (or strategic; i.e., contingent play) form. Traditional game theory treated the two as equivalent, but many experimental studies have reported data rejecting this postulated equivalence.[11] The two game forms are cognitively much different in that in the extensive form the first mover conveys to the second mover her intentions before the latter is required to choose. *Sentiments* is particularly relevant in this interpretation because intentions are central to the capacity of the

---

[10] Marco Casari and Timothy Cason (2009) observe similar behavior in a trust game with different parameters.

[11] For a discussion and several references, see Vernon Smith (2008, pp. 264–67) and for other experiment results making this comparison see Kevin McCabe, Stephen Rassenti, and Vernon Smith (1996). We note that an early draft of this 1996 paper appeared as a working paper (cited by BDMc) as Kevin McCabe, Stephen Rassenti, and Vernon Smith (1994) entitled, "Forward and Backward Rationality in Achieving Cooperation." The aborted early draft was an unsuccessful and unconvincing attempt to explain trust game cooperation in terms of forward signaling. If both players do backward induction, each can see that equilibrium play is in order. Hence, if the first mover elects not to play equilibrium, that is a signal inviting cooperation. Although uninformed by *Sentiments* at the time, the working paper reflected a struggle with similar issues that were missing in traditional game theory.

impartial spectator to form an appropriate judgment of the other person's action and, therefore, in judging an appropriate response.[12]

EXPLORING "CIRCUMSTANCES": DOES OPPORTUNITY COST MATTER IN CONVEYING INTENTIONS?

Figure 8.3(a) presents a simple trust game – the voluntary trust game – with the same game-theoretic analytical incentive structure as Figure 8.1, but with different payoffs. In single play, if the first mover chooses to end the game, each receives $20; if the first mover passes to the second mover, the latter chooses between playing right, yielding $25 for each, or playing down, yielding $15 for the first mover and $30 for the second mover. As in the trust game of Figure 8.1, the SPE is for the first mover to end the game and each collects $20 apiece. In the laboratory with 27 pairs choosing, we observe that 17 of the first movers (63 percent) pass to the second mover; an increase over Figure 8.1 – incentives matter with the first mover standing to lose less if the second mover defects on the offer to cooperate. And 11 (65 percent) of the second movers choose to play right, which is nearly twice the number, 6 (35 percent), who choose to play down. As before, many of the pairs are choosing cooperatively in a manner consistent with the Corollary on reciprocal beneficence in TMS.

Kevin McCabe, Mary Rigdon, and Vernon Smith (2003) use this game to answer the following question: How will these results be affected if in a second treatment condition the first mover cannot voluntarily choose between ending the game and passing to the second mover, with passing being required of the first mover? The "involuntary trust game" is shown in Figure 8.3(b). The second mover faces the same payoff alternatives as in Figure 8.3(a) but sees that the first mover gives up nothing – incurs no opportunity cost. Consequently, under these conditions, the impartial spectator in the second mover is prevented from forming the same intentional "kindness" judgment of the conduct of the first mover as in the first treatment. Consistent with this reasoning, under the second treatment conditions, the results from the first experiment in Figure 8.3(a) are

---

[12] Kevin McCabe, Vernon Smith, and Michael LePore (2000) argue that the better coordination in the extensive form "derives from the human capacity to read another's thoughts or intentions by placing themselves in the position and information state of the other person" (p. 4404). This attribution is not from *Sentiments* but from the "mindreading" literature that independently discovered Smith's conception of the impartial spectator. In Smith, however, "mindreading" begins with "feel-reading" in a feeling-thinking-knowing process.

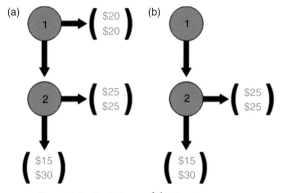

Figure 8.3. Variations of the trust game

(a) Voluntary trust game

(b) Involuntary trust game

reversed in Figure 8.3(b): now only 33 percent of the second movers choose right over down.[13] But why do one-third still appear to empathize with their paired first movers? The involuntary trust game exerts control over the action alternatives—the opportunity cost incurred—by the first mover and is visible to both in each interacting pair. To make it equivalent in all other respects to the voluntary trust game, a real first mover (i.e., no deception) is essential to make the involuntary move. Think of the first mover as acting as an agent who must follow the will of the experimenter. Apparently, this agency is a circumstance that is perceived by a minority as deserving of reward, although the agent cannot deviate from the will of the experimenter.

REPEAT-PLAY TRUST GAMES: DOES A TRUST ENVIRONMENT ENCOURAGE TRUST OR INVITE DEFECTION?

Mary Rigdon, Kevin McCabe, and Vernon Smith (2007) have also studied behavior in repeat play of the stage game in Figure 8.3(a). Their experiments examine decision behavior under two different conditions that vary only the protocols for matching subject pairs after each round of play. In both protocols, the participants are not informed as to the number of repetitions; without warning, play is stopped after twenty rounds. In the first protocol the subjects are simply re-paired at random. In the second, a

---

[13] Armin Falk, Ernst Fehr, and Urs Fischbacher (2008) also find that intentions matter in a game played in strategic (simultaneous play) form.

scoring algorithm uses their previous decisions to enable all the first movers and the second movers to be separately ranked from most cooperative to least. Then, the highest in each rank are matched with each other for the next round; the second highest are matched with each other for the next round; and so on down the list. A cooperative choice by the first mover means that he passed to the second mover; a cooperative choice by the second mover occurs whenever playing right is selected. It is very important to keep in mind that the subjects in these experiments *were not informed of the matching procedure.* In both treatments, all the participants were told simply that they would be re-paired with a person in the room each period. In all sessions there were 16 people in the room with 8 first movers (and 8 second movers) to be re-paired either at random or by application of the scoring algorithm.

If indeed "kindness begets kindness" as in Adam Smith's Corollary on reciprocal beneficence (Chapter 6), then the scoring rule allows those interacting over the twenty repetitions to "discover" by experience that they are in an environment characterized by "kindness." Over time each person's impartial spectator would be updated and reflect any experiential tendencies toward kind behavior. Rigdon, McCabe, and Smith (2007) had no assured expectation as to how effective the scoring rule would be. This is why they used a comparison control that implemented random re-pairing. An open question was how effective the two protocols would be in separating the two different pools of subjects with respect to their frequency of cooperative choice. From the perspective of Sentiments, Beneficence Proposition 1 (Chapter 6), it is especially important that people in the treatment experiments not know the scoring-matching rule. If they know the rule, then their choice is justified by deliberate self-interested utility maximization, whereas Smith's proposition requires the first mover's action to arise from beneficent trusting motives, and for the second movers to respond with no reason to think that the first mover's motives were otherwise.[14]

---

[14] Rigdon, McCabe, and Smith (2007) completed their research at the University of Arizona at the turn of the millennium, reporting it as a working paper in 2002, but publication was delayed. Why? Principally, the procedure – subjects not being informed of the rank order rule for rematching pairs – was the source of controversy in seminar presentations and in the editor-refereeing process. Both theorists and experimentalists had difficulty grasping why subjects were not provided full knowledge of the cooperative matching procedure. There is a body of theory – an irrelevant distraction from the perspective of this study – that argues that a small in-group of cooperators can invade a population of defectors, and, being able to identify each other, outperform their out-group peers. Such an experiment would seek to confirm that rational constructivist prediction. Suppose our subjects knew the circumstances of their matching and behaved more cooperatively than in the randomly

The data strongly support the primary hypothesis: the two treatment groups bifurcate significantly across repeat trials in exhibiting cooperative responses. On trials 1–5, the ratio of percent cooperative choice by the first movers in the treatment to the percent cooperation in the random control was 1.047; for the second movers, the ratio was 1.094; i.e., essentially very little treatment difference in the first five trials. But cooperation steadily improved, so that in the last five trials, 16–20, these ratios respectively were 1.944 and 1.67, corresponding to increases respectively of $(1.944/1.047) - 1 = 85.6$ percent for the first movers and $1.67/1.094) - 1 = 52.6$ percent for the second movers.

Rigdon, McCabe, and Smith (2007) also report a very pronounced regularity in the conduct of people in both treatments: the individual decisions of the first movers to trust or not, and for the second movers to respond trustworthily or not, *on the first trial* was strongly and significantly related to their subsequent tendency to show trust or trustworthy behavior in repeat interaction, whichever treatment was later experienced. Thus, we can say that in these experiments, each person, after reading the instructions and entering into the first round of play, makes a decision conditional upon their previous history and their anticipated future interactive behavior. What we learn across all the subjects is that their state of sympathetic responsiveness is marked indelibly by their first decision, and is predictive of their subsequent behavior in the remaining 19 trials. In the language of game theory, the participant is "typed" by their decision on the first trial, and their type significantly accounts for their subsequent decisions although these vary significantly with their subsequent experience and the experimental treatment condition.[15] In the language of *Sentiments*

---

re-paired group. What would be learned? Only that when it is made plain to people that in repeat interaction cooperation is individually optimal, then people are likely to choose optimally. In that case, we would learn, yet again, that people tend to maximize in games that essentially reduce rationally to games against nature. However, this experiment had a different objective. The question: What will people do if they find themselves – without being informed why – in a climate of relative cooperation, compared to a climate of relative defection? Are there forces qua rules at work in individuals that draw out cooperative tendencies? Will cooperation and profitability build experientially? Or will it deteriorate in self-loving exploitation of the good offices of others? From the hindsight perspective in *Sentiments*, will kindness beget kindness in this weak atmosphere of intentionality? The published version of the paper reflects the editor-refereeing process mixed with the motivation explained in this footnote; working papers are often better than the published version.

[15] Thomas Rietz, Roman Sheremeta, Timothy Shields, and Vernon Smith (2013) extend this finding in two directions: first to a three-person trust game environment, and second, using an independent single-trial game, as distinct from first-trial behavior in repeat play, to "type" people in the subsequent repeat play game. Cooperation in single play significantly types cooperative play in the repeat play version of the same game.

these subjects show strong propensities to act in accordance with Beneficence Proposition 1 and the Corollary on reciprocal beneficence which explains their "type." Game theory imports "types" from outside its domain, then maximizes conditionally on the types; *Sentiments* models the emergence of types as rule-followers based on fellow-feeling-thinking-knowing (Chapter 3), and is able to *deduce that the resulting norms are efficient without anyone seeking efficiency.* We know of no modern treatment that can make any such claim.

MIX THE SIGNAL OF BENEFICENCE WITH EXTORTION AND OBSERVE LESS COOPERATION

Kevin McCabe, Vernon Smith, and Michael LePore (2000) report a second variation on the game in Figure 8.1, also motivated by the BDMc investment trust game: the invest $5 trust game in Figure 8.4(a). As before, the first mover can opt out, and each receives $10. But if the first mover passes to the second mover, the first mover retains $5, investing $5, which is tripled to $15. The gain is then split evenly between the two, yielding $7.5 + $5 = $12.5 for the first mover, and $7.5 + $10 = $17.5 for the second mover; alternatively, the second mover can keep his

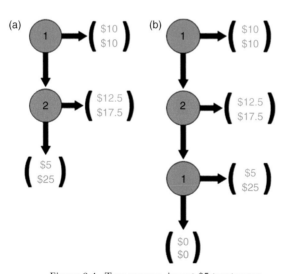

Figure 8.4. Two-person, invest $5 trust game

(a) Standard

(b) With Punishment

endowment plus all the gains ($10 + $15 = $25), leaving the first mover with the $5 retained.

Twenty-seven pairs of subjects participated in this game, with 15 (56 percent) of the first movers choosing right, 12 (44 percent) offering to cooperate by playing down; 9 (67 percent) second movers choose to cooperate, 3 (33 percent) to defect. These percentage outcomes are compatible with the data for the invest $10 trust games above, further reinforcing the general replication properties of these trust games.

Since the defection outcome is positive for both players, McCabe, Smith, and LePore (2000) introduce a structural variation in which, if the second mover defects, play returns to the first mover, who can either choose the defection payoff ($5, $25) or forfeit her $5 and deny the defection payoff to the second mover; that is, each walk away with zero from their interactive play. See Figure 8.4(b). According to Injustice Proposition 1 (Chapter 6), the hurtful action of the second mover tends to cause resentment in the first mover, and some of them are predicted to incur the cost of punishing the second mover. The positive-sum reciprocity trust game with defection in Figure 8.4(a) can escalate into the negative-sum reciprocity outcome at the bottom of Figure 8.4(b) if the second mover defects on the first mover's offer to cooperate. McCabe, Smith, and LePore (2000) report the results of 24 pairs participating in the punishment version: 12 (50 percent) of the first movers choose equilibrium play in line with the previous trust game outcomes. However, in the punishment version we find a reduction in reciprocal cooperative play by the second movers, with only 5 (42 percent) cooperating, as the defection rate more than doubles from 3 to 7 (58 percent). Moreover, 2 (29 percent) of the first movers invoke the punishment option.

We have learned that outcomes in trust games like that of Figure 8.4(a) follow from Beneficence Proposition 1: If the first mover passes to the second mover, the action is clearly intended to be beneficial, for the offer to cooperate is unconditional without sanctions of any kind. Because beneficence is always free and cannot be extorted (Beneficence Proposition 2, Chapter 6), cooperative action by the first mover invokes a response in which some two-thirds of the second movers reward the offer to cooperate by accepting it. But in the punishment version, Figure 8.4(b), the second mover can read a move down by the first mover as carrying the threat of punishment for not cooperating as an attempt to extort the cooperative outcome. An offer of cooperation under threat is not a trusting act and relieves the trustee of any moral obligation to be trustworthy. Hence, the first movers send a noisy signal, and fewer of the second movers cooperate.

Trustworthiness loses meaning where trust is in doubt. Suppose that a first mover does not act beneficently, but offers cooperation motivated by the belief that the threat of punishment would invoke a cooperative response. If the second mover defects, contrary to the belief, the first mover may feel like her bluff has been called. Resenting the threat, the second mover defects, compounding resentment in the first mover, who punishes the defection. The opportunity to realize the virtuous circle of the Corollary on reciprocal beneficence has cascaded to $0 for both. For such a subset of pairs, the potential gains from exchange, attainable through trust and trustworthiness, is entirely dissipated along with initial endowments; better for the first mover to have opted out of attempting a relationship under the structural conditions of Figure 8.4(b). This social destructiveness is thoughtfully considered in *Sentiments* (TMS, Second. II.II, p. 124–25):

Society . . . cannot subsist among those who are at all times ready to hurt and injure one another. The moment that injury begins, the moment that mutual resentment and animosity take place, all the bands of it are broke asunder, and the different members of which it consisted are, as it were, dissipated and scattered abroad by the violence and opposition of their discordant affections.

The key role played by extortion, or of its perception, in *Sentiments,* is corroborated in the punishment version of trust games, which provides the essential insight for viewing the popular ultimatum game in a new light.

References

Ariely, Dan. 2012. *The Honest Truth about Dishonesty: How We Lie to Everyone— Especially Ourselves.* New York: HarperCollins.

Berg, Joyce, John Dickhaut, and Kevin McCabe. 1995. "Trust, Reciprocity, and Social History," *Games and Economic Behavior* 10: 122–42.

Casari, Marco, and Timothy N. Cason. 2009. "The Strategy Method Lowers Measured Trustworthy Behavior," *Economics Letters* 103(3): 157–59.

Cox, James C. and Cary A. Deck. 2005. "On the Nature of Reciprocal Motives," *Economic Inquiry* 43, 623–35.

Falk, Armin, Ernst Fehr and Urs Fischbacher. 2008. "Testing theories of fairness– Intentions matter," *Games and Economic Behavior* 62(1): 287–303.

Gillies, Anthony S. and Mary L. Rigdon. 2017. "Plausible Deniability and Cooperation in Trust Games," Working paper, Rutgers University.

Gunnthorsdottir, Anna, Kevin A. McCabe and Vernon L. Smith. 2000. "Using the Machiavellian Instrument to Predict Trustworthiness in a Bargaining Game," *Journal of Economic Psychology* 23: 49–66.

Johnson, Noel and Alexandra Mislin. 2011. "Trust games: A meta-analysis," *Journal of Economic Psychology* 32: 865–89.

Mayo, Deborah. 1996. *Error and the Growth of Experimental Knowledge*. Chicago: University of Chicago Press.

McCabe, Kevin, Stephen Rassenti, and Vernon L. Smith. 1994. "Forward and Backward Rationality in the Achievement of Cooperation," Mimeo, Economic Science Laboratory, University of Arizona.

McCabe, Kevin, Stephen Rassenti, and Vernon L. Smith. 1996. "Game Theory and Reciprocity in Some Extensive Form Experimental Games," *Proceedings of the National Academy of Arts and Sciences* 93: 13421–28.

McCabe, Kevin, Mary L. Rigdon, and Vernon L. Smith. 2003. "Positive Reciprocity and Intentions in Trust Games," *Journal of Economic Behavior and Organization* 52(2): 267–75.

McCabe, Kevin and Vernon L. Smith. 2000. "A Comparison of Naïve and Sophisticated Subject Behavior with Game Theoretic Predictions," *Proceedings of the National Academy of Arts and Sciences* 97(7): 3777–81.

McCabe, Kevin, Vernon L. Smith, and Michael LePore. 2000. "Intentionality Detection and 'Mindreading': Why Does Game Form Matter?" *Proceedings of the National Academy of Sciences* 97(8): 4404–9.

Ortmann, Andreas, John Fitzgerald, and Carl Boeing. 2000. "Trust, Reciprocity, and Social History: A Re-examination," *Experimental Economics* 3(1): 81–100.

Rietz, Thomas A., Roman M. Sheremeta, Timothy W. Shields, and Vernon L. Smith. 2013. "Transparency, Efficiency and the Distribution of Economic Welfare in Pass-Through Investment Trust Games," *Journal of Economic Behavior and Organization* 94: 257–67.

Rigdon, Mary L., Kevin A. McCabe, and Vernon L. Smith. 2007. "Sustaining Cooperation in Trust Games," *Economic Journal* 117(522): 991–1007.

Smith, Adam. 1853 [1759]. *The Theory of Moral Sentiments; or, An Essay towards an Analysis of the Principles by which Men naturally judge concerning the Conduct and Character, first of their Neighbours, and afterwards of themselves. To which is added, A Dissertation on the Origins of Languages. New Edition. With a biographical and critical Memoir of the Author*, by Dugald Stewart. London: Henry G. Bohn. Available online and in electronic formats at http://oll.libertyfund.org/titles/2620.

Smith, Vernon L. 2008. *Rationality in Economics: Constructivist and Ecological Forms*. New York: Cambridge University Press.

9

The Ultimatum Game as Involuntary Extortion

Since its introduction by Werner Güth, Rolf Schmittberger, and Bernd Schwarze in 1982, the popularity of the Ultimatum Game (UG) has been comparable to, and perhaps exceeds, that of trust games.[1] In the typical UG experiment people are recruited to the laboratory in groups of size *2N*, e.g., 12 or 16, randomized into anonymous pairs, and at random one person is selected to be the Proposer (the first mover), the other the Responder (the second mover). The task of each pair is to determine the allocation of a fixed sum of money, $M, say $10 or $100 (consisting of ten $1 bills or ten $10 bills), between the two members of the linked pair according to the following rules: the Proposer in the UG offers a division ($x, $M − x) of $M made available by the experimenter; $x for Proposer, $M − x for Responder, where $0 \leq x \leq M$; the Responder chooses to accept the division offered or to reject it, in which case the outcome is zero for each ($0, $0). If people are strictly motivated by their immediate monetary self-interest, and this is common knowledge, it is evident that the Proposer would offer the minimum positive amount ($M − x = $1) and the Responder would accept it.

For thirty-five years, this model of the UG has failed to be predictive of player choices in standard versions of the game as described above. Modal and median offers are 40–50 percent of $M (mean about 45 percent); because there are so few low offers, the rejection rate is less than 10 percent, but about half of the offers below 20 percent are rejected (Colin Camerer 2003, pp. 48–56).

Economists soon postulated a utilitarian solution to solve the contradiction between theory and evidence. In the neoclassical paradigm, action was motivated by the own-regarding utility of the outcome, an assumption

[1] See Werner Güth and Martin Kocher (2014) for a review of the UG literature.

that carried over without modification into game theory. If the outcomes are other-regarding – revealed by above-equilibrium allocations to other – then these outcomes, it was thought, must be in the decision makers' utility functions. This follows given the prevailing scientific belief that action implies outcome yields utility and vice versa; hence, other-regarding behavior is observed if and only if utility functions contain other as well as own payoffs.

The simplicity of the UG explained its popularity and its attraction as a vehicle for justifying social preference explanatory themes in decision behavior. It was lauded as delivering the "death blow" to the universality of models of self-interested choice:

> The ultimatum game could hardly be simpler.... The data falsify the assumption that players maximize their own payoffs as clearly as experimental data can. Every methodological explanation you can think of (such as low stakes) has been carefully tested and cannot fully explain the results. Since the equilibria are so simple to compute ..., the ultimatum game is a crisp way of measuring social preferences rather than a deep test of strategic thinking. (Camerer 2003, p. 43)

But as we have seen, *Sentiments* offers a methodology that models the emergence of rule-following conduct among postulated strictly self-interested individuals. Such a model has indeed been excluded from "every methodological explanation you can think of" because thinking has been restricted to the modern tradition of choosing to Max-U over outcomes only.

Continuing with the Smithian line of thought, the observation that proposers make very few offers of low amounts is a predictable result if a person's action reflects the self-discipline of an impartial spectator who has acquired the socializing habit of viewing his action from the perspective of others, in this case the Responder (Principle 1, Chapter 5). In effect, each Proposer, by imagining himself a Responder, is able in most cases to anticipate and reduce the prospect of rejection. Violations are of only two types: failures of the changing-places imagination or an attempt to test its boundary.

But why, if Proposers imagine themselves in the place of Responders, do they make sure-thing offers of $5 to their respective responders? Can the only answer simply be that there is a heartfelt concern for "fair" outcomes, the meaning of which surely involves mutual voluntary agreement that unequal outcomes are not merited?

Adam Smith's answer also could not be simpler, but you have to get past utility theory as a theory of everything: Because beneficence is always free and cannot be extorted (Beneficence Proposition 2, Chapter 6). The standard experimenter protocol in which participants have no control over the circumstances of their task assures that the arbitrary power of rejection by the Responder is the cloud that hangs over every Proposer's choice, whatever the other treatment conditions studied. An early study of UG play by Robert Forsythe, Joel Horowitz, N. E. Savin, and Martin Sefton (1994) challenged the interpretation that the strong tendency toward equal-split was attributable to fairness. The authors argued that if fairness was indeed the primary explanation, then it should make no difference in the bargaining outcome if the right of rejection by the Responder is eliminated. But eliminating the Responders' right of veto makes a substantial difference; in the resulting "Dictator" game – an UG absent the right of Responder veto – Proposer offers decline from a mean of 45 percent to 23 percent. (Elizabeth Hoffman, Kevin McCabe, Keith Shachat, and Vernon Smith (1994) find that the offer rate reduces still further to 10.5 percent under double anonymity, when neither the participants nor the experimenter know what any participant does.)[2]

Neither before nor after Forsythe et al. (1994) and its related literature was causality properly investigated and established. Behavioral economists identified and measured the invisible force of fairness by waiting for the effect which the force was desired to predict: Equal-split was a definition of fair, and the immediate implication of fair behavior is to choose an equal-split; it was just as good a definition of "non-enviousness" which was on no scientific radar screens, so much did the science identify with its subjects. Hence, "fair," a name for the phenomena observed, became the reigning "theory," however empty of empirical content! Symmetrically, behavioral economists explained Responder rejections as arising from outcomes that are "unfair" (or unequal) and the impulse to punish the Proposer even at a cost to the Responder herself. These fair/unfair explanations became a special case of social preferences, the new theory of all choice behavior in trust, ultimatum and dictator games (also public good games). The ubiquity of the fair-outcome occurrence became the foundation of all social behavior.

Many important findings, however, resulted from experimental studies designed to better understand the nature of the new social preference paradigm. Misguided models in no sense mean that the experiments they

---

[2] In further examination of its robustness, it turned out that in Dictator Games, if the money given by the Proposer is earned – their own and not the experimenters – Dictator giving disappears. This was established in studies by Todd Cherry, Peter Frykblom, and Jason F. Shogren (2002) and Robert Oxoby and John Spraggon (2008), but this earned money effect is not the case for UGs as in John List and Todd Cherry (2000).

motivate are without interest. Rather experimental results in new contexts are facts, independent of their motivation, and must be accounted for in a coherent theory. As we shall see, the experiments are particularly significant in evaluating the relevance of Smith's model, which, if it is to have standing, must be consistent with the findings.

BINARY CHOICE FORMS OF THE ULTIMATUM GAME

In the pursuit of understanding, the new experimental studies quickly established that "intentions" mattered. Although not normally a utilitarian characteristic, the unpredicted finding was readily embraced as part of what one naturally should mean by preferences being social – taking account of another.[3] The finding was seen as welcome and hardly surprising, once self-interested preferences were replaced by social preferences, but the language now drifted, and we find people being described as "pro-social." Of course intentions were an integral part of Adam Smith's model of human social conduct in 1759, but it was not in the utility function. Personal as well as market relationships have a structure in which preferences play a role; it is the structure we want to capture in modeling that is in turn predictive of the richness and variation in what we observe.

Armin Falk, Ernst Fehr, and Urs Fischbacher (2003) examine intentions in a study reporting the results of a variation on the standard UG in which Proposers are constrained to offer only two alternative integer splits of 10 points.[4] The split that is fixed across all choices was (8 points for Proposer, 2 points for Responder), which is always offered against one of the following set of controlled single alternatives from which the Proposer must choose in each game (5, 5), (2, 8), (8, 2), and (10, 0). They use the "strategy method" in which Responders are required to report their decision for each of the two possible choices by the Proposer in every game.

In Table 9.1 Proposers choose to offer either the allocation in the first column or (8, 2). The Proposer's corresponding frequency of choosing to

---

[3] Imagine discovering that the "intentional," as opposed say to "impulse," purchase of an item, importantly changes the seller's behavior. Would you model the phenomena by inserting a (0, 1) parameter for intended or not into the preference function of the seller? Not if you wanted to model it usefully beyond its discovery. The behavior of the seller changes because she wants to maximize profit, and learns to display the item near the cash register, where it will not be missed while checking out of the store.

[4] Points were converted into Swiss francs at the end of all the experiments when the subjects learned the outcomes. Each point was worth 0.80 CHF. Initially all subjects (90) were assigned randomly to the role of Proposer or Responder, then played the games in varying order, learning the outcomes only after all decisions were made.

Table 9.1 *Mini-ultimatum game offers and rejections in Falk et al. (2003)*

Alternative to (8, 2) that Proposer can Offer	Frequency at which Proposers Offer (8, 2)	Proportion of (8, 2) Offers Rejected
no alternative: (8, 2)	1.00	0.180
(10, 0)	1.00	0.089
(2, 8)	0.73	0.267
(5, 5)	0.31	0.444

offer (8, 2) is shown in the second column. The frequency with which the Proposer's offer is rejected by the Responder is listed in the third column. Row one is for the case with no choice – the alternatives are identical: Responder has no choice except to offer (8, 2), but 18 percent of them are rejected! This seems to be a "kill the messenger" response, not a "punish the Responder" reaction. In row two, Proposers never offer (10, 0), but when this most generous possible alternative is available, Responders decline only 9 percent of the (8, 2) offers. These choices are hard to reconcile with social motives of dissatisfaction with the Proposer's choice, who treats the Responder in the best possible way given the experimenters' imposed constraints. When the alternative is (2, 8), 73 percent of Proposers offer the more self-interested option (8, 2) [27 percent offer (2, 8)], but the rejection rate, already at 18 percent when Proposers can only choose (8, 2), rises to 26.7 percent. When the alternative is the claimed "fair" split (5, 5), only 31 percent of Proposers offer the self-interested division (8, 2), but 44.4 percent are rejected. The argument of *Sentiments* suggests that Proposer rejections reflect a confounding of feelings inherent in the game circumstance, with the particular offer of the Proposer. The offer, conjoined with the involuntary context defined by the experimenter, subjugates the Proposer to the coercive threat of a zero payoff, corrupting the benefit interpretation of the payoffs.

Are there variations on the UG in which low offers are accepted at higher rates than reported above and elsewhere in the UG literature? The answer is yes, in a new voluntary version of the ultimatum game.

EQUILIBRIUM PLAY IN VOLUNTARY ULTIMATUM GAMES:
BENEFICENCE CANNOT BE EXTORTED

We design and report choice in new UGs in which the first mover can voluntarily signal her willingness to play the role of the Responder in a UG and thereby enable the second mover to initiate play of the UG subgame as the Proposer. In our new experiments, an outside option allows self-selection to play or not a UG, whereas in the literature, outside options have been used extensively to study expectations, offers, and rejection rates by players, but only while engaged in a UG that is required-play by the experimenter. This distinction illustrates how orthogonal is the standard utilitarian model to *Sentiments*, which is refreshingly new and predictively rich in accounting for extant empirical results as well as predicting outcomes in new test designs.

Using between-subjects treatments, we examine two new UG economic environments: (1) the standard UG for the division of a fixed sum, where the choice is between an equal split and an 11 to 1 equilibrium division – much higher than the 4 to 1 splits, normally the largest reported, and in which, if offered, rejection rates are considerable (44.4 percent in Table 9.1); (2) a variable-sum version in which the second mover chooses between an equal split of a fixed sum and an investment option, with an equilibrium outcome that doubles the original stakes. In both games, based on Beneficence Proposition 2 in Chapter 6 – "Beneficence is always free, it cannot be extorted by force" – we predict and find substantially increased support for equilibrium play in one-shot (direct response) games relative to all the received literature known to us in developed economies.[5]

Our experiment tests the interpretation that the standard UG is played by "reluctant duelists," a nontrivial condition relevant to predicting decision, and embraced by Adam Smith's model of human sociability. In particular, Smith's claim that because beneficence is always free, and cannot be extorted by force, it strategically qualifies the interpretation of payoffs in terms of the ordinary beneficence calculus of gratitude and

---

[5] In the fixed-sum version, equilibrium play has only been observed in tribal societies isolated from markets. Thus, "In some of these cultures, people did not think that sharing fairly was necessary ... and Responders accepted nearly every offer. Ironically, these simple societies are the *only* known populations who behave exactly as game theory predicts!" (Camerer 2003, p. 11). Adam Smith, well aware of the differences in such societies, viewed them as conditioned by extreme hardship: "His (a savage's) circumstances not only habituate him to every sort of distress, but teach him to give way to none of the passions which that distress is apt to excite. He can expect from his countrymen no sympathy or indulgence for such weakness. Before we can feel much for others, we must in some measure be at ease ourselves. If our own misery pinches us very severely, we have no leisure to attend to that of our neighbor" (TMS, Fifth.(I).II, p. 297). Note Smith's reference to what the individual can expect from his countrymen, where sociability may reign, but by a different pattern of emergent rules. Smith had a general model of human sociality, independent of cultural-specific features, although he writes mostly from eighteenth-century Britain. See the discussion in answer to his rhetorical question: "What different ideas are formed in different nations concerning the beauty of the human shape and countenance?" (TMS, Fifth.(I).I, p. 288).

reward. We use the proposition in Chapter 8 to explain why trust games with an option to punish defection from a first mover's offer to cooperate, send a mixed signal of intent to the second mover, and substantially reduce the acceptance of offers to cooperate. What is the significance of this critical feature for the UG?

One perspective harkens back to a classic paper by Daniel Ellsberg (1956), "Theory of the Reluctant Duelist," in which Ellsberg argues that minimax strategies are not satisfactory solutions to zero-sum games, because if that were the solution to playing the game, and a person has the option to refuse play, then "he would never play," always preferring zero for sure to any possibility of loss (1956, p. 922). Hence, zero-sum game theory, which had led to the "general" minimax strategy solution, was a theory that applied only to reluctant dualists – "The psychology of a timid man pressed into a dual" (Ellsberg 1956, p. 923). Not being allowed to refuse play, such games necessarily involved reluctant players, hence the name of Ellsberg's classic paper.[6] The UG is a constant-sum, strict opposition game (one participant can only gain at the expense of the other), exactly as in zero-sum games.[7]

The other perspective, arising in the vast literature on the UG, argues that rejections of low offers are an emotional response stemming from anger.[8] Emotion, or more specifically, passion, sentiment, and fellow-feeling, underlies Adam Smith's concepts of beneficence and injustice, arising not from a utilitarian analysis, but from our rule-following adaptation to learning from our social experience.[9]

---

[6] "One might well ask: Why bother to play the game at all, if one prefers the certainty of zero to the chance of winning or losing? This question once was put to a prominent game theorist; his unconsidered reply, presumably intended as no more than a partial answer, was that in many situations one must play a game, even against one's wishes" (Ellsberg 1956, p. 922). But this concedes Ellsberg's point, that the whole sound and fury of the Neuman-Morgenstern "general solution" was the special case where participants could not refuse play.

[7] Thus in traditional game theory: "In a constant sum game, the sum of all players' payoffs is the same for any outcome. Hence, a gain for one participant is always at the expense of another.... Since payoffs can always be normalized, constant sum games may be represented as (and are equivalent to) zero sum games in which the sum of all players' payoffs is always zero." See https://en.wikipedia.org/wiki/Zero-sum_game.

[8] Madan Pillutla and Keith Murnighan (1996); Kathleen O'Connor, Carsten De Dreu, Holly Schroth, Bruce Barry, Terri Lituchy, and Max Bazerman (2002); Alan Sanfey, James Rilling, Jessica Aronson, Leigh Nystrom, and Jonathan Cohen (2003); Erte Xiao and Daniel Houser (2005); and Mascha van't Wout, René Kahn, Alan Sanfey, and André Aleman (2006).

[9] "It is altogether absurd and unintelligible to suppose that the first perceptions of right and wrong can be derived from reason, even in those particular cases upon the experience of which the general rules are formed. These first perceptions, as well as all other experiments upon which any general rules are founded, cannot be the object of reason, but of

EQUILIBRIUM PLAY IN ULTIMATUM STAGE GAMES:
VOLUNTARY PLAY WITH GAINS FROM EXCHANGE

A further indication of the "reluctant duelist" source of inhibitions in the standard UG is provided by an experiment in which this coercive element is replaced with a voluntary mutual interaction that ends with a stage game identical to the UG, but with radically different outcomes.

Motivated by eBay selling procedures, Timothy Salmon and Bart Wilson (2008) provide a game-theoretic model, and test its predictions, in which subjects engage in a two-stage process: First, a seller who has two identical units of an item, offers a single unit for purchase by multiple competing buyers in a typical ascending price (English) auction. The seller then makes a take-it-or-leave-it offer of her second unit to the bidder with the highest losing bid (second highest of the bid prices). If the offer is accepted, the buyer makes a profit equal to the difference between his randomly drawn value and the seller's offer price. If the offer is refused, both the seller and the buyer receive zero earnings from that unit. This is an ultimatum stage game. In a treatment with two bidders, 12 of 273 offers, or 4.4 percent are rejected; 93 of the offers exceed the buyer's losing final bid, but only 6 are refused. The median buyer profit is only 61 cents earned on these offers. In a second treatment four buyers compete in the auction, and sellers make 111 profitable offers to their corresponding second high bid buyers; only four, or 3.6 percent are rejected, and the median buyer profit is 39 cents. These outcomes provide strong support for subgame perfect equilibrium in the second stage UG.

This version of the UG reflects not only voluntarism but also gains from exchange; it is a voluntary variable-surplus ultimatum game, suggesting that we need to test not only for the effect of voluntarism, but also the added effect of gains from exchange.

The variable-surplus connection is further indicated in experiments by Lawrence Fouraker and Sidney Siegel (1962, p. 218–19) who, two decades prior to the innovation of Güth, Schmittberger, and Schwarze (1982), studied bilateral monopoly bargaining in which, in a two-stage process, a monopoly seller quotes a take-it-or-leave it price for the sale of units to a monopsony buyer who responds with the quantity to be purchased at that

immediate sense and feeling. It is by finding in a vast variety of instances that one tenor of conduct constantly pleases in a certain manner, and that another as constantly displeases the mind, that we form the general rules of morality. But reason cannot render any particular object either agreeable or disagreeable to the mind for its own sake" (TMS, Seventh.III.II, p. 470).

price. The (Bowley) equilibrium price and quantity is for an ultimatum game with a variable surplus depending on the price and quantity chosen by the seller Proposer and the buyer Responder. Both players have complete information under a single-trial protocol that jointly determines their payoffs. Since the buyer is free to respond with a quantity choice of zero units, and is well-motivated to do so if the price is too high, this is an ultimatum game with a variable joint surplus to be divided by the monopolists. Moreover, the seller has a prominently available price at which there is a corresponding quantity that the buyer can choose that yields an equal split profit at the Pareto optimal division of the joint surplus. None of ten sellers choose the equal split price; all choose prices at (or near) the equilibrium price. Seller earned profit varies asymmetrically from 2.2 to 3.6 times the buyer's profit.

VOLUNTARY ULTIMATUM GAMES FOR THE DIVISION OF A FIXED SUM AND OF A VARIABLE SUM

Figure 9.1 displays the two extensive form games in our experiment. In Figure 9.1(a) the first mover, elects either to play right, yielding the minimum unit of account ($1, $1) for each person, or to play down, volunteering to enter the fixed-sum UG as the Responder. In Figure 9.1 (b), the first mover elects either to play right, yielding ($1, $1), or to play down, volunteering to enter the variable-sum UG as the Responder. Playing down by the first mover guarantees that she will earn more than $1 in either game as she will decide whether or not to reject the second mover's proposed split. We implement the signal, "voluntary play," as a choice by the Responder; we could have implemented it as a choice by the Proposer, or both could be given the opt-out alternative before the UG stage begins. We assume, as in the above auction and the bilateral monopoly experiments, that the important element is that the people have a sense of voluntary control in the ultimatum stage game. Thus, almost all retail consumer goods are sold at fixed, posted, take-it-or-leave-it prices. But only volunteer buyers walk into the vender's store or visit his internet site, and there is no requirement that a buyer must buy – surely perceived by both buyer and seller as a completely voluntary process. Indeed, this is the structure of the choice sequence that we present in Figures 9.1 in contrast to the standard UG.

We recruited forty-eight pairs of undergraduate participants at Chapman University to participate in the fixed-sum voluntary UG and forty-nine other pairs to play the variable-sum version. No student had any

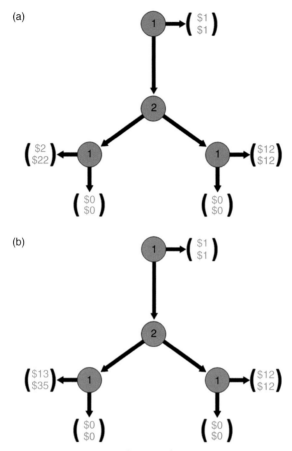

Figure 9.1. Voluntary ultimatum games

(a) $24 fixed sum

(b) 2 x $24 variable sum (gains from exchange)

prior experience in an extensive or normal form game, though many had experience in at least one prior economic experiment. Participants played the extensive form game only once and, in addition to their payoffs, as shown, received seven dollars for showing up on time. For the experiment instructions, see the appendix in Smith and Wilson (2017).

Figure 9.2 reports the results. Notice that 6 percent in Figure 9.2(a) and 8 percent in Figure 9.2(b) volunteer not to play their respective UGs. In standard UG protocols offering choice between equal-split and a single alternative, Proposers typically do not offer splits less than (80 percent for Proposer, 20 percent for Responder). If the split (80, 20) is offered,

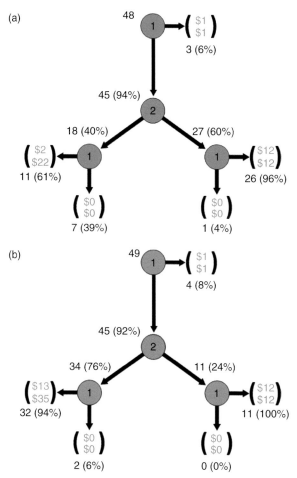

Figure 9.2. Results from voluntary ultimatum games

(a) $24 Fixed Sum

(b) 2 x $24 Variable Sum (Gains from Exchange)

it is rejected nearly half the time (Camerer 2003). Our alternative is much more extreme: the subgame perfect equilibrium of ($22 for Proposer, $2 for Responder) constitutes a split of (92 percent, 8 percent); and we find *more* subgame perfect play than has been reported in the literature for *larger, more generous* splits: 40 percent of our Proposers offer (92 percent, 8 percent), with 61 percent of Responders *accepting* an offer of only 8 percent of the pie. In comparison, Falk, Fehr, and Fischbacher (2003, p. 24) report that 31 percent of Proposers offer (80 percent, 20 percent) against equal split, and the rejection rate is 44 percent. Van't et al. (2006, p. 566) present stand alone, single offers sequentially for rejection or acceptance. They find that all equal split offers are accepted, and offers of 10 percent of the fixed sum (€4.5, €0.5) are rejected at a rate of 80 percent. Simon Knight (2012, p. 11) reports an experiment in which the "common offer" of Proposers are presented to Responders and "offers of ... 12.5% of the pot ... were rejected about 80% of the time." Finally, John List and Todd Cherry (2000) study both low stakes ($20) and high-stakes ($400) repeat-play (distinct pair matching, 10 trials) ultimatum games, and report that "27.4% (74 out of 270 subjects) of the offers in the high-stakes treatment were less than 25%; of these 74 offers, 55.4% (41/74) were rejected" (p. 14, 17). In trial 10, however, unconditional rejection rates had fallen to 14.7 percent, from their high, 44.4 percent, on trial 2.

In Figure 9.2(b) 76 percent of the Proposers offer the unequal split of ($35, $13) or (73 percent, 27 percent) and a whopping 94 percent of the Responders accept it. These results are entirely consistent with the high acceptance rates and low offers in Salmon and Wilson (2008). No prior experiment for involuntary, fixed sum UG division has reported such a high percentage of Proposers offering, and such a high percentage of Responders accepting, unequal splits this large in a one-shot game. Voluntarily engaging in an interaction with gains from exchange leads to high rates of subgame perfect equilibrium play with unequal outcomes.

PRUDENCE PREVAILS IN THE ABSENCE OF EXTORTION

In Adam Smith's model of human social conduct, actions are governed by context-dependent rules based on experience and the human capacity for mutual sympathetic fellow-feeling. The model leads to general propositions that predict actions depending on their intended benefit or hurt, and thereby require common knowledge that all are self-interested: that more is beneficial, less is hurtful. In judging an action as beneficial, however, Smith proposes that it must be free of coercion, for the presence of coercion means that the common gratitude-reward response invoked by beneficence is nullified. Applied to ultimatum games this proposition implies that the failure to observe equilibrium play is not a failure of the self-interest axiom, but rather is a consequence of the standard protocol that involves involuntary exposure to the coercive threat of veto – a condition under which the calculus of benefit (and gratitude) fails to be relevant. The origin of the gratitude-benefit calculus is in our experience of mutual fellow feeling and voluntary consent. We cannot presume that people in an ultimatum game are comfortable in the unfamiliar positions of the extorter or the extorted. The Falk et al. (2003) participants nicely illustrate that tension across the imposed binary choices they make, and which are replicated by others in differing protocols. By this reckoning, the systematic error has been in interpreting the data as strong and unambiguous support for an outcome preference for fairness/equality. Accordingly, we design new constant-sum and variable-sum versions in which the first mover has an outside option that, if not chosen, allows her to signal her willingness to be the responder in an ultimatum game. The results support equilibrium play at rates substantially in excess of any reported in the large UG literature. In trust games, Smith's model of beneficence explains why self-interested agents willingly choose to share monetary gains jointly; in ultimatum games, it explains why self-interested agents unwillingly choose to share monetary gains under threat of extortion. In each case it is the circumstances that matter, given the outcome choices and not only the outcomes themselves.

Why are the Salmon and Wilson (2008) results so strikingly different relative to the standard ultimatum game? Because, in our interpretation of *Sentiments*, the ultimatum game for awarding the second unit is not a game of extortion mixed with beneficence from receiving a windfall. Rather, the second unit is a game of prudence with an immediate prior defining history, and the context that invokes the virtue of prudence is distinct from those that call for the virtues of beneficence or justice (TMS, Part Sixth). There is no open-ended question as to whether the seller is being beneficent enough with his offer to the buyer because she's not beneficently splitting a windfall with the buyer. She's prudently attempting to sell the second unit of a commodity to a buyer who couldn't pay as much as some other buyer for the first unit. We observe that there is simply no intentional beneficence to assess in a seller's take-it-or-leave-it offer.

Likewise, there is also no room for resentment of the seller's offer, because "resentment seems to have been given us by nature for defence, and for defence only" (TMS, Second.II.I, p. 113). In the UG, seen as a reluctant game of extortion, a Proposer may go too far in extracting money from the windfall and thus an offer of $2 may "prompt us to beat off the mischief which is attempted to be done to us, and to retaliate that which is already done" (TMS, Second.II.I, p. 113). But in the Salmon and Wilson markets, where is the mischief on the part of the seller? The buyer has just revealed that he is unwilling to name and pay a price as high as someone else, and in the process he has revealed approximately how much he is willing to spend. So, when faced with "take it or leave it," the buyer takes it nearly every time – happy rather than resentful of the opportunity which he knew he would have as part of the experimental protocol. Notice, however, in comparing observations from the two different experimental designs that the process is governed by "fairness" in the sense of the rules of conduct given the circumstances, not whether the outcomes are fair; i.e., equal in magnitude for each player.

Paul Pecorino and Mark Van Boening (2010) embed the ultimatum game in the context (psychologists call it a "frame") of a litigation dispute. A plaintiff and a defendant are bargaining over how to split the cost savings of avoiding a court trial, $0.75 to the plaintiff and $0.75 to the defendant. To avoid this cost, the defendant makes a pretrial settlement offer to the plaintiff. If the plaintiff accepts the settlement offer, neither incurs the trial costs. The plaintiff receives the offer as payment, and the defendant incurs the cost of his wrongdoing (which is subtracted as a lump sum given to him by the experimenter). If the plaintiff rejects the offer, then the plaintiff receives a judgment from which the trial costs are subtracted, and the defendant incurs the trial cost and the cost of judgment. In the baseline comparison treatment, a Proposer and a Responder play a traditional ultimatum game with $M = \$1.50$. Both versions are repeated for 10 rounds.

In the embedded UG, the median offer by the defendant is 8 percent of $1.50, or 12¢. In Pecorino and Van Boening's (2010) replication of the traditional ultimatum game, the median Proposer offer is 50 percent of $1.50, or 75¢. For offers in the range 0–25¢, 23 percent of the offers are rejected in the litigation game and 100 percent in the traditional game. Thus, defendants offer less and plaintiffs accept more often than their counterparts in the traditional ultimatum game. How does the *Sentiments* framework help us understand this? In the litigation game, the motives are no longer mixed. The proposing defendant is attempting to avoid a loss with an offer to the plaintiff which corresponds to the plaintiff avoiding the cost of a trial. While the experimenter has thrown them into a dispute, albeit an unavoidable one (which might explain the high rejection rates of 21–25 percent), mutually avoiding a cost is not a matter of beneficence on the part of the defendant.[10] In the litigation game, prudence in the form of accepting an offer equal to her opportunity

---

[10] Nancy Buchan, Rachel Croson, Eric Johnson, and George Wu (2005) observe similar differences between ultimatum games over gains versus losses, though to not such a stark extent.

cost is a virtue for the plaintiff, and not a matter of how beneficent the defendant is in his offer. Regardless of what happens, the defendant is minimizing the depletions from his upfront windfall.

References

Buchan, Nancy, Rachel Croson, Eric Johnson, and George Wu. 2005. "Gain and Loss Ultimatums," in *Advances in Behavioral and Experimental Economics*, John Morgan (ed.). San Diego, CA: Elsevier, 1–24.

Camerer, Colin F. 2003. *Behavioral Game Theory*. Princeton, NJ: Princeton University Press.

Cherry, Todd L., Peter Frykblom, and Jason F. Shogren. 2002. "Hardnose the Dictator," *American Economic Review* 92(4): 1218–21.

Ellsberg, Daniel. 1956. "Theory of the Reluctant Duelist," *American Economic Review* 46(5): 909–23.

Falk, Armin, Ernst Fehr and Urs Fischbacher. 2003. "On the Nature of Fair Behavior," *Economic Inquiry* 41 (1): 20–26.

Fehr, Ernst and Urs Fischbacher. 2002. "Why Social Preferences Matter – The Impact of Non-Selfish Motives on Competition, Cooperation and Incentives," *Economic Journal* 112 (478) Conference Papers, pp. C1–C33.

Forsythe, Robert, Joel L. Horowitz, N. E. Savin, and Martin Sefton. 1994. "Fairness in Simple Bargaining Experiments," *Games and Economic Behavior* 6(3): 347–69.

Fouraker, Lawrence and Sidney Siegel. 1962. *Bargaining Behavior*. New York, NY: McGrawHill.

Güth, Werner and Martin G. Kocher. 2014. "More than Thirty Years of Ultimatum Bargaining Experiments: Motives, Variations, and a Survey of the Recent Literature," *Journal of Economic Behavior and Organization* 108: 396–409.

Güth, Werner, Rolf Schmittberger, and Bernd Schwarze. 1982. "An Experimental Analysis of Ultimatum Bargaining," *Journal of Economic Behavior and Organization* 3(4): 367–88.

Hoffman, Elizabeth, Kevin McCabe and Vernon L. Smith. 1996. "On Expectations and the Monetary Stakes in Ultimatum Games," *International Journal of Game Theory* 25(3): 289–301.

Knight, Simon J. G. 2012. "Fairness or Anger in Ultimatum Game Rejections?" *Journal of European Psychology Students* 3: 2–14.

List, John A. and Todd L. Cherry. 2000. "Learning to Accept in Ultimatum Games: Evidence from an Experimental Design that Generates Low Offers," *Experimental Economics* 3: 11–29.

O'Connor, Kathleen M. Carsten K.W. De Dreu, Holly Schroth, Bruce Barry, Terri R. Lituchy, and Max H. Bazerman. 2002. "What We Want to Do Versus What We Think We Should Do: An Empirical Investigation of Intrapersonal Conflict," *Journal of Behavioral Decision Making* 15(5): 403–18.

Oxoby, Robert J. and John Spraggon. 2008. "Mine and Yours: Property Rights in Dictator Games," *Journal of Economic Behavior and Organization* 65(3–4): 703–13.

Pecorino, Paul and Mark Van Boening. 2010. "Fairness in an Embedded Ultimatum Game," *Journal of Law and Economics* 53: 263–87.

Pillutla, Madan M. and J. Keith Murnighan. 1996. "Unfairness, Anger, and Spite: Emotional Rejections of Ultimatum Offers," *Organizational Behavior and Human Decision Processes* 68(3): 208–24.

Salmon, Timothy C. and Bart J. Wilson. 2008. "Second Chance Offers Versus Sequential Auctions: Theory and Behavior," *Economic Theory* 34: 47–67.

Sanfey, Alan G., James K. Rilling, Jessica A. Aronson, Leigh E. Nystrom, and Jonathan D. Cohen. 2003. "The Neural Basis of Economic Decision-making in the Ultimatum Game," *Science* 300(13): 1755–58.

Smith, Adam. 1853 [1759]. *The Theory of Moral Sentiments; or, An Essay towards an Analysis of the Principles by which Men naturally judge concerning the Conduct and Character, first of their Neighbours, and afterwards of themselves. To which is added, A Dissertation on the Origins of Languages. New Edition. With a biographical and critical Memoir of the Author, by Dugald Stewart.* London, UK: Henry G. Bohn. Available online and in electronic formats at http://oll.libertyfund.org/titles/2620.

Smith, Vernon L. and Bart J. Wilson. 2017. "*Sentiments*, Conduct, and Trust in the Laboratory," *Social Philosophy and Policy* 34(1): 25–55.

van't Wout, Mascha, René S. Kahn, Alan G. Sanfey, and André Aleman. 2006. "Affective State and Decision-Making in the Ultimatum Game," *Experimental Brain Research* 169(4): 564–68.

Xiao, Erte and Daniel Houser. 2005. "Emotion Expression in Human Punishment Behavior," *Proceedings of the National Academy of Sciences* 102(20): 7398–401.

10

Designing, Predicting, and Evaluating New Trust Games

The motivation in Chapter 8 was to reexamine the original theory-falsifying discoveries in the light of our subsequent study of *Sentiments*. It was postdiction, a "back-prediction" exercise in which past results are reexamined and re-explained via a completely different model than that which motivated the original work. We now put *Sentiments* to work in a new generation of trust games to reexamine trust and trustworthiness and motivate new game designs and tests unique to the Smithian framework of analysis, with its significant implications for understanding human society at large.

Methodologically, the scientific focus is to engage in forward prediction exercises. In particular we shall find that several propositions in *Sentiments* lead naturally to new testable hypotheses that are novel in the sense that we find it difficult to imagine anyone formulating these designs and testing them in the absence of the specific background, motivation, and model provided in *Sentiments*. Traditional theory does not naturally facilitate these new designs. The ability to generate novel new experiments and predict their outcomes has been claimed by some to constitute the hallmark of progressive science. But there is no science of the methodology and conduct of science. All the action is in the conversation, the persuasion, the perceived truth in the evidence science uncovers. New theory is sometimes particularly convincing if it both explains previous observations and predicts new results not within the imaginable embrace of the old theory.[1] Thus Relativity Theory easily subsumed all the empirical content of Newtonian Physics and led to confirmed new predictions not

---

[1] In contemplating why, we are reminded that "what is new and singular, excites that sentiment which, in strict propriety, is called Wonder; what is unexpected, Surprise; and what is great or beautiful, Admiration" (Smith 1795, p. 33).

imaginable by the Newtonians. Newton for his age had accomplished the same intellectual breakthrough.[2]

We begin by introducing a new trust game, the Baseline Trust (BT) game, and associated nodal payoffs that are direct extensions of the "Invest $10" game we introduced in Chapter 8. All the experiment results we report in this chapter will be design variations on the Baseline Trust game. The discussion will give particular attention to using *Sentiments* to interpret player actions as signals and responses to signals depending on the available alternatives in each game. Context, in the sense of the set of all action alternatives including outcomes, is all-important in *Sentiments,* and our experience with the new games brings new appreciation for the prominence and content of this feature in Smith's theory.

When we introduce and motivate new games and proceed to test new hypotheses, the results, as is common, often raise new unanswered questions, because the experimental environment, though a special case, is also richer in decision interpretation possibilities than the theory. We have seen how the failure of Max-U in the small group experiments of the 1980s–1990s led to new experiments attempting to find out why. New questions suggest new designs and corresponding tests. Where appropriate, we follow that exploration in the new tests because the potential learning from such exercises much exceeds each particular finding.

We will close the chapter by evaluating the performance of two primary games as mini-societal representations of Smith's concept of beneficence and justice – the two great socializing forces that, as Smith teaches us, define our humanity. We ask how effective are the rules that people follow in achieving individual and joint total welfare levels (efficiency), as measured by monetary earnings. Think of the experiments as two-person small-world personal exchange cultures in which people apply the rules they follow in life to this unfamiliar context.

BASELINE TRUST GAME

The decision nodes, move sequence, and outcome payoffs in dollars define the Baseline Trust game shown in Figure 10.1, which also displays the action outcomes for 49 pairs of subjects. The game is directly comparable to the original "Invest $10" trust game, Figure 8.1, which we discussed in

---

[2] For discussion of these methodology-of-science issues, see Vernon Smith (2008, Chapter 13).

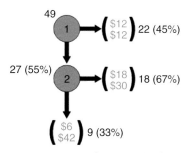

Figure 10.1. Baseline Trust (BT) game

Chapter 8. Similarly, because of synergy – gains from the exchange – think of playing down by the first mover as an investment of $12, which is tripled to $36. The investment gross gain is split evenly if the second mover plays right yielding the outcome ($18 for the first mover, $30 for the second mover); but if the second mover defects the payoff 2-tuple is ($6, $42).

The game-theoretic equilibrium of the game is for the first mover in his self-interest to move right at the top, conditional on the assumption of self-interested action by the second mover; for if the second mover were to play down, the outcome ($6, $42) constitutes a loss of $6 for the first mover. We observe that 55 percent (27/49 = 0.55) of the first movers violate the equilibrium prediction, and 67 percent (18/27 = 0.67) of the second movers violate the conditional. These violations strongly replicate our previous results; namely, coordination in achieving the cooperative outcome ($18, $30) as against the traditional predictions in which each player chooses their payoff dominant strategy.

The results support Beneficence Proposition 1 (Chapter 6): if the first mover does something good (play down) for the second mover because he wants to do something good for the second mover, the first mover's playing down appears, with nothing further needed, to deserve reward by the second mover.

Let's use this proposition and the *Sentiments* model to explicate and interpret the results; i.e., by imagining how people might perform (think about, or follow autonomously) their task in the manner that Smith does in modeling humans interacting as real people, and not abstract, "as if" own or social utility maximizing agents.[3]

---

[3] Of course there is always an as-if element in the interpretation of data, but we refer here to the conduct-action model of people interacting in the task as Smith envisions their rule-governed interaction.

DESCRIBING TRUST/TRUSTWORTHY ACTION

If a first mover in Figure 10.1 foregoes the equilibrium safe action ($12, $12) and moves down, he is intentionally choosing a path vulnerable to defection by the second mover who, under the cloak of anonymity and subject to no external sanctions – only internal "self-command"[4] – is free to choose in her strict self-interest the outcome ($6, $42). Hence, the action by the first mover signals beneficence toward the second mover and is quite properly motivated (e.g., is in no way an unconditional greedy action), as required by Beneficence Proposition 1. If the second mover cooperates, the payoff to the first mover increases by 50 percent but more generously increases the payoff to the second mover by 150 percent, relative to the equilibrium. If the participants each see themselves as the other sees them, the first mover, imaging himself in the position of the second mover may appreciate that he would feel gratitude for this action. If the second mover is similarly motivated, she can reward the first mover's action by playing right, yielding ($18, $30). Hence, the first mover might reasonably expect a reward response for his action from a like-minded person, subject to self-command, by imagining how generous he must appear from the perspective of the second mover. Similarly, the second mover can expect to reward the first mover by imagining herself in that position and empathizing with his good intentions.[5] Empirically,

---

[4] Recall the role of self-command in achieving one's normative social duty: "The man who acts according to the rules of perfect prudence, of strict justice, and of proper benevolence, may be said to be perfectly virtuous. But the most perfect knowledge of those rules will not alone enable him to act in this manner: his own passions are very apt to mislead him; sometimes to drive him and sometimes to seduce him to violate all the rules which he himself, in all his sober and cool hours, approves of. The most perfect knowledge, if it is not supported by the most perfect self-command, will not always enable him to do his duty.

[5] In the explicit language of our axioms, principles, definitions, and propositions in Chapters 5 and 6:

- By Principle 1, the second mover self-examines his own sentiments after the first mover moves down because the first mover wanted to do something good for the second mover.
- By Assumption 1, the first mover is the object of gratitude because the first mover's moving down is the object of gratitude.
- By Axiom 1, the second mover fellow feels with the sentiments of the first mover.
- By Axiom 2, the second mover applies his sense of propriety to judge the fellow-felt sentiments of the first mover.
- When judging the first mover's sentiments,

under these parameter conditions, Beneficence Proposition 1 beats the predictions of the traditional neoclassical game theoretic model: 45 percent (22/49) right play vs 100 percent predicted for the first mover; only 33 percent (9/27) play down vs 100 percent predicted for the second mover.[6]

Observe that the second movers defect at a lower frequency (0.33) than do the first movers (0.45). Why? And what are the implications of this finding? Two-thirds of the second movers know with certainty the action of their counterpart and respond by choosing to cooperate. Consequently, two-thirds of the sample population choose actions that are in harmony with Beneficence Proposition 1 and with the exercise of self-command (Principle 1, Chapter 5). Since the subjects are randomly assigned to the player roles we can estimate that two-thirds of the first movers share the same standard of conduct as the second movers and, if assigned the second mover role, would choose to cooperate in response to an offer to cooperate. But in the first mover position he faces great uncertainty as to whether he and his matched counterpart are like-minded in the rule-following sense of Beneficence Proposition 1. Hence, we can estimate that on average 12 percent (0.67–0.55) of the first mover equilibrium choices of ($12, $12) would have offered cooperation were it not for the added uncertainty as to their counterpart type in this single play protocol.

- the second mover thinks that the first mover did not have to move down, i.e., the second mover thinks that the sentiments of the first mover are proper;
- the second mover wants to think good things about the first mover because of this, i.e., the second mover approves of the sentiments of the first mover; and
- the second mover feels something good when she thinks about all of this.

By definition of gratitude, the second mover feels gratitude towards the first mover for having moved down.

- By Axiom 0, the second mover knows that the first mover is made better off if he moves right.
- By Axiom 3, the second mover is prompted immediately and directly by gratitude to reward the first mover by moving right.
- Thus by the Desert Lemma, the first mover's moving down appears to deserve the reward of the second mover moving right.
- By Principle 4, the second mover wants to be praiseworthy and does not want to be blameworthy, i.e., the first mover's moving down appears, with nothing further needed, to deserve the reward of the second mover moving right.

[6] These odds overwhelmingly reject the classical model and bring into question the suppositions and mode of analysis on which it is based.

COMPARATIVE ANALYSIS OF THE TRUST GAME:
TRADITIONAL VERSUS *SENTIMENTS* MODEL

Using common knowledge of the self-interest as modeled by Smith, based on the human capacity to feel, think, and know, we summarize the backward induction leading to action for a mature rule-following socialized person. This analysis, from the perspective of the actor/ players as represented in *Sentiments*, is shown in the right column of Table 10.1; the left column states the traditional backward induction analysis in which all actions are based on common knowledge of self-interested actors, and who always choose actions to maximize own outcome payoff.

Table 10.1 *Comparison of backward induction in the baseline trust game*

Traditional Analysis: Action to Maximize Own Payoff	Smithian Analysis: Action Based on Hurt, Benefit, Intent, Imagining Other, Rule-following, and Self-command.
1. Common knowledge that all people are strictly self-interested, non-satiated.	1. Common knowledge that all people are strictly self-interested, non-satiated.
2. Own payoff outcomes alone matter in choosing action by each player.	2. Action determined by who is hurt or benefits from an action, and an inference of intent.
3. Determine each player's choice in reverse sequence of play.	3. Intentions inferred from opportunity cost of action taken, given hurt and benefit.
5. If the first mover passes to the second mover, the latter is motivated to move down.	4. Rule-Following: Intentional Beneficence→Gratitude→Reward; (Intentional Hurt→Resentment→Punishment).
6. The first mover's best strategy is to move right, the "equilibrium" of the game.	5. Apply backward induction to the game tree to determine who is hurt or benefits from an action at each node and to judge intent.
	6. Each person's "impartial spectator" imagines herself in the role of the other in judging intent and probable responses.
	7. Forward play is a signaling game – a conversation – that conveys intent.
	8. If the first mover would cooperate in the second mover role, will the second mover see it in the same way if given opportunity to act?
	9. Will the second mover cooperate, given unambiguous signal of the first mover's beneficial intentions?

ADDING AN OPTION TO PUNISH "WANT OF BENEFICENCE"

Beneficence Proposition 2 predicts that – given the option – the second mover will choose not to punish the first mover for neglecting to play down. We make this option available by altering the BT Game. In the new game, if the first mover decides to choose the equilibrium outcome, play passes to the second mover who either selects the equilibrium or elects to punish the first mover with a reduced payoff. If the punishment action is to be credible in registering resentment and disapproval, the second mover should be willing to incur a cost. Figure 10.2 displays the new game, in which the second mover can reduce the first mover's payoff by $2 at a cost to herself of $2. We also display the observed choice outcomes. Previously, we reported the outcomes for 25 pairs in which 15 of the first movers chose right play, but none of the counterpart second movers chose to punish this action (Vernon Smith and Bart Wilson 2017, Figure 4b). It is unprecedented in these games for a test of any prediction model to yield zero contrary falsifying observations.[7] To add confidence in this finding, we subsequently increased sample size, and report here the observations for an independent additional 13 pairs (indicated by 25 + 13 at node 1).[8] In both samples, Beneficence Proposition 2 perfectly predicts that no one feels motivated by resentment to register their disapproval of the first mover in choosing not to offer cooperation.

The natural social order, it seems, is that people feel implicit respect for the right of first movers to decline an opportunity to initiate beneficent actions, given the set of action opportunities in Figure 10.2. In this experiment, in an unfamiliar context, we observe a general rule of propriety (Beneficence Proposition 2) reinforced by mutual voluntary consent – an everyday ongoing process in society.

In our earlier reported experimental tests of Beneficence Proposition 2, we found that adding the option to punish the want of beneficence (a) changed the frequency of playing down by the first mover and (b) altered the frequency of cooperative right play by the second mover (Smith and Wilson 2017, Figure 4b versus 4a). In the BT game (Figure 10.1), we observe 55 percent of the first movers play down, but in the PWB game

---

[7] Experimental observations speak not only to the reliability of a theory but also to the reliability of the experiment as a test of the theory. So, even if a theory is reliable, its first tests may yield unfavorable outcomes because of experimental protocol inadequacy, parameter choice and other sources of observational variance.

[8] Implicitly, in increasing sample size, we anticipate the post-experiment conversation among experimentalists, which always should focus on much more than significance levels.

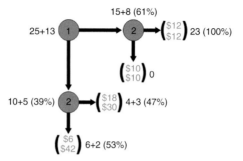

Figure 10.2. Punish Want of Beneficence (PWB) game

(Figure 10.2), the presence of the additional node with option to punish decreases the frequency of cooperative offers. Only 40 percent (10/25 = 0.40) of the first movers choose to risk a cooperative response by the second mover. The first movers reveal that the offer to cooperate is less desirable given that the second mover is able to punish failure to offer it. In Figure 10.2 the increase in the sample size is an opportunity to replicate this observation. The initial results hold true: only 5 of 13 new first movers offer to cooperate. Pooling, we observe 39 percent (15/38 = 0.39) of the first movers offer to cooperate, a non-trivial decrease from 55 percent in BT. In comparison with BT, the PWB context shifts the first mover choices toward equilibrium play, a shift that is to their benefit given the effect of the changed context on the responses of the second movers. In other words, unlike us, the experimenters (who made no prior prediction), the first movers in the experiment appear to anticipate the untrustworthiness of the second movers in this game.

Now consider an analysis of the PWB game from the perspective of the second mover using Smith's framework. We have argued that a move down by the first mover in Figure 10.1 unambiguously implies a properly motivated act of beneficence toward the second mover. But playing down in the PWB game of Figure 10.2 sends an impure mixed signal. The second mover, who reads the meaning in the first mover's actions based on her new action alternatives, may now read the first mover when playing down, not as expressing an unmitigated act of beneficence but as avoiding the prospect of punishment contingent on right play at the top. Hence, the second movers, feeling comparatively less gratitude than they would in BT, may be more likely to play down themselves. Comparing Figures 10.1 and 10.2, the second movers indeed choose to defect more frequently in the PWB game than in the BT game. We observe an increase in defections by the second movers from 33 percent in the BT game to 53 percent (8/15 = 0.53) in PWB. This finding reinforces the credibility of Smith's repeated emphasis on the importance of context in reading intentions: the meaning signaled by an action depends critically upon the action *not taken* and its outcomes. Further tests reported below support this important point.

BUT DO THE SUBJECTS SEE IT AS WE (AND SMITH) SEE IT?

The PWB game modifies the core game by introducing the conjunction of two changes: whatever the choice of the first mover, the second mover now controls end-play; *and* the second mover is afforded the option to punish the first mover for failing to offer cooperation. Could the first movers' actions be affected by the first condition, "loss of control," and not only the punishment option. To unpack the change in meaning implied by the costly punishment option introduced by PWB, we ran subjects independently in the No Punish Pass (NPP) game in Figure 10.3. The purpose was to test the assumption that NPP is perceived as identical to the core BT game. According to the traditional analysis, this is patently obvious, but our past record as experimentalists qua theorists concerning what is "obvious" has been found wanting. Is it so perceived by the subjects? The outcomes are displayed for twenty-five pairs in the original experiments (Smith and Wilson 2017, Figure 7a) plus thirteen new independent pairs.

There is no significant or important difference between the frequencies of playing down by the first movers in NPP (20/38 = 0.53) and in BT (0.55). The defection rate by the second movers actually decreases but seems to be within the sampling variation that we have become accustomed to in trust

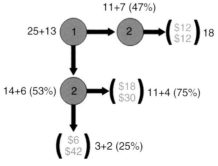

Figure 10.3. No Punish Pass (NPP) game

games: 5/20 (25 percent) in NPP vs 33 percent in BT.[9] So, yes, what we think we see appears also to correspond with what the subjects see. And, as we had supposed, it is indeed the introduction of the PWB option at the top of the tree in Figure 10.2 that explains why the results changed in the cooperative subgame.

COMMENTARY ON THE STUDY OF "WHAT IS NOT"

As a counterfactual experimental treatment, the PWB game allows us to measure the effect of a hypothetical rule on observed conduct. Punishing the want of beneficence is a rule of "what is *not*" (Hayek 1973, p. 17). It does not emerge as a community convention because, as explained by Adam Smith, the want of beneficence does no real and positive harm.[10] Thus, if Beneficence Proposition 2 holds, introducing the opportunity to punish the want of beneficence interferes with, or distorts, reading the motives of one's counterpart, particularly in a situation stripped of the normal contextual (face-to-face) cues that we rely upon to make such assessments. Actions signal intentions and motivations in *Sentiments*, and are not just inert if-and-only-if determiners of outcomes. So perhaps we should not have been surprised at the sensitivity of the conduct of both players in the PWB game. (Except to parse the cause, we needed the NPP game results). This observation reminds and humbles the hypothesizing social scientist that the human taste for a particular tenor of conduct is a rather sensitive and complicated palate; it also demonstrates how experimental tests can provide more specific content for the model in *Sentiments*.

INTRODUCING PUNISHMENT FOR INJUSTICE

We test Injustice Proposition 1 by introducing a punishment option in the BT game for the first mover who moves down, contingent on the second mover moving down. This is the Punish Injustice (PI) game shown in Figure 10.4. If the first mover moves down, and the second mover defects on the intentional offer to cooperate, then play passes back to the first mover, who can choose the cooperative outcome or, at a cost to himself,

---

[9] Thus Kevin McCabe and Vernon Smith (2000) report a defection rate of 25 percent for a sample of 24 undergraduates in the "invest $10" trust game.

[10] We can imagine all sorts of beneficence in our favor, but punishing the want of it invites resentment from those whose circumstances we do not fully know. They might not agree that their beneficence to us is appropriate given the context, or we might not know that they are incapable of being beneficent to us.

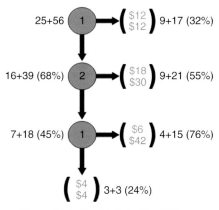

Figure 10.4. Punish Injustice (PI) game

punish the first mover by selecting the outcome ($4, $4). To defect on a properly motivated good-faith act of beneficence – the first mover playing down – is surely quite improper and hurtful. Hence, Injustice Proposition 1 predicts that the first mover will resent the second mover for playing down. Whether the resentment will be great enough to invoke punishment will likely depend upon how costly the punishment option is.

For the low-cost/high-punishment parameterizations in Figure 10.4, we observe that 24 percent (6/25 = 0.24) of the first movers invoke the punishment option. The sample size is thinned this deep into the tree but large enough to motivate the question: Why is it that we do not observe *more* than 24 percent of the first movers punishing defection? It costs only $2 of $6 to impose a loss of $38 of $42 on the second mover for her blameworthy failure to respond cooperatively. The answer, we suggest, is captured in Smith's carefully articulated concept of the fair, as well as impartial, spectator. The rules of fair play require the punishment to be appropriate – to be reasonable in fitting the resentment to the infraction. Therefore, if many first movers impartially judge the second movers misstep, and see the punishment as excessive, they will be loath to impose such a high punishment for defection. The impartial spectator is not vindictive (TMS, First.I. V, p. 27):

We admire that noble and generous resentment which governs its pursuit, of the greatest injuries, not by the rage which they are apt to excite in the breast of the sufferer, but by the indignation which they naturally call forth in that of the impartial spectator; which allows no word, no gesture, to escape it beyond what this more equitable sentiment would dictate; which never, even in thought, attempts any greater vengeance, nor desires to inflict any greater punishment, than what every indifferent person would rejoice to see executed.

Comparing the outcome in Figure 10.4 with that in Figure 10.1, we find that introducing the option to punish defection changes play at both nodes relative to the BT game. Let's see how well the *Sentiments* model helps us to understand why introducing a dominated node (which changes nothing in the traditional analysis) has repercussions beyond the added node.

As in our test of Beneficence Proposition 2 in the PWB game, adding the prospect of punishing the second mover if she defects, changes the meaning signaled by the first mover's offer to cooperate. In the PI game the first mover's offer to cooperate implicitly reserves the right to punish the second mover in the event she does not accept. Hence, a first mover is more likely to play down in Figure 10.4 than in Figure 10.1 if he sees the risk of defection as being reduced. Indeed, comparing outcomes in the two figures, the rate at which the first movers play down increases from 55 percent to 64 percent (16/25 = 0.64).[11] Several of the equilibrium first movers in BT would now choose to play down; some will be in our estimated 12 percent of equilibrium first movers who were rule-following cooperative types in BT but were marginally put off by uncertainty as to their counterpart types. From the second mover's perspective, however, a move down by the first mover is no longer an unambiguous signal of beneficence in the PI game. From Beneficence Proposition 2, beneficence is "always free, it cannot be extorted" and something cannot be considered freely given if it is coupled with the right to punish nonacceptance – in effect, an extortion. Hence, for the second mover, under this interpretation, there is the suggestion of coercive intent in the PI game that is not present in the BT game. Whereas in the BT game, 67 percent of the second movers respond

---

[11] In Ernst Fehr and Bettina Rockenbach (2003), when the threat of punishment is conveyed in advance of the offer to cooperate, cooperation is reduced. However, their interpretation of why sanctions fail to elicit cooperation is quite different from that in *Sentiments*. It is true that people react negatively to coercive threats, and selfish, grasping behavior, but it is not because they are not self-interested. Rather, they learn to follow fair-play *rules* that control such actions in their social relations. Such conduct builds directly on knowledge that people are self-interested. In civil society people achieve mutual relational benefits from voluntarily entering into contracts that penalize deviant unilateral actions. Consistent with this interpretation, Elinor Ostrom, James Walker, and Roy Gardner (1992) explore sanctions and other mechanisms to facilitate cooperation in a public goods game, and find that the highest performing mechanism combines pre-play communication with the choice by vote to accept a sanctioning mechanism.

cooperatively, in PI the response declines to 56 percent.[12] Both the first movers and the second movers make judgment errors that are directly attributable to the increased ambiguity of trustful intent conveyed by the first movers who move down. The second movers discount or under-estimate the trustfulness of the first mover's motive for action, and the first movers underestimate the extent to which they are misread by their paired counterparts, compromising their credibility; otherwise, fewer rather than more would offer to cooperate relative to BT.

Why are we observing these judgment errors? What has failed, we would suggest, is common knowledge, or agreement, that if the first mover plays down, and the second mover defects, then the first mover has the right to punish the action – a right of defense. If that were common knowledge, we would expect more first movers to play down, as we do, but also fewer second movers reading the play as a deficiency in trust, or threat of reprisal, and therefore providing an excuse for not being trustworthy. Suppose we think of first movers as consisting of three perception-motivation types who exercise beneficence, coercion, or self-defense. Only the first types move down in BT. The decreased response of second movers appears to be a reaction based on coercive threat. Since they gain from defection, Smith might say it is self-deceit, a failure of self-command. Indeed, there is an incentive to misread the signal. Note the contrast with how people saw punishment for want of beneficence. It was "natural" for people to recognize no such right, but there was an incentive not to punish.

By comparison with the BT game, Smith's model helps us to understand the increase in offers to cooperate in a one-shot game as well as the reduced acceptance rate in the PI game. But in repeat interaction any reluctance of the first movers to offer cooperation in the no-punish BT game can be reduced if the second mover is observed to cooperate whenever it is experimentally offered on a previous trial. Or, if the second mover defects, the first mover can signal disapproval (relative punishment) by playing the equilibrium strategy on the next trial. Similarly in the PI game, if the second mover cooperates, the first mover can offer cooperation again on the next trial and reinforce her trustworthiness. If he offers cooperation, and the second mover defects, then he invokes the punishment option and immediately repeats his offer to cooperate on the next trial. In this way, second mover coercion types can be "taught the lesson of property" to respect the merits of cooperation. Kevin McCabe, Stephen Rassenti, and

[12] Similarly, in Ernst Fehr and John List (2004) the punishment option reduces the trust-worthiness of both business CEOs and student subjects in a single-play protocol.

Vernon Smith (1998) compare repeated games using the same partners, with and without the option to punish defection in the cooperative sub-game. In both games, cooperation increases over repetitions, but the game with the option to punish defection in the subgame converges more rapidly than the one without. Hence, if the BT and PI games are repeated, we would expect PI to outperform BT, but with cooperation increasing in both. What is different from McCabe et al. (1998), besides payoffs and tree structure, is that we now have Smith's rigorous model of sociability.

The PI game encapsulates the fundamental strategic interaction features of human sociability: voluntary, intentional actions that benefit another, may be rewarded in subsequent actions because of the gratitude felt by the recipient. This is the source of social harmony in which kindness begets kindness. Or such action may be exploited for personal gain by people who are insensitive to the goodwill intended and to the hurt suffered by the benefactor, whose feelings of resentment may give cause to punish the evil done by the improperly hurtful response. The punishment option is central to limiting and discouraging deliberately hurtful actions, and thereby achieving justice. It also holds the possibility of escalating into a destructive cascade of mutual annihilation.

INTRODUCING AN OPTION TO SWEETEN THE REWARD FOR BENEFICENT ACTION

There is a corollary to Beneficence Proposition 1 that we test with a new design:

Beneficence Corollary 1: The greater the sense of gratitude the greater the deserved reward.[13]

We implement a test of Beneficence Corollary 1 by adding a node conditional on the second mover moving right in the BT game. The additional option returns play to the first mover, who can either choose the cooperative outcome shown in Figure 10.1 or, at a cost to herself, show any unusual gratitude, if she feels it, by increasing the payoff of the second mover. Smith predicts its use only if our initial

---

[13] "Though the mere want of beneficence seems to merit no punishment from equals, the greater exertions of that virtue appear to deserve the highest reward. By being productive of the greatest good, they are the natural and approved objects of the liveliest gratitude" (TMS, Second.II.I, p. 117). A parallel corollary is associated with Injustice Proposition 1. Resentment is proportioned to the evil inflicted, and punishment is proportioned to the resentment felt.

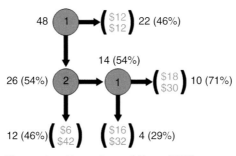

Figure 10.5. Bonus Reward Trust (BRT) game

parameterization of the reward to cooperation is inadequate; hence, it is an internal "validity" check on our choice of the payoffs to cooperative coordination.[14] The Bonus Reward Trust (BRT) game, shown in Figure 10.5, simply gives the first mover the option of transferring $2 of her payoff to the account of the second mover. Figure 10.5 reports the results.

We first check to see if adding the opportunity for the second mover to enhance the reward of the first mover for offering cooperation materially changes cooperative play at node 1. It does not. We observe 55 percent down play in Figure 10.1, and 54 percent (26/48 = 0.54) in Figure 10.5. But at the second node, the second movers play right less often: 67 percent in the BT game, decreasing to 54 percent (14/26 = 0.54) in the BRT game. Also notable is the nontrivial 29 percent (4 in 15) of the first movers who are willing to sweeten the payoff to the second movers for their cooperative responses. The implication for these first movers is that the externally imposed rewards to mutual cooperative play provided by the experimenter are inadequate for expressing the contribution of the second movers to the bargain. The just action deserves more than specified in our parameterizations! But why this largesse? Gross irrationality? Smith would attribute it to the impartial spectator, a metaphor for monitoring self-command; in particular for achieving praiseworthy, and avoiding blameworthy, end states. One can postulate, using the Smithian framework, that such subjects

---

[14] Social science theories, including game theory, are too imprecise to tell you how to parameterize or quantify test designs. Parameter choice – for example, absolute and relative payoff levels – are part of the "practice" of experimenters, and when exploring new territory are commonly varied to establish the sensitivity of the results to their variation. In such exercises we study/measure the effect of different contexts on incentives. Based on self-interested incentives, Smith provides a qualitative model of sociability, and experiments empirical measurement.

feel strongly that the explicit (experimenter-controlled) reward in the cooperative outcome is inadequate.

In the traditional game-theoretic analysis, such actions are unthinkable and are dismissed or even eliminated by construction. The questions such actions answer would never be asked. Hence, yet again, we see the relevance of *Sentiments* to the twenty-first century study of human sociability. People show that they care enough about dominated actions to choose them. What makes *Sentiments* relevant for all time is that its propositions involve the choice of dominated actions, actions that emerge naturally out of mutual fellow-feeling, thinking, and knowing.

ENABLING EITHER OF THE PUNISHMENT OPTIONS

In the PWB and PI games we have seen that adding a punishment option for failure to offer cooperation or, alternatively, for defecting on an offer to cooperate, changes the frequency of play at other nodes. But suppose an expanded game includes options to punish either of these choices. Will the availability of both options rebalance and restore play to comparability with the original BT game in Figure 10.1 or raise new questions? The game and frequency of play at each node in shown in the Punish Either (PE) game of Figure 10.6.

The greatest change is in the action of the first movers: equilibrium choice falls from 45 percent in BT to 30 percent in PE, the lowest frequency we have so far observed. The prospect of the second mover punishing

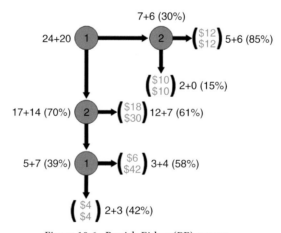

Figure 10.6. Punish Either (PE) games

failure to offer cooperation, combined with the first mover being able to punish the second mover if he refuses to accept cooperation, lures a higher proportion of the first movers into offering cooperation. Elsewhere in the tree there is little attention-getting change. We do, finally, pick up two (15 percent) mavericks (rogues would have shown up in PWB game!) who punish the failure to act beneficently. A bit smaller proportion of the second movers, 61 percent, reduced somewhat from 67 percent, cooperate by playing right. The punishment rate for defection increases, but the sample (5/12 = 42 percent) is very small.

UPSHOT

With the predictive failure of Max-U(*own payoff*), as it applied to trust games in the 1980s and 1990s, experimental and behavioral economists offered social preference, Max-U(*own payoff, other's payoff*) and reciprocity explanations of the results. Neither of these adaptations positioned us to think outside the bounds of our accustomed utilitarian and exchange frameworks of thought. Max-U had served well-enough the observational demands of decision in market supply and demand experiments under perfect enforcement of property, but not in the interactive world of personal social exchange. That world required a plethora of new experiments designed to understand why the postulated mapping from action to outcome to utility was so sensitive to the particular context. However, none of the new efforts to improve understanding were guided by a comprehensive theory of human sociability as had been provided in *Sentiments* wherein individual actions are signals of rule-governed relational conduct, where context matters because it gives meaning to outcomes. Nor was it influenced by any of the rare and more contemporary work that had echoed *Sentiments,* as in Frank Knight's dictum, "the economist meets the problem of conduct and motive at every point and stage of his work" (Knight 1925, p. 374).

We demonstrate that foundational propositions from *Sentiments* anticipate both the initial observations in trust games and many of the subsequent explorations of the role of intentions in accounting for these observations. Moreover, we show that the propositions make new testable predictions that are well beyond the vision of traditional theory because the propositions deal directly with the dominated actions ruled out as irrelevant by traditional theory.

Sentiments is about the ethical rules that constitute the character of an inherently sociable person who strives for a better life, and it has predictive power where Max-U(*own payoff*) fails decisively. This great book is the foundation for lost insights into a quintessentially humanistic science of economics.

References

Fehr, Ernst and John List. 2004. "The Hidden Costs and Returns of Incentives – Trust and Trustworthiness among CEOs," *Journal of the European Economic Association* 2: 743–71.

Fehr, Ernst and Bettina Rockenbach. 2003. "Detrimental Effects of Sanctions on Human Altruism," *Nature* 422: 137–40.

Hayek, F. A. 1973. *Law Legislation and Liberty.* Vol. I, *Rules and Order.* Chicago, IL: University of Chicago Press.

Knight, Frank H. 1925. "Economic Psychology and the Value Problem," *Quarterly Journal of Economics* 39(3): 372–409.

McCabe, Kevin, Stephen Rassenti, and Vernon L. Smith. 1998. "Reciprocity, Trust and Payoff Privacy in Extensive Form Experimental Games," *Games and Economic Behavior* 24: 10–23.

McCabe, Kevin and Vernon L. Smith. 2000. "A Comparison of Naïve and Sophisticated Subject Behavior with Game Theoretic Predictions," *Proceedings of the National Academy of Sciences* 97: 3777–81.

Ostrom, Elinor, James Walker and Roy Gardner. 1992. "Covenants with and without a Sword: Self-Governance Is Possible," *American Political Science Review* 86(2): 404–17.

Smith, Adam. 1982 [1795]. "The History of Astronomy," in *Essays on Philosophical Subjects.* Indianapolis, IN: Liberty Fund, 33–105.

Smith, Adam. 1853 [1759]. *The Theory of Moral Sentiments; or, An Essay towards an Analysis of the Principles by which Men naturally judge concerning the Conduct and Character, first of their Neighbours, and afterwards of themselves. To which is added, A Dissertation on the Origins of Languages. New Edition. With a biographical and critical Memoir of the Author, by Dugald Stewart.* London, UK: Henry G. Bohn. Available online and in electronic formats at http://oll.libertyfund.org/titles/2620.

Smith, Vernon L. 2008. *Rationality in Economics: Constructivist and Ecological Forms.* New York, NY: Cambridge University Press.

Smith, Vernon L. and Bart J. Wilson. 2017. "*Sentiments*, Conduct, and Trust in the Laboratory," *Social Philosophy and Policy* 34(1): 25–55.

11

Reconsidering the Formal Structure of Traditional
Game Theory

The initial predictions of experimental ultimatum and trust games were derived from game theory. The replicable results of these experiments were decisively contrary to the equilibrium predictions of the theory. The research consequence was to launch empirical investigations designed to reveal the anatomy of that failure. As is their wont in such circumstances, scientists look for hints of new and better principles by altering the experimental conditions in search of results that enhance an understanding of why the original predictions failed. In this case, informal but influential conjectures guided the new explorations. Notions of outcome fairness and social preferences guided new ultimatum and trust game experiments, and, by analogy with gains from market exchange, the concept of reciprocity in trust games. Economists found evidence against fairness by asking how the results changed by eliminating the Responders right of veto.[1] Indeed, offers declined substantially in this treatment, named the Dictator Game (DG), but Proposers still were generous enough to breathe life into a large literature on this new game, interpreted as showing the strength of the "social" element in homegrown preferences. This trend was undeflected by experiments showing that DG results were an artifact of unearned money supplied by the experimenter – a class of games for studying how generous people were with the experimenter's money.[2] Beliefs about relevance did not change. Rather, the DG became a widely used tool for exploring social distance (for example, Elizabeth Hoffman, Kevin McCabe and Vernon L. Smith 1996a), and by those pursuing the Social Preference paradigm. Numerous variations on

---

[1] Robert Forsythe, Joel Horowitz, N. E. Savin, and Martin Sefton (1994). See, e.g., p. 99.
[2] Todd Cherry, Peter Frykblom, and Jason Shogren (2002) and Robert Oxoby and John Spraggon (2008).

the UG quite clearly showed that context was very important in shifting the data and was a more important treatment condition than payoff level.[3] In studies of both the UG and the TG, intentions mattered.[4] The behavioral and experimental community greatly expanded the evidence to be comprehended but without developing a correspondingly comprehensive model that was generally accepted. Most, but not all, were comfortable with coalescing around social preference forms of modeling and thinking.

This chapter is for readers interested in the mathematical formalization of human conduct. In the first section of the chapter, based on Joel Sobel (2005), we begin with a brief summary of the traditional game-theoretic model toward showing where it failed in these games. Then we introduce the reparative modifications in this framework that allow the concept of social preferences to accommodate the falsifying evidence. Finally, we indicate how Adam Smith's model provides a different means of interpreting Sobel's framework to achieve this end.

In the second section, we provide a characterization of an individual's choice problem in a one-shot interaction in which the individual's choice is rule-governed by propriety. The choice is a rule that maps context into an outcome. Each context defines an outcome, and the motivation stems from Smith's concept of seeking praise (avoiding blame) and praiseworthiness (avoiding blameworthiness). The intention is to generalize and complement the trust game analysis we provided in the right column of Table 10.1.

Neither of these constructions is complete, an end beyond what we are able to deliver now. However, each confronts the elements addressed with a different formulation directly out of *Sentiments* and is surely the first step in a more complete Smithian reformulation.

THE TRADITIONAL GAME DYNAMIC

Suppose that individual $i = 1, \ldots, n$ takes an action, x_i, in a stage game to maximize

$$Z_i(x) = (1 - d)u_i(x) + dV_i(H(x)), \tag{1}$$

where $x = (x_1, \ldots, x_i, \ldots, x_n)$ are strategy choices by n players, $1 > d > 0$, d is the discount rate, $H(x)$ is the history of play, u_i is i's self-interested

---

[3] Elizabeth Hoffman, Kevin McCabe, Keith Shachat, and Vernon Smith (1994), Elizabeth Hoffman, Kevin McCabe and Vernon Smith (1996b), and Colin Camerer (2003).
[4] See, e.g., Armin Falk, Ernst Fehr, and Urs Fischbacher (2003) and Kevin McCabe, Mary Rigdon, and Vernon Smith (2003).

"utility" outcome from the choice x_i in the stage game, and V_i is the value to i of play continuation. (In the discussion below our examples are for $n = 2$ persons.)

$Z_i(x)$ is interpreted as the criterion of judgment for decision-making by i in a single sequential repetition of the same stage game with the same well-identified other. $Z_i(x)$ is described as i's discounted current plus future utility in a pairing created by the experimenter. Hence, $H(x)$ includes all past play history, as well as the shadow of i's anticipated future history of play with other. As described by Sobel (2005, p. 412):

Repeated-game theory incorporates strategic context, not by changing preferences but by changing the way people play. In order to obtain equilibria distinct from repetitions of equilibria of the underlying static game, the history of play must influence future play. History does not influence preferences, but it does influence expectations about behavior.

To achieve this, actions may take the form of punishments and rewards, contingent on actions by other that shape the self-interested behavior of other, and enable i to maximize her long-term self-interest over the horizon of the repeated game.

In this development, V_i is an endogenous function of the history of play. If V_i is positive and d is sufficiently large (near enough to 1), then in maximizing $Z_i(x)$, i must take care not to spoil her future interaction with this particular other person by her choice in the present. This concern for the future, in traditional repeated game theory, exhausts the content of actions that are social; i.e., her sociality is defined and confined relative to her historical and anticipated future interactions with the particular person with whom she interacts.

PROPOSED SOCIAL PREFERENCES MODIFICATION

In game theory, repetition is essential for long-term strategic success in achieving cooperative results, but laboratory experiments have long recorded significant levels of cooperation in single plays of a stage game in which the anonymous players forego a larger payoff for themselves in favor (or in expectation) of a cooperative outcome. Therefore, as noted by Sobel (2005, p. 411), "because laboratory experiments carefully control for repeated-game effects, these results need a different explanation." That is, in a single play of the stage game, a rational i is *assumed* to set $V_i = 0$ when matched with an unknown other person and therefore is presumed to be a "stranger" who person i cannot identify and thereby build on any relevant past personal history. Hence, both *i* and the other are predicted to choose self-interest maximizing dominant outcomes, whatever the circumstances defined by the game.

The "different explanation" commonly offered for experimentally observed cooperative outcomes is the postulate of other-regarding or "social preferences" that rationalize the observed behavior by each player attributing own utility to money assigned to other, as well as money assigned to one's self in a single play of the stage game (or formally equivalent envious disutility if other has more). In such an explanation, any generosity, positive or negative, has been accounted for by simply augmenting the decision-maker's utility function in an appropriate way. As we have already indicated, the "if" in the scientific proposition "if preferences are social, then choices will be other-regarding" is replaced by "if and only if." It is the latter interpretive proposition that has been widely adopted by theorists and experimenters since the predictive failures of game theory started to accumulate. *But the consequence is to give up any attempt to model relationships.* The Folk Theorem of traditional repeated game theory did that, precisely and elegantly, for strictly self-interested players by allowing that a cooperative outcome could emerge endogenously, in the players' mutual self-interest, out of their entwined history. The model, however, could only predict defection in a single-play version of the players' interaction. Moreover, in the trust game of Figure 10.1 we report a robust two-thirds of second movers violating that prediction, and 55 percent of their first-mover (and stranger) counterparts anticipate that violating action. A just so utility function rescues the failed prediction without providing a clue to its roots in human social development and subverts rather too much in leaving un-modeled any role for repeat interaction.

RECONSIDERATIONS OF ONE-SHOT PLAY BASED ON *SENTIMENTS*

Adam Smith's model of human social interaction requires a different formulation of Sobel's framework. The process does not alter the utility function but modifies how people relate to each other over time. Hence, it preserves the game-traditional idea that the interaction is about the players' relationship, not their preferences. People are self-interested, but "no man is an island." History matters because the rules governing fair-play conduct depend upon intentions and upon the effect of alternative actions on who benefits or is hurt.

In (1), if H is "history," one's entire cultural and past social experience must inform the action taken. An action is intelligible only in reference to moral judgments in past and anticipated future interactions. Smith's program in *Sentiments* provides a pathway that includes a continuation value – call it $W_i(H(x))$ – where the stage game is to be repeated and also sympathetically modifies the self-interested first term, $u_i(x)$, in equation (1). Moreover, W_i is now based on expected future *conduct, both own and other, and not only on outcomes*.

In *Sentiments*, individuals are motivated to seek praise and praiseworthiness, and to avoid blame and blameworthiness, in all social interactions. Moreover, in judging her own conduct, a person i will implicitly imagine that conduct as subject to examination by a fair and impartial spectator. Her actions will vary with circumstances, based on experience, but require that her conduct serve personal long-term (reputational) ends across a wide variety of human social encounters. When she knows little of a particular other she may be cautious, and more preserving of immediate Stoic care for herself, but she knows it is another human, recruited from a group whose characteristics may not be that dissimilar from her own, and she relies on self-command principles that have served her well on average in the past. Her action x_i will generate a current value that we will designate $U_i(x|H_i(0))$, where $H_i(0)$ is her current entry-level personal historical state (after reading the instructions of the experiment). U_i values i's conduct in taking immediate action x_i. Part of that valuation is the resulting payoffs. However, the value attained is derived from the judgment of the Impartial Spectator as to the propriety of her action, including that the payoffs *are deserved and justified by the circumstances*.

That our description of $U_i(x|H_i(0))$, captures baseline elements in Smith's criterion for weighing the present against the future by a prudent person, under the self-commanding judgment of the Impartial Spectator, is evident in the following quotation (TMS, Sixth.I, p. 314):

In his steadily sacrificing the ease and enjoyment of the present moment for the probable expectation of the still greater ease and enjoyment of a more distant but more lasting period of time, the prudent man is always both supported and rewarded by the entire approbation of the impartial spectator, and of the representative of the impartial spectator, the man within the breast. The impartial spectator does not feel himself worn out by the present labour of those whose conduct he surveys; nor does he feel himself solicited by the importunate calls of their present appetites. To him their present, and what is likely to be their future situation, are very nearly the same: he sees them nearly at the same distance, and is affected by them very nearly in the same manner. He knows, however, that to the persons principally concerned, they are very far from being the same, and that they naturally affect *them* in a very different manner. He cannot therefore but approve, and even applaud, that proper exertion of self-command, which enables them to act as if their present and their future situation affected them nearly in the same manner in which they affect him.

Instead of equation (1) we now have a sympathy-derived criterion of action

$$S_i(x) = (1 - d)U_i(x|H_i(0)) + dW_i(H(x)). \tag{2}$$

$W_i = 0$ in an advertised one-shot stage game, but max $S_i(x)$ does not reduce to max $Z_i(x)$; that would occur only for an i raised in isolation from all contact with other humans, or who is otherwise barren of all socialization: "To a man who from his birth was a stranger to society, the objects of his passions, the external bodies which either pleased or hurt him, would occupy his whole attention" (TMS, Third.(I).I, p. 162).

When $W_i > 0$, equation (2) allows action to accommodate the knowledge that the interaction will be repeated and thereby enables the relationship with other to be influenced by possible futures that the two are able to create beyond the self-command principles that would apply to a single encounter which already contains baseline considerations of futurity as in the above quote from *Sentiments*. Under repetition, judgments by the Impartial Spectator of each person in their shared interaction cause updates conditional on how each reads the intentions conveyed sequentially by the other.

In the previous section, we explain the high level of cooperation in the stage trust game by postulating that the individual maximizes her utility conditional on other-regarding social preferences as her criterion of choice. Here we explain cooperation by postulating with Smith a socialized individual who chooses an action conditional on her own past internalization of a rule-following history of interaction with other like-developing individuals. Her action is other-regarding because of rule-following norms she shares with her counterpart. However, to evoke the appropriate rule of action, she uses common knowledge that both she and her counterpart are self-interested.

FROM GAME STRUCTURE TO ACTION IN USING
THE PRINCIPLES IN *SENTIMENTS*

Think of an action, a_i, by individual i as depending on i's judgment of its propriety, given the action's contextual circumstances:

$$a_i(Propriety|C) = \alpha_i(C) \cdot PR + \beta_i(C) \cdot PR \cdot PW + \gamma_i(C) \cdot PW + \delta_i(C), \quad (3)$$

where PR and PW are (0, 1) indicator variables, respectively, that action is praised by others (1), or not (0), and is praiseworthy (1), or not (0); and α_i, β_i, γ_i and δ_i are nonnegative functions that weight PR and PW in determining the propriety of the action. In the second term, PW leverages PR, while the third term expresses the sentiment that PW may yield stand-alone value (self-command), distinct from PR, even where no praise is possible. For example, in double anonymity experiments, weight is still given to PW even where no one can know your decision (see James Cox and Cary Deck, 2005). A positive weight is given further credence by the results comparing voluntary and involuntary versions of a trust game in which 1/3 of the Player 2s share gains with their Player 1 counterparts in the absence of any signal of Player 1 intentions. See our summary of McCabe et al., (2003) in Chapter 8, Figure 8.3.

Let $C(m_1, m_2)$ be the circumstances including game structure, choice alternatives, and the vector of all nodal payoffs (m_1, m_2) allowing the signal to be deciphered. An action is based on conduct that is more or less appropriately conditional on circumstances, where the action chosen best satisfies or "fits" a socially mediated criterion. The additive function, $\delta_i(C)$, independent of the social indicators, allows socially unmitigated "self-interest" to be expressed – in *Sentiments* this motive always has an important stoic role. Where i cannot infer the intent of other and reward beneficence, then $\alpha_i(C) = \beta_i(C) = 0$, and $\delta_i(C)$ looms larger than otherwise in determining the action chosen, but this is still mediated by a positive weight for PW.[5]

An expression similar to equation (3) applies to a hurtful action subject to blame/blameworthiness.

Equation (3) defines a rule for i; *viz*, i's choice of an action given $C(m_1, m_2)$ and the self-command weights (judgments) i places on PR and PW. Simultaneously, there exists in i's social world a convention ("custos") defining what "people will go along with" for the choice of α_i,

---

[5] See Kevin McCabe, Mary Rigdon, and Vernon Smith (2003, p. 273) and Chapter 8, figure 8.3(b), where 33 percent of the second movers are choosing right, consistent with praiseworthiness.

β_i, γ_i and δ_i subject to the same conditionals. If i's choice is out of order, he or she will receive corrective feedback ("disapprobation"). Hence, *Sentiments* is primarily about the adaptation of individuals to what is "fit and proper." The model is open ("vague") concerning the inertial processes whereby the demands of social conventions emerge and change through time, but there is an implication of evolutionary change and adaptation.

Sentiments offers an abstract definition of equilibrium in rule space based on unanimous agreement as to the validity of a norm: given the circumstances of an action, the actor normatively deserves reward when every impartial spectator, every indifferent bystander, and every reasonable person entirely goes along with and agrees that the actor is the proper object of gratitude and therefore of reward. And likewise the actor deserves punishment when all agree that the actor is the proper object of resentment (TMS, Second.I.II).

"FAIRNESS" EQUILIBRIA OR AGREEMENT ON BENEFICENCE PROPOSITION 1 AND INJUSTICE PROPOSITION 1?

In response to the results in ultimatum and other experimental games of the 1980s, Matthew Rabin (1993) offered techniques and theorems showing how the results can be obtained as a Fairness equilibrium, a concept he introduces and relates to the Nash equilibrium. The basic idea builds on the framework developed in John Geanakoplos, David Pearce, and Ennio Stacchetti (1989), who modify conventional game theory to allow payoffs (utility) to depend on players' beliefs and not only on their actions. Note that the utility dimension is quite contrary to *Sentiments*, but it preserves the game-theoretic relation between action and utility: Action → Outcome → Utility, where Outcome/Utility involves the conjunction of belief and material consequence. Thus, Rabin's formulation begins with two "stylized facts: (A) People are willing to sacrifice their own material well-being to help those who are being kind. (B) People are willing to sacrifice their own material well-being to punish those who are being unkind" (Rabin 1993, p. 1282).

Rabin's facts (A) and (B) are, respectively, imprecise forms of Beneficence Proposition 1, and Injustice Proposition 1 derived by Smith from more elementary considerations, and used by Smith to explain characteristic features of the civil order of a (free) society. For Rabin, fairness involves the beliefs (A) and (B), and his results demonstrate "mutual-max" outcomes, wherein each person maximizes the other's material payoff, given the other person's behavior. But there are also "mutual-min" outcomes wherein, given the other person's behavior, each person minimizes the other's material payoffs. A Nash equilibrium, either a mutual-max outcome or mutual-min outcome, is a fairness equilibrium. People believe that it is "fair" to reward good conduct and punish bad conduct. Hence, in the Baseline Trust game (Figure 10.2) the second mover chooses the cooperative outcome (maximizes the first mover's payoff) if the first mover passes to the second mover. In the Punish Injustice game (Figure 10.4), the first mover minimizes the payoff to the second mover, given that the latter defects on the first mover's offer to cooperate. In *Sentiments* maturation involves learning to follow the rules; not doing so is a violation of fair play.

Rabin's approach rationalizes the empirical results by inserting other as well as own payoff in each utility function (a form of "altruism"), and is akin to *Sentiments* in operating on the role of social belief in modifying the utility of outcomes. Missing in Rabin, however, is a systematic treatment of the source of belief modification and of the forms that it takes. As in *Sentiments* people must be strictly self-interested because what constitutes sacrifice or kindness in Rabin must be common knowledge.

EQUILIBRIUM, THE PERSON OF YESTERDAY, AND THE PERSON OF TODAY

Experiments with the Joyce Berg, John Dickhaut, and Kevin McCabe's 1995 trust game vary the (average) age of the subjects (8, 12, 16, 22, 32 and 68).[6] The average amount sent by trustors is monotone increasing in age (except for age 68), and similarly for the average amounts returned by trustees. These results are in accord with the social maturation articulated by Smith, who explicitly makes exception for children. For example, in the chapter "Of the Influence and Authority of Conscience" (TMS, Third. III. p. 203–4), he asserts that the very young child is without self-command, and while its more disrupting outcries may be restrained for their own ease, generally the parents are indulgent toward the child. When old enough for school, or to engage its equals, the child soon encounters no such indulgent partiality. But the child

naturally wishes to gain their favour, and to avoid their hatred or contempt . . . and it soon finds that it can do so in no other way than by moderating, not only its anger, but all its other passions, to the degree which its play-fellows and companions are likely to be pleased with. It thus enters into the great school of self-

---

[6] Matthias Sutter and Martin Kocher (2007, Table 2, p. 372).

command, it studies to be more and more master of itself, and begins to exercise over its own feelings a discipline which the practice of the longest life is very seldom sufficient to bring to complete perfection.

In game-theoretic terms, Smith is describing an interaction between an individual and others in which reputations are formed and captured in the form of general rules mapping context into outcomes and are shaped across the games of life by rewards that are responses to feelings of gratitude and by punishments that are provoked by resentment.

Stephen Meardon and Andreas Ortmann (1996) pioneer in showing that *Sentiments* provides a sophisticated analysis of the reputational discipline of action that serves self-interested individuals. It is opportunity-costly to allow your social interactions to be governed by uncontrolled passive passions like resentment and hatred as against willful active passions of generosity and compassion; consequently, self-command emerges out of the crucible of experience. They model the rationality of self-command as a reputational equilibrium in which active principles can eventually overcome the deleterious effects of the immediate passions in the actions taken. They specifically build on Smith's within-person developmental tension between "two selves," as it were: "The man of yesterday and the man of today" who is reevaluating his earlier conduct, but with "payoffs" for motivation based in praise and praiseworthiness, and the avoidance of blame and blameworthiness. Their interaction game is between the man of today and the man of tomorrow, in which the transformation of the child occurs in the great school of self-command. This is the mechanism whereby we learn "to go along with" our friends and neighbors. Such achievements are subject to error, imperfection, and failure as well as success. A static utility function does not capture that process, which involves a dynamic and uncertain mutual transformation of relationships over time, consistent with self-interested individuals.

References

Berg, Joyce, John Dickhaut, and Kevin McCabe. 1995. "Trust, Reciprocity, and Social History," *Games and Economic Behavior* 10: 122–42.

Camerer, Colin F. 2003. *Behavioral Game Theory*. Princeton, NJ: Princeton University Press.

Cherry, Todd L., Peter Frykblom, and Jason F. Shogren. 2002. "Hardnose the Dictator," *American Economic Review* 92(4): 1218–21.

Cox, James C. and Cary A. Deck. 2005. "On the Nature of Reciprocal Motives," *Economic Inquiry* 43, 623–35.

Falk, Armin, Ernst Fehr, and Urs Fischbacher. 2003. "On the Nature of Fair Behavior," *Economic Inquiry* 41(1): 20–6.

Forsythe, Robert, Joel L. Horowitz, N. E. Savin, and Martin Sefton. 1994. "Fairness in Simple Bargaining Experiments," *Games and Economic Behavior* 6(3): 347–69.

Geanakoplos, John, David Pearce, and Ennio Stacchetti. 1989. "Psychological Games and Sequential Rationality," *Games and Economic Behavior* 1: 60–79.

Hoffman, Elizabeth, Kevin McCabe, Keith Shachat, and Vernon L. Smith. 1994. "Preferences, Property Rights, and Anonymity in Bargaining Experiments," *Games and Economic Behavior* 7(3): 346–80.

Hoffman, Elizabeth, Kevin McCabe and Vernon L. Smith. 1996a. "Social Distance and Other Regarding Behavior in Dictator Games," *American Economic Review* 86(3): 653–660.

Hoffman, Elizabeth, Kevin McCabe and Vernon L. Smith. 1996b. "On Expectations and Monetary Stakes in Ultimatum Games," *International Journal of Game Theory* 25 (3): 289–301.

McCabe, Kevin, Mary L. Rigdon, and Vernon L. Smith. 2003. "Positive Reciprocity and Intentions in Trust Games," *Journal of Economic Behavior and Organization* 52(2): 267–75.

Meardon, Stephen J. and Andreas Ortmann. 1996. "Self-Command in Adam Smith's *Theory of Moral Sentiments*: A Game-Theoretic Reinterpretation," *Rationality and Society* 8(1): 57–80.

Oxoby, Robert J. and John Spraggon. 2008. "Mine and Yours: Property Rights in Dictator Games," *Journal of Economic Behavior and Organization* 65(3–4): 703–13.

Rabin, Matthew. 1993. "Incorporating Fairness into Game Theory and Economics," *American Economic Review* 83(5): 1281–1302.

Smith, Adam. 1853 [1759]. *The Theory of Moral Sentiments; or, An Essay towards an Analysis of the Principles by which Men naturally judge concerning the Conduct and Character, first of their Neighbours, and afterwards of themselves. To which is added, A Dissertation on the Origins of Languages. New Edition. With a biographical and critical Memoir of the Author,* by Dugald Stewart. London, UK: Henry G. Bohn. Available online and in electronic formats at http://oll .libertyfund.org/titles/2620.

Sobel, Joel. 2005. "Interdependent Preferences and Reciprocity," *Journal of Economic Literature* 93: 392–436.

Sutter, Matthias and Martin G. Kocher. 2007. "Trust and Trustworthiness across Different Age Groups," *Games and Economic Behavior* 59: 364–82.

12

Narratives in and about Experimental Economics

Man has developed rules of conduct not because he knows but because he does not know what all the consequences of a particular action will be.
F. A. Hayek (1976, pp. 20–21)

Life as it is lived is made up of narratives, stories that we talk about as experiences. Much of the elaboration of experience is about the circumstances, the setting, because we see that as essential to conveying an accurate sense of the lived experience. We create a narrative based on our memory of the experience, which in reality, consists in what is left over afterwards.

The modern tradition in modeling is to extract from life scenarios what we believe is the "essence" of the behavior, of the phenomena that we are trying to characterize in terms of its general (context-free) elements. Newtonian physics was a striking success in separating the science of motion from our intuitive experience of it, a tradition carried much further by Einstein. In economics we have followed that modeling tradition since the late nineteenth century. We studied models of decision by a hypothetical individual in the context of opportunity cost at the margin and discovered new insights about markets, prices, the extended order of cooperation, and equilibrium. Experimental economics began its career by starting with these models. We have stories about markets, but we reduce them to a certain kind of theoretical essence. Then we go to the laboratory with simple austere instructional statements that put the attention on this abstract essence – well justified we think because we want to minimize noise relative to that essence. The results, as luck would have it, turn out to be remarkably robust across multilateral impersonal markets. Indeed, something essential seems to have been captured. The "luck" turned out to be informative, especially in the light of subsequent experiments. Reducing markets to their supposed structural supply and demand essence in the lab is predictive; the subjects do not bring so much "baggage from their life experiences" into the lab that it upsets the strong predictive content of the structure.[1]

All that changed with the study of two-person games – such as ultimatum and trust games in the 1980s and 1990s. Max-U, which had worked so well in the supply-and-demand structure of markets, failed in games believed to be far simpler and more transparent than the markets. The subjects were importing baggage from life that, on average, was serving them far better than Max-U. Overnight, context emerged as important, although the language did not change. It was still all about "decisions and behavior," a Max-U hangover. What is striking about *Sentiments* is that the framework of thought, the language used, and the role of narrative are all so different from the modern tradition in economics: a framework that is comfortable with the complexity of the patterns of action in "simple" ultimatum and trust games. *Sentiments* articulates a rigorous model: complex but rich in narrative. That is relevant to its main message because, unlike traditional theorizing, a major up-front analytical proposition is that context matters. The results are driven by fellow-feeling, which arises from imagining what another might feel. It does not concern behavior in its modern sense of choosing, of deciding. Rather it is about action as part of conduct. The word *conduct* suggests a pattern, a manner, a certain fitness between pattern followed and pattern expected. Neither outcomes nor goals are defined only by a particular point in payoff space. The word *action* suggests involvement, emersion, and activity in relating to an environment that includes others. Even if an action is one-dimensional, there are alternatives, now and in the future, depending

---

[1] All the early laboratory market experiments were about the exchange of items that had the non-re-tradable characteristics of perishables – technically, non-durable goods and services. These markets were stable in the lab and stable in the economy. In such markets there cannot exist a discrepancy between value in use or consumption, and value in resale. However, when experimentalists turned to the study of asset trading – durable re-tradable goods – that accustomed stability became as elusive in the lab as it was in the economy; compare the market for hamburgers or haircuts with the market for houses or securities. See chapter 2 in Steven Gjerstad and Vernon Smith (2014) for a summary of experiments with the two kinds of markets.

on action now with some other who is part of the relationship. Context allows experienced memory to enter as instances that trigger the propriety of conduct; consequences are in the future conditional on the actor's relationship with others.

The typical two-person sequential action single-play experiment takes as its essence "the payoffs and moves" – who moves when and who gets what. This form of mechanical "essence" does not see the game as an instance in human relationships, often intricate and related to narrative memories. We know, of course, that the participants in an experiment cannot be expected to see it as the experimenter-theorist sees it. We ask only if the views are equivalent in observation. But they are not equivalent in observation, which is why it is hazardous to tinker with the utility function or other parts rather than examine an alternative thought framework. Adam Smith did that for us. Moreover, he was equally committed to the development of a system of thought consistent with observations on human sociality, not just a series of antidotal (and anecdotal) ex post rationalizations.

NARRATIVIZING THE TRUST GAME

As a first approximation for understanding these human concepts of trust, trustworthiness, and spite, economists begin with the assumption that agents have complete symmetric information over all contingencies, which lends itself to tidy logic and, hence, full explanations. The everyday use of these concepts, however, is not limited to the concrete circumstances of this provisional assumption. We also trust someone not just when we know what the payoffs may be but as a general rule. That is what we mean when we say that we trust someone with our life. Likewise, we say that someone is trustworthy, not only because he did not take advantage of us on a specific occasion, but because it is in his character to be trustworthy in unforeseeable circumstances, come what may (TMS, Part Third). Often that is why we trusted him in the first place. But how is it that someone personally unknown to us comes to be trustworthy for the very first time? It depends on the circumstances of time and place. It depends upon his character. It depends upon the story that leads up to the encounter. Or does it?

Game theory strips the "narrative" down to outcomes and a causal structure of actions, which are known in advance – a reduction in the spirit of Max-U. Players in this game employ strategies based upon immediate or anticipated future benefit. In a head-to-head, zero-sum interaction, reducing the problem to this essence predicts reasonably well, for the actions and consequent payoffs dominate the content of the narrative. Even here, as we saw in Chapter 9, the head-to-head fixed sum ultimatum game results are altered significantly by the simple Smithian device of introducing voluntary play. But in a positive sum world with the possibilities for trust, the narratives imposed by the mind are commonly too rich to be distilled down to players, actions, and a mapping of actions into payoffs. Our human minds rely on rules of conduct to cope with these fickle circumstances, particularly when the precise consequences of our actions are unknown.

Jan Osborn, Bart Wilson, and Bradley Sherwood (2015) take the payoffs and the order of moves in the Punish Injustice game (see Figure 10.4) and embed it in a narrative form. Participants read a story. In the relationship, opportunities arise later and they do not know the payoffs before they get there. The information state is different from the usual extensive form game (EFG) tree, and the people in the experiment are part of an explicit story. Osborn, Wilson, and Sherwood (2015) compare how people conduct themselves in the sterile EFG environment of Chapter 10 to how they conduct themselves when they are, instead, acting as a participant in a narrative, making decisions as a character in a story.

EXPERIMENTAL DESIGN AND PROCEDURES

Unlike an EFG in which participants see all potential outcomes and the paths to those outcomes, the narrative reveals only one decision node at a time, thus eliminating the opportunity for backward induction. The participants become characters in the world of a story that unfolds in front of them. When characters make a decision, they do not know that it may end the game or pass the next decision to the other character. All they know is that they are furthering the story as the three short pages of simple instructions inform them:

Welcome (page 1)
Today you will participate as a character in a story. The story will unfold as two characters make decisions. The decisions made by you and another person seated in this laboratory will determine how much money you will earn. Your earnings will be paid to you privately, in cash, at the end of your story.

The Story (page 2)

You and the other character will jointly determine the plot, resulting in a set of payoffs. When it is time to make a decision, two buttons will appear, each designating an action to take in the story.

At the end of the story, you will be paid at the rate of US$1 per 1,000 story dollars. For example, if you end with $9,000 in the context of the story, you will be paid US$9.

Your story may conclude before or after participants around you. When your story comes to an end, please wait quietly until you are called to the window to be paid.

Ready to Begin (page 3)

If you have any questions, please raise your hand, and a monitor will come by to answer them. If you are finished with the instructions, please click the START button. The instructions will remain on your screen until everyone has clicked the START button. We need everyone to click the START button before the story can begin.

In a typical EFG experiment, like those in Chapters 8–10, two strangers without a personal history interact in what they may or may not contextualize as a personal, social interaction. The first decision in narrativizing the game is choosing the setting for the story. Osborn et al. deliberated between either setting the scene as an interaction between explicit strangers or between two characters personally known to each other. Supposing that characters known to each other might be more likely to reach the ($18, $30) outcome than in EFG experiments, they set the scene with two characters who have a history with each other. Failing to observe more ($18, $30) outcomes in this context would be that much more informative.

Osborn, Wilson, and Sherwood then place these two characters familiar with each other in a plotline that is readily relatable to undergraduate participants and ask the first mover to take one of two actions, one of which ends the story with the ($12, $12) outcome and the other which passes the decision-making to the other character. They do not assign a name to the participant reading the story; he or she is simply referred to as "you." Each participant's counterpart, however, is referred to as "Taylor," a name without gender specification. Figure 12.1 displays the story for the first decision node. The first mover's perspective is on the left and the second mover's on the right.

Unlike in an EFG, where it is basically up to the participants whether to travel the tree with a notion of "we are in this together" or "I'm in this for myself," Osborn et al. embed the two characters as coworkers in a collaborative relationship. To further emphasize the collaboration, the

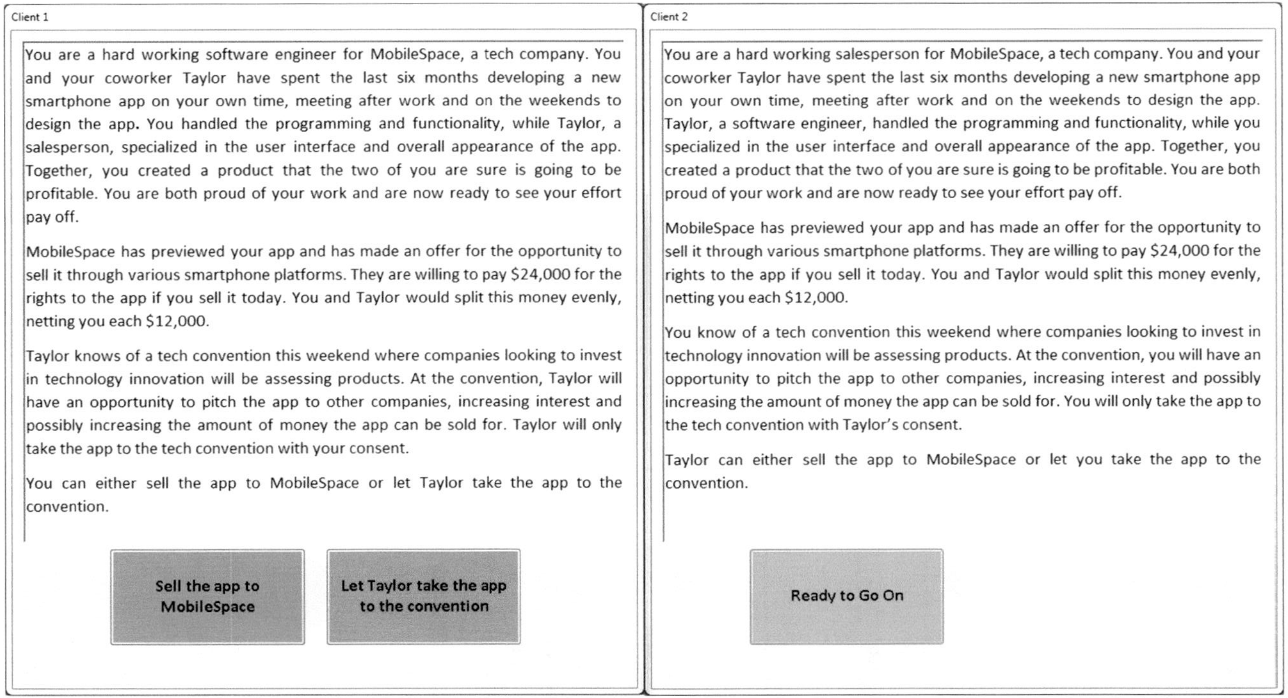

Client 1

You are a hard working software engineer for MobileSpace, a tech company. You and your coworker Taylor have spent the last six months developing a new smartphone app on your own time, meeting after work and on the weekends to design the app. You handled the programming and functionality, while Taylor, a salesperson, specialized in the user interface and overall appearance of the app. Together, you created a product that the two of you are sure is going to be profitable. You are both proud of your work and are now ready to see your effort pay off.

MobileSpace has previewed your app and has made an offer for the opportunity to sell it through various smartphone platforms. They are willing to pay $24,000 for the rights to the app if you sell it today. You and Taylor would split this money evenly, netting you each $12,000.

Taylor knows of a tech convention this weekend where companies looking to invest in technology innovation will be assessing products. At the convention, Taylor will have an opportunity to pitch the app to other companies, increasing interest and possibly increasing the amount of money the app can be sold for. Taylor will only take the app to the tech convention with your consent.

You can either sell the app to MobileSpace or let Taylor take the app to the convention.

| Sell the app to MobileSpace | Let Taylor take the app to the convention |

Client 2

You are a hard working salesperson for MobileSpace, a tech company. You and your coworker Taylor have spent the last six months developing a new smartphone app on your own time, meeting after work and on the weekends to design the app. Taylor, a software engineer, handled the programming and functionality, while you specialized in the user interface and overall appearance of the app. Together, you created a product that the two of you are sure is going to be profitable. You are both proud of your work and are now ready to see your effort pay off.

MobileSpace has previewed your app and has made an offer for the opportunity to sell it through various smartphone platforms. They are willing to pay $24,000 for the rights to the app if you sell it today. You and Taylor would split this money evenly, netting you each $12,000.

You know of a tech convention this weekend where companies looking to invest in technology innovation will be assessing products. At the convention, you will have an opportunity to pitch the app to other companies, increasing interest and possibly increasing the amount of money the app can be sold for. You will only take the app to the tech convention with Taylor's consent.

Taylor can either sell the app to MobileSpace or let you take the app to the convention.

| Ready to Go On |

Figure 12.1. Narrative of first mover's decision node

two characters jointly develop an app on their own time outside of work. Each character participates equally in the development of the app, and each is responsible for a specific portion of the app. Thus, it is a joint effort that generates the total value of the app. Note that we purposefully state that the value of the app could possibly increase without providing any monetary specifics. In contrast to an EFG, the story only hints at the possibility of a better offer for the app. The characters must discover on the fly the total value of the app. In the EFG, it is public knowledge that the first mover may end up with a lower payoff by not initially ending the game. Thus, without being aware of such a possibility, we hypothesize that a greater proportion of first movers will "let Taylor take the app to the convention" than first movers play down in the extensive form trust game.

Action buttons, which always begin with a verb, express the characters' agency in the context of the story, much like the option to flip between pages in the Choose Your Own Adventure series. For each pair of participants, the computer randomly determines the order in which the options to act are presented to the pair. The first (second) option is always presented as the left (right) button, and we block the color of the left button, blue or orange, across all pairs. The character who does not have a decision to make must click on the green "Ready to Go On" button. Only after both participants have clicked a button does the story simultaneously advance for the pair.

The decision for the second mover is how to allocate who receives what portion of the new offer from another company (see Figure 12.2). The participants can always click back to reread how they arrived at subsequent decision nodes.

Notice that at this decision node, the paths and payoff outcomes are exactly the same as in Baseline Trust game (see Figure 10.1). The first mover has foregone ($12, $12) and the second mover is deciding between ($18, $30) and ($6, $42). The above story complicates the recognition of beneficence by explicitly stating that the new offer is due to the second mover's distinct portion of the joint effort. Thus, the narrative, unlike an austere EFG, justifies why the second mover receives more money in the ($18, $30) outcome that rewards beneficence. But does it justify ($6, $42)? At this point in the extensive form trust game *without* punishment, both participants know that this decision is final. In contrast, in the extensive form trust game *with* punishment (Punish Injustice game, Figure 10.4), both know that the first mover will have to sanction ($6, $42) by foregoing ($4, $4) at the next decision node. In the

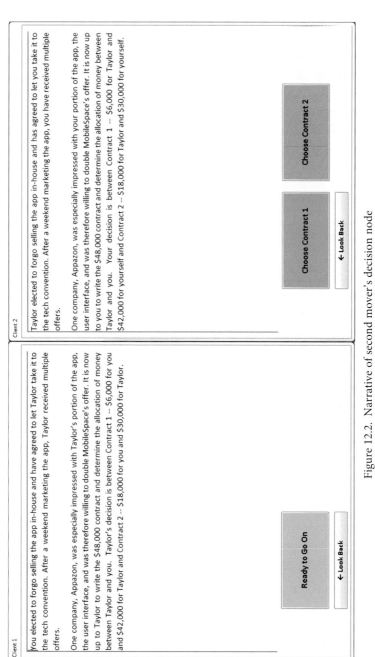

Client 1

You elected to forgo selling the app in-house and have agreed to let Taylor take it to the tech convention. After a weekend marketing the app, Taylor received multiple offers.

One company, Appazon, was especially impressed with Taylor's portion of the app, the user interface, and was therefore willing to double MobileSpace's offer. It is now up to Taylor to write the $48,000 contract and determine the allocation of money between Taylor and you. Taylor's decision is between Contract 1 -- $6,000 for you and $42,000 for Taylor and Contract 2 -- $18,000 for you and $30,000 for Taylor.

Ready to Go On

← Look Back

Client 2

Taylor elected to forgo selling the app in-house and has agreed to let you take it to the tech convention. After a weekend marketing the app, you have received multiple offers.

One company, Appazon, was especially impressed with your portion of the app, the user interface, and was therefore willing to double MobileSpace's offer. It is now up to you to write the $48,000 contract and determine the allocation of money between Taylor and you. Your decision is between Contract 1 -- $6,000 for Taylor and $42,000 for yourself and Contract 2 -- $18,000 for Taylor and $30,000 for yourself.

Choose Contract 1

Choose Contract 2

← Look Back

Figure 12.2. Narrative of second mover's decision node

Figure 12.3. Story ending for the ($18, $30) outcome

narrative, though, both participants know only that the second mover is choosing between ($18, $30) and ($6, $42) and that the story may or may not end with either decision. Does Beneficence Proposition 1 apply for the second mover?

This is a realistic middle-ground case that an extensive form game cannot readily accommodate. Sure, we could create a new unformaliz-able EFG experiment in which the second mover clicks on the ($6, $42) outcome and then a new decision node for the first mover suddenly appears in its stead. *Oops, you thought you had clicked on ($6, $42) but, no, now the first mover decides.* But how would we explain how the decision-making in the game tree works without deceiving the participants? Even supposing that we could find such delicate but not contorted statements to explain the story-free exercise, the subjects are going to be asking themselves, why and what (the heck) is going on? There is nothing for the participant to cleave to. In a narrative, we can preempt questions stemming from vertigo, thereby allowing the participants to focus on the decision of interest. The story grounds the participants. It is a basis on which to predicate their thinking.

If the second mover chooses ($18, $30), the characters receive a one sentence ending to the story (see Figure 12.3). The order of the two outcomes is randomly presented to the pair and the colors of the button blocked across half of the pairs.

If the second mover chooses ($6, $42), the story continues, and the first mover has another decision to make (see Figure 12.4). The key principle for the narrative design at this juncture in the story is to present a plausibly unforeseeable opportunity for the first mover to punish the second mover for not choosing ($18, $30). Notice that their employer has come forward in the meantime and is willing to represent the first mover. Taking the second mover to court is a deliberate and explicitly meaningful action for carrying out resentment. The costs of suing and winning justify to the characters a loss of $40. As with the previous decision nodes, the order of the two actions is randomly presented to the pair and the colors of the button blocked across half of the pairs.

The outcomes of this decision node and the path to it are the same as those in the third and final decision node of the Punish Injustice game. Injustice Proposition 1 predicts that because the second mover is harming the first mover (giving a payoff less than $18 or $12) the second mover deserves punishment by the first mover. Recall

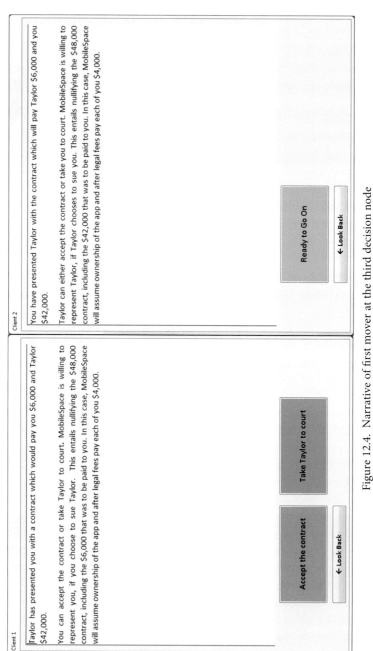

Figure 12.4. Narrative of first mover at the third decision node

that in Figure 10.4, only 25 percent of the first movers choose ($4, $4).

Our ex post facto speculation in Chapter 10 is that both participants know, even before the first mover plays down, that the second mover can also play down. Thus, when the decision reaches the second mover, he may be daring the first mover to choose ($4, $4). In other words, the second mover is not harming the first mover because the first mover knows from the get-go that the second mover may play down. In the narrative this is not the case. The first mover does not know that the second mover will be presented with a choice to harm the first mover, and the second mover does not know that the first mover will have the opportunity to punish the second mover after having explicitly chosen ($6, $42). Notice also that in the PI game, the second mover literally chooses a branch in the tree, but in the narrative the second mover actually chooses a contract paying out ($6, $42). The question is, in the heat of the moment, will a greater proportion of first movers in the narrative resent a perceived harm and punish the second movers by choosing ($4, $4) over ($6, $42) than in the extensive form trust game with punishment? Obviously, there is a key difference that the story may go on and the EFG will not, but that difference is part and parcel of what we are exploring. Does Injustice Proposition 1 apply for the first mover?

If the first mover takes Taylor to court, the first (second) mover reads the following conclusion to the story: "You (Taylor) sued Taylor (you). MobileSpace owns the app and you have received a check in the amount of $4,000. The End." And if the first mover accepts the contract, the story similarly ends this way: "You accepted the contract and have received a check in the amount of $6,000. The End." Correspondingly, the story concludes for the second mover with "Taylor accepted the contract, and you have received a check in the amount of $42,000. The End."

To simultaneously test the robustness of their results and whether a slight modification to their narrative alters the conduct of our participants, holding everything else constant, Osborn et al. conducted a second narrative treatment. The Narrative 2 treatment replaces just three little words with two new ones at the second decision node only. By using the same story for the first decision node, we can assess the

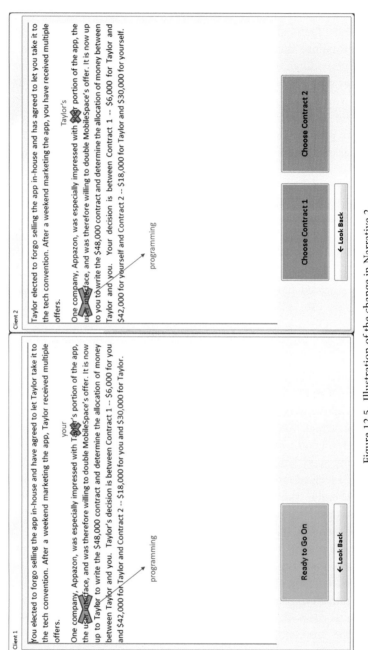

Figure 12.5. Illustration of the change in Narrative 2

robustness of the decisions on the first page with another set of participants. Figure 12.5 illustrates the small change to the story. The aim is, *ceteris paribus*, to differently draw the future into the desires expressed at the second decision node by crediting the first mover's efforts to the app as the reason for the doubled offer. The hypothesis is that a greater proportion of second movers will choose the contract for ($18, $30) in accordance with Beneficence Proposition 1.

This treatment is central to the thesis of the experiment and should not be mistaken for a framing effect that economists often summarily dismiss. A framing effect is a pattern of judgment whereby people differently respond to different hypothetical situations that are logically equivalent.[2] This change in the narrative is not a framing effect because the two narratives are not logically equivalent. The payoffs are identical and the possible actions are identical, but the newly discovered present as caused by the immediate past is decidedly not. The open research question is whether the Beneficence Proposition 1 at the second decision node differently draws the future into the expression of the present actions.

RESULTS

We compare the participants' organic decisions growing out of the story with those from Chapter 10 in which the participants have nothing to cleave to except the bare structure of the game. In the Baseline Trust game, 45 percent of the first movers immediately end the game. In the two narrative stories, only 11 out of 48 (23 percent) and 8 out of 48 (17 percent) of first movers choose to "Sell the app to MobileSpace," ending the game. Knowing that there is a possibility of greater joint value and without explicitly knowing that they could do worse than $12, more first movers take the leap and let the second mover take the next action in the story. The narrative has established a relationship at this node, the two characters living within a world of shared participation in the development of the app, thus furthering the trust, even in a situation where potential outcomes are unknown.

Upon seeing the remaining results of an experiment, it is tempting to claim, "'Of course, it had to happen like that.' Whereas we ought to

---

[2] See, e.g., Amos Tversky and Daniel Kahneman (1981).

think: it may have happened *like that* – and also in many other ways"
(Ludwig Wittgenstein 1980, p. 37e). So in what follows, Osborn et al.
take the unconventional approach of using the reader's predictions
about what their subjects do to synthesize the conclusions of the
experiment. In other words, the readers choose their own adventure
through the results, culminating in one of eight possible lessons learned
from the experiment.

What do we learn from the experiment by presenting the results in
such a way? If at this moment you cannot predict what you will learn
from this experiment because you do not even know what outcomes
are possible nor the actions you will have to take to realize them,
then the focal question becomes, what story are you telling yourself to
pick the next page to turn to? How do you make the decision that
you do with an unforeseeable future? How are you thinking about
Adam Smith's propositions? Not only do we learn from this experiment how Adam Smith's Beneficence Proposition 1 and Injustice
Proposition 1 work or do not work in this experiment, we learn
how to invert the very way we think about games in economics;
i.e., we learn how Adam Smith would humanly think about games.
Like Adam Smith, we begin by incorporating feeling, thinking, and
knowing in a narrative to which we then consider how Adam Smith's
propositions apply. At this point, the reader who dwells on the actual
results misses the point of the project and the presentation of it:
What are the abstract rules of conduct for the narrative by which the
participants in our experiment act with an unforeseeable future, and
what are the abstract rules for the narrative by which the reader of
economic science thinks about rules of conduct?

If you think that 46 percent of the second movers in Narrative 1 and
70 percent in Narrative 2 choose the ($18, $30) contract, go to page 187.

If you think that 46 percent of the second movers in Narrative 1 and
90 percent in Narrative 2 choose the ($18, $30) contract, go to page 189.

If you think that 73 percent of the second movers in Narrative 1 and
70 percent in Narrative 2 choose the ($18, $30) contract, go to page
191.

If you think that 73 percent of the second movers in Narrative 1 and
90 percent in Narrative 2 choose the ($18, $30) contract, go to page
193.

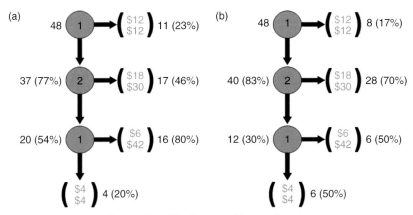

Figure 12.6. The first possible set of results

(a) Narrative 1

(b) Narrative 2

Even though a greater proportion of first movers let the second mover take the next action in Narrative 1 than in an EFG, a smaller proportion of second movers, 46 percent, choose ($18, $30). In EFG experiments, 67 percent of second movers play right. The net result is that nearly the same proportion of Narrative 1 and EFG pairs, 35 percent and 33 percent, respectively, achieve a payoff improvement for both people over the first mover simply ending the story unwittingly or the EFG wittingly.

Comparing the two narrative treatments, the small change in words has a large impact on the proportion of second movers who choose the ($18, $30) contract. *In Narrative 2, 70 percent of the second movers, i.e., 24 percentage points more, reward the first movers' action of beneficent tendency.* It clearly matters whose effort is responsible for doubling of the joint value of the app.[3] The consummate consequentialist might be tempted to conclude because the second version of the story restores the results of the observed proportion of second mover play in extensive form trust game experiments that the motive of the second movers in EFG trust games is to reward the first mover for her contribution to doubling the pie. That leap, which ignores the different epistemic conditions of the narrative and EFG games, cannot account for why 46 percent still choose the ($18, $30) contract in the first narrative. What our narrative experiments expose is the possibility that two individuals in an EFG might disagree on who is "responsible" for the pie doubling.[4] Is it the first mover or the second mover? The silence of the tree is deafening.

[3] It also indicates how closely the participants read the story. How many words were changed?
[4] See Bart Wilson (2010).

When the second movers in our narrative do not know that there is a possibility of 50 percent increase in payoff for the first mover playing down, they conduct themselves differently than when the payoffs are laid out beforehand in the EFG. The first movers do not know what payoffs lie ahead if they decide not to sell right away, and when the second movers know that the first movers do not know what lies ahead, the second movers are less inclined to reward the first movers with the ($18, $30) contract when it becomes a possibility. In an EFG experiment first movers play down because they see that the second mover can increase her own payoff by 50 percent, for we do not presume that the first mover wishes to lower her payoff by 50 percent. When the decision is passed to the second mover in Narrative 1, however, the second movers know the first movers did *not* know what might come of it, and 21 percentage points fewer of them (67–46 percent) feel no need to reward the first movers with the ($18, $30) contract. They take the ($6, $42) contract instead. For 54 percent of the second movers, the Beneficent Proposition 1 does not appear to apply. This is, of course, complicated by the story line that another company is particularly impressed with the second mover's contribution to the app design and is, therefore, willing to double the offer. In accepting Contract 1, "$6,000 for Taylor and $42,000 for you" the Beneficent Proposition 1 fails to predict how these participants conduct themselves, for now the first mover has less than the initial $12,000. How do the corresponding 20 first movers respond to the ($6, $42) contract? Is offering the ($6, $42) contract an action of a hurtful tendency?

In Narrative 1, only 4 out of 20 (20 percent) first movers at the third decision node punish the second movers for choosing the ($6, $42) contract. We find that when a smaller proportion of the second movers choose the ($6, $42) contract, a greater proportion 6 out of 12 (50 percent) punish the second mover in Narrative 2. Unlike the Narrative 1 treatment, Narrative 2 supports both Beneficent Proposition 1 and Injustice Proposition 1 in the world of the story. When the first mover's contribution to the design of the app is that which results in a doubling of MobileSpace's offer, the second mover rewards the first mover's action of a beneficent tendency when she chooses ($18, $30) over ($6, $42). The gratitude towards the first mover results in the second mover choosing the highest payoff presented for the first mover. A hurtful tendency would be evidenced by reducing the first mover's payoff when it is her contribution that resulted in more money. And such an action as an approved object of resentment, Smith predicts, prompts punishment. The story, in this case, evokes Injustice Proposition 1, 50 percent of the time when first movers punish the second mover's decision to take the contract for ($6, $42).

Go to page 195.

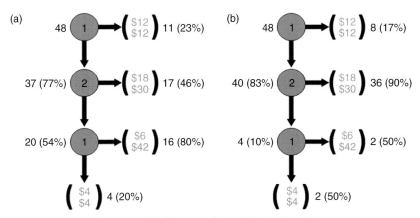

Figure 12.7. The second possible set of results

(a) Narrative 1

(b) Narrative 2

Even though a greater proportion of first movers let the second mover take the next action in Narrative 1 than in an EFG, a smaller proportion of second movers, 46 percent, choose ($18, $30). In EFG experiments, 67 percent of second movers play right. The net result is that nearly the same proportion of Narrative 1 and EFG pairs, 35 percent and 33 percent, respectively, achieve a payoff improvement for both people over the first mover simply ending the story unwittingly or the EFG wittingly.

The small change in words has a tremendous impact on the proportion of second movers who choose the ($18, $30) contract. *In Narrative 2, 90 percent of the second movers, i.e., 44 percentage points more, reward the first movers' action of beneficent tendency.* It matters dramatically whose effort is responsible for doubling the joint value of the app.[5]

Four previous extensive form trust game experiments *each* find that two-thirds of second movers reward the beneficence of first movers. In Narrative 2, 90 percent of second movers conform to Beneficence Proposition 1. Rare is the result in experimental economics in which 36

---

[5] It also indicates how closely the participants read the story. How many words were changed?

of 40 participants make the same decision when such a result is ex ante uncertain. Moreover, 75 percent (36 out of 48) of all pairs end up at the ($18, $30) outcome. How many pairs in extensive form trust games realize the equivalent of the ($18, $30) outcome? Merely one-third. Our second narrative generates a conformity of welfare-improving conduct that EFG's do not and starkly suggests, in comparison to the first narrative, that the higher variance of outcomes in EFG experiments stems from a disagreement on who is "responsible" for the pie doubling.[6] Is it the first mover or the second mover? The silence of the tree is deafening.

In Narrative 1, only 4 out of 20 (20 percent) first movers at the third decision node punish the second movers for choosing the ($6, $42) contract. The flip side of the stark result at the second decision node is a dearth of data at the third node for Narrative 2. Even though only 4 second movers choose the ($6, $42) contract, 2 first movers (50 percent) punish.

The Narrative 2 treatment clearly supports Beneficent Proposition 1 in the world of the story. When the first mover's contribution to the design of the app is that which results in a doubling of MobileSpace's offer, the second mover rewards the first mover's action of a beneficent tendency when she chooses ($18, $30) over ($6, $42). The gratitude towards the first mover results in the second mover choosing the highest payoff presented for the first mover. A hurtful tendency would be evidenced by reducing the first mover's payoff when it is her contribution that resulted in more money. And such an action as an approved object of resentment, Smith predicts, prompts punishment. The story, in this case, conforms to the Injustice Proposition 1, 50 percent of the time when first movers punish the second mover's decision to take the contract for ($6, $42).

Go to page 195.

---

[6] See Bart Wilson (2010).

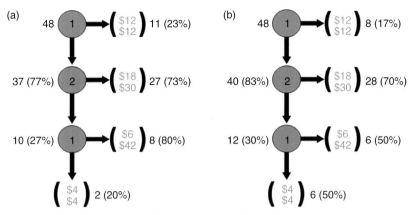

Figure 12.8. The third possible set of results
(a) Narrative 1
(b) Narrative 2

While a greater proportion of first movers let the second mover take the next action than in an EFG, a comparable proportion of second movers, 73 percent, choose ($18, $30) in Narrative 1. In EFG experiments, roughly the same proportion of second movers, 67 percent, play right. The net result is that a greater proportion of narrative pairs, 56 percent versus 33 percent in EFG pairs, achieve a payoff improvement for both people over the first mover simply ending the story unwittingly or the EFG wittingly.

When the second movers in Narrative 1 do not know that there is a possibility of 50 percent increase in the payoff for the first mover playing down, they conduct themselves just as they do when the payoffs are laid out beforehand in the EFG. The first movers do not know what payoffs lie ahead if they decide not to sell right away, and when the second movers know that the first movers do not know what lies ahead, the second movers still reward the first movers with the ($18, $30) contract when it becomes a possibility. In an EFG experiment, first movers play down because they see that the second mover can increase her own payoff by 50 percent and the second mover's payoff by 250 percent, for we do not presume that the first mover plays down to lower her payoff by 50 percent. When the decision is passed to the second mover in the Narrative 1, however, the second movers know the first movers did *not* know what might come of it and yet 73 percent of them reward the first movers with the ($18, $30) contract. They do not take the ($6, $42) contract. The Beneficence Proposition 1 appears to apply for all but 27 percent of the second movers despite the complication in the story line that another company is particularly impressed with the second mover's contribution to the app design and is, therefore, willing to double the offer.

The small change in words has virtually no impact on the proportion of second movers, who choose the ($18, $30) contract. In Narrative 2, 70 percent of the second movers reward the first movers' action of beneficent tendency. *It matters rather little whose effort is responsible for doubling the joint value of the app.*

In Narrative 1, only 2 out of 10 (20 percent) first movers at the third decision node punish the second movers for choosing the ($6, $42) contract. In Narrative 2, when the same proportion of the second movers choose the ($6, $42) contract, a greater proportion 6 out of 12 (50 percent) punish the second movers. Resentment appears to grow when the first mover's effort is responsible for increasing the joint value of the project. *In sum, apart from the first mover's decision to let the second mover act, there is little evidence of any difference between our narratives, and little evidence between our narratives and the traditional EFG experiment.*[7] Does this mean that narratives do not matter in trust games? The answer depends upon whether (a) you believe that payoffs are all that matter and that it matters little that the future is unforeseeable, or (b) you simply conclude that this narrative does not matter for this game.

Go to page 195.

---

[7] The critic who expected that the change in Narrative 2 wouldn't matter might claim that it indicates how inattentively the participants read the story in both experiments. How many words were changed?

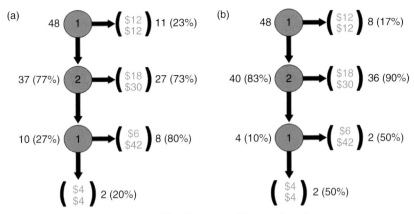

Figure 12.9. The fourth possible set of results

(a) Narrative 1

(b) Narrative 2

While a greater proportion of first movers let the second mover take the next action than in an EFG, a comparable proportion of second movers, 73 percent, choose ($18, $30) in Narrative 1. In EFG experiments, roughly the same proportion of second movers, 67 percent, play right. The net result is that a greater proportion of narrative pairs, 56 percent versus 33 percent in EFG pairs, achieve a payoff improvement for both people over the first mover simply ending the story unwittingly or the EFG wittingly.

When the second movers in Narrative 1 do not know that there is a possibility of 50 percent increase in the payoff for the first mover playing down, they conduct themselves just as they do when the payoffs are laid out beforehand in the EFG. The first movers do not know what payoffs lie ahead if they decide not to sell right away, and when the second movers know that the first movers do not know what lies ahead, the second movers still reward the first movers with the ($18, $30) contract when it becomes a possibility. In an EFG experiment, first movers play down because they see that the second mover can increase her own payoff by 50 percent and the second mover's payoff by 250 percent, for we do not presume that the first mover plays down to lower her payoff by 50 percent. When the decision is passed to the second mover in the Narrative 1, however, the second movers know the first movers did *not* know what might come of it and yet 73 percent of them reward the first movers with the ($18, $30) contract. They do not take the ($6, $42) contract. The Beneficence Proposition 1 appears to apply to all but 27 percent of the second movers despite the complication in the story line that another company is particularly impressed with the second mover's contribution to the app design and is, therefore, willing to double the offer.

The small change in words has a tremendously large impact on the proportion of second movers who choose the ($18, $30) contract. *In Narrative 2, 90 percent of the second movers reward the first movers' action of beneficent tendency.*[8] It clearly matters whose effort is responsible for doubling of the joint value of the app.[9]

Four previous extensive form trust game experiments *each* find that two-thirds of second movers reward the beneficence of first movers. In Narrative 2, 90 percent of second movers conform to Beneficence Proposition 1. Rare is the result in experimental economics in which 36 of 40 participants make the same decision when such a result is ex ante uncertain. Moreover, 75 percent (36 out of 48) of all pairs end up at the ($18, $30) outcome. How many pairs in extensive form trust games realize the equivalent of the ($18, $30) outcome? Merely one-third. Our second narrative generates a conformity of welfare-improving conduct that EFG's do not and starkly suggests, in comparison to the first narrative, that the higher variance of outcomes in two-person EFG experiments stems from a disagreement on who is "responsible" for the pie doubling.[10] Is it the first mover or the second mover? The silence of the tree is deafening.

In Narrative 1, only 2 out of 10 (20 percent) first movers at the third decision node punish the second movers for choosing the ($6, $42) contract. The flip side of the stark result at the second decision node is a dearth of data at the third node for Narrative 2. We find that only 4 second movers choose the ($6, $42) contract, and 2 of them (50 percent) punish.

The Narrative 2 treatment clearly 2 supports Beneficent Proposition 1 in the world of the story. When the first mover's contribution to the design of the app is that which results in a doubling of MobileSpace's offer, the second mover rewards the first mover's action of a beneficent tendency when she chooses ($18, $30) over ($6, $42). The gratitude towards the first mover results in the second mover choosing the highest payoff presented for the first mover. A hurtful tendency would be evidenced by reducing the first mover's payoff when it is her contribution that resulted in more money. And such an action as an approved object of resentment, Smith predicts, prompts punishment. The story, in this case, conforms to Injustice Proposition 1, 50 percent of the time when first movers punish the second mover's decision to take the contract for ($6, $42).

Go to page 195.

---

[8] We reject the null hypothesis of equal proportions ($z = 1.9$, p-value = 0.0265, one-tailed test).
[9] It also indicates how closely the participants read the story. How many words were changed?
[10] See Bart Wilson (2010).

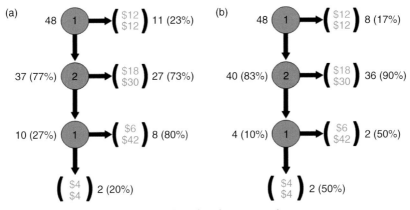

Figure 12.10. Actual results of narrativized experiment

(a) Narrative 1

(b) Narrative 2

If you are arriving to this page from page 194, then you have correctly anticipated the actual results of both narrative treatments. Figure 12.10 summarizes the actual results for the two narrative treatments. If you are not arriving from page 194, the summary implications of our findings for the two treatments are discussed on pages 193–4.

LIFE IS INDEFINITE AND ALWAYS IN FLUX

As capable as humans are of kindness by advancing mutual good, they are equally capable of effecting and ready in designing mischief. To contend with the capriciousness of the human primate, rules of conduct arose in the small band or tribe, by experience and tradition, to regularize and order human interaction.[11] In the face of an unknowable future, we rely on rules of conduct to guide us as the momentaneous present is revealed. Human beings do not simply express behavior; i.e., act under specified conditions like amoral molecules in a flask. Rather, we conduct ourselves accordingly in relation to the circumstances in which we suddenly find ourselves. If by creating laboratory experiments our goal is to understand human conduct against this hurly-burly background of human action, then including that which is essentially human – the stories we tell ourselves to make

[11] F. A. Hayek (1973, 1988).

meaning of our experience – is as much a part of economics as the science of pecuniary interests that currently pervades the discipline.

Moreover, economic scientists no more set aside their humanness when contemplating the conduct of experimental participants than the participants themselves do when they enter the laboratory. The results do not speak in their own voice to the readers; the readers themselves discover the meaning of the observations. Their own voices echo through the results. And that is the spirit in which Osborn, Wilson, and Sherwood present their results to the reader. An economic experiment is ultimately about testing what we expect of it, our own way of interpreting the facts, our own assumptions about how we think the narrative of the world works. Thus, each unexpected fact that we encounter is an opportunity to work on our own way of seeing things. Discovery is irreversible, whether it is by a participant in the laboratory reading an interactive story for real, salient payoffs or by the reader of economic science. A discovery changes the narrative; it changes what a person knows. There is no going back. But what does not change is the rule of conduct applicable to the particular circumstances of time and place. Strict logical performance, however, is reversible and thus is antithetical for studying moments of discovery and our human conduct therein. Rules of conduct are our footholds on the shores of unanticipated reality.

References

Gjerstad, Steven and Vernon L. Smith. 2014. *Rethinking Housing Bubbles: The Role of Household and Bank Balance Sheets in Modeling Economic Cycles.* New York, NY: Cambridge University Press.

Hayek, F. A. 1973. *Law, Legislation and Liberty,* Volume 1: *Rules and Order.* Chicago, IL: University of Chicago Press.

Hayek, F. A. 1976. *Law, Legislation and Liberty,* Volume 2: *The Mirage of Social Justice.* Chicago, IL: University of Chicago Press.

Hayek, F. A. 1988. *The Fatal Conceit.* Chicago, IL: University of Chicago Press.

Osborn, Jan, Bart J. Wilson, and Bradley R. Sherwood. 2015. "Conduct in Narrativized Trust Games," *Southern Economic Journal* 81(3): 562–97.

Tversky, Amos, and Daniel Kahneman. 1981. "The Framing of Decisions and the Psychology of Choice," *Science* 211(4481): 453–8.

Wilson, Bart J. 2010. "Social Preferences are not Preferences," *Journal of Economic Behavior and Organization* 73: 77–82.

Wittgenstein, Ludwig. 1980. *Culture and Value.* Peter Wench (trans.) and G. H. von Wright and H. Nyman (eds.). Chicago, IL: University of Chicago Press.

13

Adam Smith's Program for the Study of Human Socioeconomic Betterment

From Beneficence and Justice to the *Wealth of Nations*

Smith's theory of justice is a development that follows from his two propositions on injustice, which are the counterpart opposites of the two propositions on beneficence. Whereas beneficence is about propriety, injustice is about impropriety. First, we have Injustice Proposition 1, in which improperly motivated actions of a hurtful tendency alone deserve punishment because of the resentment they provoke in those hurt by the actions and in every fair and impartial spectator; and second, we have Injustice Proposition 2, in which foregoing actions of a hurtful nature does not merit reward. Just as failure to be beneficent in a particular action, or "want of beneficence," is not a proper source of resentment, and subject to punishment, so failure to engage in deliberately hurtful actions, "want of injustice," is not properly a general subject of reward.

Resentment supplies the foundation in feeling and thinking for the emergence of justice (and of property) from human experience as summarized in Injustice Proposition 1. Smith begins his articulation of the nature and role of resentment in establishing the truth of Beneficence Proposition 2, wherein Smith explains why we do not feel motivated to punish people purely because they fail to show beneficence toward us. Nature arms us with resentment for defense, and this is its unique channeling function. Resentment serves us by safeguarding justice, protecting innocence, motivating us to beat off and retaliate against mischief, making the offender repent of his offense, and others to fear committing like offenses. Resentment is reserved for all such purposes, "nor can the spectator ever go along with it when it is exerted for any other" (TMS, Second. II.I, p. 113).[1] Consequently, "the mere want of the beneficent virtues,

---

[1] Smith illustrates this in his *Lectures on Jurisprudence*: "Years ago the British nation took a fancy (a very whimsical one indeed) that the wealth and strength of the nation depended

though it may disappoint us of the good which might reasonably be expected, neither does nor attempts to do, any mischief from which we can have occasion to defend ourselves" (TMS, Second.II.I, pp. 113–14).

The trust game test results we reported for "want of beneficence" (Figure 10.2) were observations of actions taken in an unfamiliar environment that, by hypothesis, is subject to Smith's principle. The data provide fresh credibility for Smith's insistence that this pattern of conduct is a virtue that experience has deeply instilled in us. Not a single second mover took action in the trust game to punish the failure to offer cooperation by their counterpart first mover.

Contrastingly distinct from the virtue of beneficence is justice, the violation of which causes real and positive hurt (with improper motivation) and provokes resentment. Smith evaluates actions from their intersubjective origins in which the hurtfulness of the outcomes orders the intensity of the resentment. Smith thereby reverses the utilitarian path from outcomes to internal disutility, going to the "roots of action." Samuel Alexander summarizes the Smithian process (1933, pp. 249–50):

> We disapprove theft because we wish to keep our property and sympathise with the similar desire of the person robbed, and have no sympathy with the robber because we do not ourselves want to rob. The "impartial spectator" represents in an ideally imagined person the "pitch" to which the wants and impulses of all can be tuned; the word is Adam Smith's own.... I have no doubt that Adam Smith has touched the matter on its quick, as anyone may verify for himself who asks why stealing is wrong. Does he first think of the uncertainty and pain produced by that conduct, or does he not disapprove because he himself feels the resentment of others.... But he who goes to the impulses from which the action proceeds goes to the roots of action, and not merely to its issues.

The same intersubjective process gives rise to the control of actions through punishment, the setting of penalties. Society, and not only the sufferer, goes along with the violence used to avenge hurt caused by deliberate acts of injustice; even more do they go along with actions to prevent, turn back, and restrain offenders from hurting their neighbors

---

entirely on the flourishing of their woolen trade, and that this could not prosper if the exportation of wool was permitted. To prevent this it was enacted that the exportation of wool should be punished with death. This exportation was no crime at all, in natural equity, and was very far from deserving so high a punishment in the eyes of the people; they therefore found that while this was the punishment they could get neither jury nor informers. No one would consent to the punishment of a thing in itself so innocent by so high a penalty. They were therefore obliged to lessen the punishment to a confiscation of goods and vessel" (Smith 1766, pp. 104–5).

(TMS, Second.II.I, p. 113). As Smith says in the *Lectures on Jurisprudence*, "the end of justice is to secure from injury" (1766, p. 199).

The important conceptual implication of these principles is that justice is a negative virtue, defined negatively by a process that restricts, and hinders us from hurting our neighbor. That is, justice is the infinite (uncountable) set of actions not disapproved, avenged, and discouraged with penalties for their violation. Justice defines property. Justice is the freedom to take any action not specifically excluded.

PUNISHMENT IS PROPORTIONED TO RESENTMENT

As the greater exertions of beneficence merit larger rewards, so the greater the injustice of an action the more it is resented, and the greater the punishment to avenge and discourage further infraction: "As the greater and more irreparable the evil that is done, the resentment of the sufferer runs naturally the higher; so does likewise the sympathetic indignation of the spectator, as well as the sense of guilt in the agent" (TMS, Second.II.II, p. 121).

Death being by far the greatest loss a person can suffer, murder is the worst of all crimes that can be committed against another individual, and an advanced society sees such loss as deserving of capital punishment.[2] To be deprived of our property by theft or robbery is next in order of personal loss and of punishment. Finally, in this ordering is the loss of what we had expected from breach of contract.

---

[2] In his more expansive *Lectures on Jurisprudence*, Smith observes that capital punishment is the mark of an advanced national civil order within the larger society. We quote in full to convey Smith's remarkable observational sense of evolution and social change in the role of government in response to the affairs of the larger order of society. It was, however, about resentment all the way up to civil law. "But amongst barbarous nations the punishment has generally been much slighter, as a pecuniary fine – the reason of this was the weakness of government on those early periods of society, which made it very delicate of intermeddling with the affairs of individuals. The government therefore at first interposed only in the way of mediator, to prevent the ill consequences that might arise from those crimes in the resentment of the friends of the slain. For what is the end of punishing crimes, in the eyes of the people in this state? The very same as now of punishing civil injuries, viz the preserving of the public peace. The crimes themselves were already committed, there was no help for that; the main thing therefore the society would have in view would be to prevent the bad consequences of it. This therefore they would not attempt by a punishment, which might interrupt it. For it was not till a society was far advanced that the government took upon them to cite criminals and pass judgment on them" (Smith 1766, p. 106). Smith continues with an illustrative case from the Iroquois in America.

Why does Smith teach us that punishment is greater for loss of property than for violation of contract? Why should it matter whether a thief steals $1,000 from me, or that a store charges me $1,000 for a television that does not work? Because of Principle 2 (Chapter 5), the asymmetry between gains and losses in our social and economic well-being, which, in turn, derives more fundamentally from the universal human experience of asymmetry between feeling something good and feeling something bad. To be deprived of that which we have acquired by the earnings of our labor and investment is a greater loss than to be deprived only of the potential gain we had expected from our transactions with others. The violator of our person and property must be made to feel the magnitude of the loss imposed by such actions and be deterred from further violations against others. Accordingly, in history, in Smith's time, and down to the present, theft and robbery are criminal infractions, while violations of contract are civil infractions, albeit subject to recovery, but are not criminal.

For Smith the big picture of civil society bulks large with the sharp legal distinction between violation of property and of contract, a distinction that emanates from the principle of asymmetry between gains and losses, a universal human experience. The principle, derived directly by Smith from the asymmetry between our experiences of joy and sorrow, and found in behavioral research by Daniel Kahneman and Amos Tversky, were independent discoveries that gives enriched new meaning to each. In this respect, as in others, *Sentiments* was a work in social psychology for all time.

NEGATIVE JUSTICE IN *SENTIMENTS* AND PROPERTY IN *WEALTH*

In Smith's conception, as we construct it from the patterns in his thought and analysis in *Sentiments* and subsequently in *Wealth*, justice is the large residue of unspecified actions left over after introducing sanctions that penalize hurtful actions. Punishment is levied in proportion to the hurt, and supports incentive compatibility, but that is not why people do it.[3]

The fair and impartial spectator achieves fairness in the game of life by calling and penalizing fouls that, by consent, we agree are particularly resentful, but that are also inimical to human socioeconomic betterment. A man must control his self-interest, bringing it

---

[3] By "incentive compatibility" we refer to individual incentives being compatible with increasing the economic welfare of the group as a whole.

down to something which other men can go along with.. . . In the race for wealth, and honours, and preferments, he may run as hard as he can, and strain every nerve and every muscle, in order to outstrip all his competitors. But if he should justle, or throw down any of them, the indulgence of the spectators is entirely at an end. It is a violation of fair play, which they cannot admit of. This man is to them, in every respect, as good as he. (TMS, Second.II.II, p. 120)[4]

But the larger economic effects encourage freedom of access under equality of opportunity rules of engagement.

Anna Wierzbicka (2006) notes that the original antonym of *fair* was *foul*, not *unfair*, as in a fair or foul ball in the rules of baseball, or the British phrase "through means fair or foul." Either they have crossed a line with their actions, or they have not; as with batting in baseball, our conduct is either within the wide bounds of fair play or it is foul. Imagine civil life as a large playing field of action in which people are free to move anywhere, in any direction, try any new actions, so long as they avoid the foul bound-aries of play. Such a civil life is Smith's vision of the liberal order that encourages new products, services, innovations in technique, and, in our time, the internet and social media proving that in a market economy, the demand for expressions of sociality were never greater.

THE TWO PILLARS OF SOCIETY: BENEFICENCE THE ORNAMENT AND JUSTICE THE FOUNDATION

Nature has fitted the human species to live, to subsist, in society only. All of us require one another's assistance. Society flourishes where that mutual support is provided in the reciprocity of gratitude and friendship bound together in good offices of affection and esteem (TMS, Second.II.III, pp. 124–25).

Even in the absence of such conditions, the society may subsist in a less happy and agreeable form, simply from a "sense of its utility . . . upheld by a mercenary exchange of good offices according to an agreed valuation" (TMS, Second.II.III, p. 124).[5] No society, however, can "subsist among

---

[4] Following the convention of his time, Smith always refers to the male gender. What were his views on women? In his *Lectures on Jurisprudence*, Smith discusses the greater penalty for adultery by the wife than the husband, wherein the usual justification "was to prevent a spurious offspring being imposed upon the husband.. . . The real reason is that it is men who make the laws with respect to this; they generally will be inclined to curb the women as much as possible and give themselves the more indulgence" (1766, p. 147).

[5] Recall earlier, that in discussing the harmony of the benevolent passions, happiness far exceeds the "little services" expected to flow from that state; here he is referring to an association defined by an agreed exchange of such services (TMS, First.II.IV, p. 53).

those who are at all times ready to hurt and injure one another. The moment that injury begins, the moment that mutual resentment and animosity take place, all the bands of it are broke asunder, and ... dissipated and scattered abroad by the violence and opposition of their discordant affections" (TMS, Second.II.III, pp. 124–25).

Beneficence is thus less critical to the support of society than justice is. Where injustice prevails, the society is in peril of destruction. While "nature ... exhorts mankind to acts of beneficence ... she has not thought it necessary to guard and enforce the practice of it by the terrors of merited punishment in case it should be neglected. It is the ornament which embellishes, not the foundation which supports the building, and ... was ... sufficient to recommend, but by no means necessary to impose. Justice, on the contrary, is the main pillar that upholds the whole edifice" (TMS, Second.II.III, p. 125).

EQUILIBRIUM VERSUS ALTERNATIVE PATHS TO COOPERATION: BENEFICENCE OR PUNISH INJUSTICE

Suppose we create an environment in which an individual first mover can self-select between the game-theoretic equilibrium, beneficence, and justice. To choose the game-theoretic equilibrium is to choose not to play either of Smith's two pillars of society. In Chapter 9 we expand choice in the context of the ultimatum game (UG), and find that voluntary UGs yield results quite different from the standard protocol. How will those choosing to play in one of the personal exchange societies self-select between them? In addition, how will the type signal inherent in the agent's choice effect outcomes? Our final design provides the first mover with a tripartite choice among equilibrium and either of two alternative paths to cooperation; i.e., two subgame routes to cooperation. One based on a beneficent society, Beneficence Proposition 1, the other based on a just society, Injustice Proposition 1. For Smith these are the two defining features of civil society. The second is the foundation pillar, the first but an ornamental pillar.

Our a priori reasoning and predictions are as follows. In Figure 10.4, introducing the option to punish defection from the first mover's offer to cooperate serves to muddy the information content in the offer relative to the Baseline Trust (BT) game in Figure 10.1. The consequence is an increase in offers to cooperate, or "trust," but trustworthiness declines because the signal can be interpreted as coercive – a negative sentiment in Smith's model that people do not like to experience in their social relationships. If this is a correct interpretation, then we can test it by allowing first movers to choose clean-signaling paths; either a beneficent path, or a threat-of-punishment path, to mutual betterment. In this new context the second movers who are offered cooperation, can observe the self-selecting choice between subgames made by their first mover counterparts. First movers who play right more purely signal their beneficence, in comparison with the Baseline Trust game, by not choosing the punish-injustice branch. Trustworthiness and the proportion of pairs cooperating should increase. Similarly, playing left implies that beneficent types have been filtered leaving cooperators who condition their cooperation on the option to punish defection. Therefore, second mover cooperation should decrease while defections increase relative to the Punish Injustice (PI) game. The first movers' threat fails to work, and so the punishment rate should rise. Also for the first time we get a measure of the proportions of the sample willing to show intentional beneficence, and those wanting the assurance of punishing intentionally hurtful behavior.

Figure 13.1 displays the new design and reports the results. First, and not part of our a priori reasoning or prediction, equilibrium choice by first movers drops to the lowest reported level, 20 percent, in any of the trust literature we know of (except in the narrative version of the trust game in Chapter 12). The important implication is that we have many more first movers attempting mutual betterment – about one-third more – than heretofore observed. The one-third more eschew the security of equilibrium choice, and who, we infer, expect to do at least as well as in equilibrium.[6] Potentially, this is wealth increasing, or efficiency enhancing, because equilibrium play is not where the money – the joint value – is. Of the 80 percent of first movers who offer to cooperate, they split 5 to 3 in favor of justice over beneficence. Smith says that the virtue of justice is more important than the virtue of beneficence, and the subjects vote decisively with their feet in the same direction. Half of the second movers are trustworthy under justice; as predicted this is a decline, but only slightly from 55 percent in the Punish Injustice treatment. Half defect and, as expected, committed to the use of threat, first movers follow through when it fails, as punishment increases from 24 percent in the Punish Injustice game to 50 percent in the Beneficence/Punish Injustice (B/PI) choice game. But contrary to prediction, in the beneficence branch, trustworthiness

---

[6] This is a choice under the veil of social ignorance for this particular game; i.e., having no previous experience in trust games the subjects have only their life experiences to guide their tripartite choice among subgames.

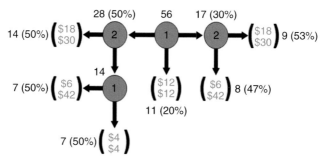

Figure 13.1. Beneficence/Punish Injustice (B/PI) game

declines to 53 percent from 67 percent in the Baseline Trust game. The greater purity of the signal is not heard, or at least not its pitch, in the new context of expanded choice.

What payoffs do the participants attain under each of the two-person mini-societies: Baseline Trust, Punish Injustice, and Beneficence/Punish Injustice treatments?

Payoffs are a measure of how well the rules that people use to make choices serve their ability to attain individual welfare, as measured by their monetary earnings. Under beneficence in the Baseline Trust game, the first mover's must earn at least $12 from cooperation for it to pay, which they will do on average if the defection rate by second movers is less than 50 percent. Second movers earn at least $30 in the cooperative branch. Under injustice in the Punish Injustice game, earnings of both people are the same as under beneficence in the absence of punishment. If defection is punished, their payoffs fall from ($6, $42) to ($4, $4).

In Table 13.1 we compute the earnings of each player type in the cooperative branch subgames under the three treatments. Second movers fare uniformly better than equilibrium in cooperative branch play, and first movers fare worse only in the justice left branch of the Beneficence/Punish Injustice game ($11.50). Branch conditional efficiencies are total pair earnings as a percent of $48 (the maximum). Total efficiency is the equilibrium and cooperative branch total earnings, weighted by the proportions of people ending in these states. Thus,

Efficiency (BT) = [(22/49)($12 + $12) + (27/49)($14 + $34)]/$48 = 0.776
Efficiency (PI) = [(26/81)($12 + $12) + (55/81)($12.33 + $31.31)]/$48
　　　　　　 = 0.778
Efficiency (B/PI) = [(11/56)($12 + $12) + (17/56)($12.35 + $35.65)
　　　　　　　　 + (28/56)($11.50 + $26.50)]/48 = 0.798

Table 13.1 *Player earnings and efficiencies for beneficence, justice, and beneficence/justice branches by game*

Game of Personal Exchange	First mover Earnings	Second mover Earnings	Branch Efficiency	Total Efficiency
Beneficence (BT)	14.00	34.00	100.0%	77.6%
Justice (PI)	12.33	31.31	90.9%	77.8%
Beneficence (B/PI: right)	12.35	35.65	100.0%	79.8%
Justice (B/PI: left)	11.50	26.50	79.2%	

FROM MORAL SENTIMENTS TO THE EXTENDED ORDER OF MARKETS, SPECIALIZATION, AND WEALTH CREATION

In Chapter 1 of *Wealth*, Smith describes the "division of labor" – specialization – as the creative productive source of a society's wealth. Specialization, though, "is not originally the effect of any human wisdom, which foresees and intends that general opulence to which it gives occasion" (WN, p. 25). This first principle of human economic action has unintended consequences, and is driven by a force not sensibly visible to the great mass of people who cooperate in achieving its ends. That driving force is Smith's primary axiom in *Wealth*: "It is the necessary, though very slow and gradual consequence of a certain propensity in human nature which has in view no such extensive utility; the propensity to truck, barter, and exchange one thing for another" (WN, p. 25). Smith is aware of the axiomatic nature of exchange. He indicates his awareness in the next sentence but speculates on a deeper cause: "Whether this propensity be one of those original principles in human nature, of which no further account can be given; or whether, as seems more probable, it be the necessary consequence of the faculties of reason and speech, it belongs not to our present subject to enquire."

Smith does not need to speculate further than to turn to his first book and read: "Actions of a beneficent tendency, which proceed from proper motives, seem alone to require reward; because such alone are the approved objects of gratitude, or excite the sympathetic gratitude of the spectator" (TMS, Second.II.I, p. 112), and then extend its elements.[7]

---

[7] Nowhere in *Wealth* does Smith refer to *Sentiments*. In the general introduction to *Wealth*, the editors offer a connection, suggesting that Smith's "work on economics was designed to follow on his treatment of ethics and jurisprudence, and therefore to add something to the sum total of our knowledge of the activities of man in society. To this extent, each of the

An exchange is a mutually beneficent action in which you offer to give me a good *A*, and I reciprocally give tangible evidence of my "gratitude" by offering to give you the reward of good *B*. In Chapter 6, we made this reinterpretation qua substitution in our Corollary: human beings reciprocate beneficence.

In *Wealth*, trade in markets for goods and services are extensions of human sociality developed in *Sentiments*, except that in the former, we make immediate or contractually pledged payments in compensation for the items provided to us by others, and in like manner we expect compensation from others for what we provide and deliver to them. Being voluntary, the result does not depend on the intermediation of gratitude to produce a future reward. Each simultaneously feels net gratitude in receiving more in value than they give up. *All such trades are an exchange of gifts in the beneficence sense, that each has to give in order to receive.* Indeed, this is the precise language Smith uses: "Give me that which I want, and you shall have this which you want, is the meaning of every such offer; and it is in this manner that we obtain from one another the far greater part of those good offices which we stand in need of" (WN, p. 26).[8] Smith does not say, "Let me take that which I want from you, and you may take this which you want from me."[9]

The intellectual indebtedness of *Wealth* to *Sentiments* is greater than mere beneficence. We also need justice. We need all the trappings of Smith's conception of the classical liberal order, an immense playing field with clear foul boundaries within which people are empowered by the freedom to discover. That conception derives from negative justice, which

---

three subjects can be seen to be interconnected, although it is also true to say that each component of the system contains material which distinguishes it from the others. One part of Smith's achievement was in fact to see all these different subjects as parts of a single whole, while at the same time differentiating economics from them. Looked at in this way, the economic analysis involves a high degree of abstraction which can be seen in a number of ways. For example, in his economic work, Smith was concerned only with some aspects of the psychology of man and in fact confined his attention to the self-regarding propensities" (WN, pp. 18–19). Our perspective in the text is more integrative.

[8] We have used experiments to determine if people can discover trade under sparse information conditions. They are informed only as to how to move objects of value and to earn monetary rewards. Some groups discover trade, and their village chat room records show that they use the language of "giving," not trading, when they strike an exchange between each other. "You give me red [things], and I will give you blue [things]." Similarly, "taking" without consent is quickly identified by their spontaneous references to "stealing" (Erik Kimbrough, Vernon Smith, and Bart Wilson 2010, pp. 213–14).

[9] For an experiment exactly on this point, see Hillard Kaplan, Eric Schniter, Vernon Smith, and Bart Wilson (2018).

is developed in *Sentiments*. But it reaches its fullest meaning and significance only when we consider the two books as an organic whole, for as Smith informs us by way of grand summary in *Wealth*: "Every man, as long as he does not violate the laws of justice, is left perfectly free to pursue his own interest his own way, and to bring both his industry and capital into competition with those of any other man, or order of men" (WN, p. 687). To grasp the meaning of "justice," "own interest," "own way," and to understand why the justice conditional appears before the verb, it is necessary to study *Sentiments*. For the science of economic betterment in the twenty-first century to be a study of humankind, it must likewise be an inquiry into human social betterment.

References

Kaplan, Hillard S., Eric Schniter, Vernon L. Smith, and Bart J. Wilson. 2018. "Experimental Tests of the Tolerated Theft and Risk-Reduction Theories of Resource Exchange," *Nature Human Behaviour* 2(6): 383–88.

Kimbrough, Erik O., Vernon L. Smith, and Bart J. Wilson. 2010. "Exchange, Theft, and the Social Formation of Property," *Journal of Economic Behavior and Organization* 74(3): 206–29.

Smith, Adam. 1853 [1759]. *The Theory of Moral Sentiments; or, An Essay towards an Analysis of the Principles by which Men naturally judge concerning the Conduct and Character, first of their Neighbours, and afterwards of themselves. To which is added, A Dissertation on the Origins of Languages. New Edition. With a biographical and critical Memoir of the Author, by Dugald Stewart.* London, UK: Henry G. Bohn. Available online and in electronic formats at http://oll.libertyfund.org/titles/2620.

Smith, Adam. 1982 [1766]. *Lectures on Jurisprudence.* Indianapolis, IN: Liberty Fund.

Smith, Adam. 1981 [1776]. *An Inquiry into the Nature and Causes of the Wealth of Nations.* Vol. 1 and 2. Indianapolis, IN: Liberty Fund.

Wierzbicka, Anna. 2006. *English: Meaning and Culture.* New York, NY: Oxford University Press.

Index

Printed in the United States
By Bookmasters